THE
HISTORY OF
SWEDEN

THE HISTORY OF SWEDEN

Byron J. Nordstrom

The Greenwood Histories of the Modern Nations
Frank W. Thackeray and John E. Findling, Series Editors

Greenwood Press
Westport, Connecticut • London

Library of Congress Cataloging-in-Publication Data

Nordstrom, Byron J.
 The history of Sweden / Byron J. Nordstrom.
  p.   cm.—(Greenwood histories of the modern nations, ISSN 1096–2905)
  Includes bibliographical references and index.
  ISBN 0–313–31258–3 (alk. paper)
  1. Sweden—History. I. Title. II. Series.
 DL648.N67   2002
 948.5—dc21   2001058643

British Library Cataloguing in Publication Data is available.

Library of Congress Catalog Card Number: 2001058643
ISBN: 0–313–31258–3
ISSN: 1096–2905

First published in 2002

Greenwood Press, 88 Post Road West, Westport, CT 06881
An imprint of Greenwood Publishing Group, Inc.
www.greenwood.com

Printed in the United States of America

The paper used in this book complies with the
Permanent Paper Standard issued by the National
Information Standards Organization (Z39.48–1984).

10 9 8 7 6 5 4 3 2 1

Copyright Acknowledgments

Map of Sweden's Historic Provinces reprinted from Sweden: The Nation's History. The University of Minnesota Press, 1977, p. 439. Used with permission of the estate of Franklin D. Scott.

Contents

Series Foreword

The Greenwood Histories of the Modern Nations series is intended to provide students and interested laypeople with up-to-date, concise and analytical histories of many of the nations of the contemporary world. Not since the 1960s has there been a systematic attempt to publish a series of national histories, and, as series editors, we believe that this series will prove to be a valuable contribution to our understanding of other countries in our increasingly interdependent world.

Over thirty years ago, at the end of the 1960s, the Cold War was an accepted reality of global politics, the process of decolonization was still in progress, the idea of a unified Europe with a single currency was unheard of, the United States was mired in a war in Vietnam, and the economic boom of Asia was still years in the future. Richard Nixon was president of the United States, Mao Tse-tung (not yet Mao Zedong) ruled China, Leonid Brezhnev guided the Soviet Union and Harold Wilson was prime minister of the United Kingdom. Authoritarian dictators still ruled most of Latin America, the Middle East was reeling in the wake of the Six-Day War and Shah Reza Pahlavi was at the height of his power in Iran. Clearly, the past thirty years have been witness to a great deal of historical change, and it is to this change that this series is primarily addressed.

With the help of a distinguished advisory board, we have selected nations whose political, economic and social affairs mark them as among the most important in the waning years of the twentieth century, and for each nation we have found an author who is recognized as specialist in the history of that nation. These authors have worked most cooperatively with us and with Greenwood Press to produce volumes that reflect current research on their nation and that are interesting and informative to their prospective readers.

The importance of a series such as this cannot be underestimated. As a superpower whose influence is felt all over the world, the United States can claim a "special" relationship with almost every other nation. Yet many Americans know very little about the histories of the nations with which the United States relates. How did they get to be the way they are? What kind of political systems have evolved there? What kind of influence do they have in their own region? What are the dominant political, religious and cultural forces that move their leaders? These and many other questions are answered in the volumes of this series.

The authors who have contributed to this series have written comprehensive histories of their nations, dating back to prehistoric time in some cases. Each of them, however, has devoted a significant portion of the book to events of the past thirty years, because the modern era as contributed the most to contemporary issues that have an impact on U.S. policy. Authors have made an effort to be as up-to-date as possible so that readers can benefit from the most recent scholarship and a narrative that includes very recent events.

In addition to the historical narrative, each volume in this series contains an introductory overview of the country's geography, political institutions, economic structure and cultural attributes. This is designed to give readers a picture of the nation as it exists in the contemporary world. Each volume also contains additional chapters that add interesting and useful detail to the historical narrative. One chapter is a thorough chronology of important historical events, making it easy for readers to follow the flow of a particular nation's history. Another chapter features biographical sketches of the nation's most important figures in order to humanize some of the individuals who have contributed to the historical development of their nation Each volume also contains a comprehensive bibliography, so that those readers whose interest has been sparked may find out more about the nation and its history. Finally, there is a carefully prepared topic and person index.

Readers of these volumes will find them fascinating to read and useful in understanding the contemporary world and the nations that comprise it.

As series editors, it is our hope that this series will contribute to a height-ened sense of global understanding as we embark on a new century.

Frank W. Thackeray and John E. Findling
Indiana University Southeast

Preface

I have tried to avoid using too many terms, letter abbreviations, and acronyms in this book. *Government* is a word that might create some confusion. Until the modern period (c.1800), *government* referred to the handful of men who ran the country. In Sweden, this was usually the monarch and his or her closest advisors. In a few instances, when the heir to the throne was a minor, a regency was in charge. In the nineteenth century it was still primarily the king who ruled, but the term *government* took on an increasingly formal meaning. The office of prime minister (*statsminister*) developed, and the prime minister and the men who headed the various administrative departments, the *ministers*, comprised the Government, with a capital G. In 1998 Sweden's Government had twenty members. Another potentially confusing word is *Riksdag*, what the Swedes call their parliament. These two words are used interchangeably throughout the book. Also used are a few of the more common acronyms: EFTA (European Free Trade Association), EU (European Union), GDP (gross domestic product), LO (*Landsorganisationen*, or the Swedish Confederation of Trade Unions), and SAF (*Svenska Arbetsgivareföreningen*, or the Swedish Federation of Employers).

I have tried to provide in many cases both the English and the Swedish names for organizations or the titles of books. Readers will note that Swedish has three more letters than the standard English alphabet: *å, ä,* and *ö*. A

Map 1. Sweden and the Baltic.

long *Å/å* sounds like the *o* in fort; a short *å* sounds like the *o* in yonder. A long *Ä/ä* sounds like the *ai* in air; the short *ä* like the *e* in best. The *Ö/ö* is a bit more complicated. Its sound sometimes depends on the letter that follows it. When followed by an *r*, it is long and sounds like the *u* in fur. Short, it is like the *e* in her. Other differences in Swedish pronunciation I will leave to language experts to explain.

Some confusion may arise from how I have spelled some names. Through the nineteenth century Carl, for example, was spelled with a *k*. So it is Karl XII, for example, but Carl XVI Gustaf. Similarly, the *v* in Gustav is now an *f*.

There are many who deserve thanks for their help in the preparation of this book. Completion of the project would have been impossible without the superb scholarship of my colleagues in Sweden, Denmark, Finland, Iceland, Norway, the United States, and the United Kingdom. This work is based on their research and publications. Special thanks also go to my wife, Janet, for her editorial comments, patience, and encouragement; to Roland Thorstensson, Roger McKnight, Dag Blanck, Terje Leiren, and Paul Levine for help with specific aspects of Swedish history I know little about; to the Swedish Institute, several ministries of the government and branches of the armed forces, and many organizations in Sweden for the superb informational materials they make available in print and on the Internet; and to Stewart P. Oakley, who wrote the 1966 Praeger volume in this series and was my friend, mentor, and colleague.

Timeline of Historical Events

1520s–1593	Lutheran Reformation
1541	Publication of the Gustav Vasa Bible
1544	Sweden becomes a hereditary monarchy
1562	Extension of protection to Riga, which marks the beginning of the Swedish Baltic Empire
1593	Uppsala Decree confirms Sweden's Lutheranism
1619	Refounding of Göteborg
1630	Sweden enters the Thirty Years' War
1632	Gustav II Adolf is killed at Lützen
1638	Founding of New Sweden colony in North America
1648	End of the Thirty Years' War
1654	Kristina abdicates and leaves Sweden
1655	End of the New Sweden Colony
1658	Sweden's Baltic Empire reaches its peak
1680–1693	Introduction of absolutism under Karl XI
1700–1721	The Great Northern War
1709	Battle of Poltava
1718	Death of Karl XII
1719–1772	Era of Liberty
1792	Assassination of Gustav III
1809	Coup against Gustav IV
	Constitution of 1809
	Loss of Finland to Russia
1814	Swedish–Norwegian dynastic union
1842	Compulsory education law
1845	Beginning of era of mass migration
1848	Sweden escapes revolution
1862	Local government reform
1866	Four Estates of the *Riksdag* replaced by a two-chamber system
1867	Alfred Nobel invents dynamite
1879	Sundsvall strike
1898	Swedish Confederation of Trade Unions founded
1902	Swedish Employers' Federation founded
1902	Three-Day General Strike
1905	End of the Swedish-Norwegian Union
1909	Universal male suffrage

1909	General Strike
1914	Farmers' March and Palace Yard Speech
1914–1918	Sweden's neutrality in World War I
1917	Parliamentarism accepted by Gustav V
1918	Universal and equal suffrage for both houses of parliament
1917–1932	Period of minority parliamentarism
1931	Ådalen Demonstration
1932	Ivar Kreuger suicide
1932–1976	Social Democrats govern (except for June–October 1936)
1932–1939	Development of the "People's Home"
1939–1945	Sweden's "neutrality" in World War II
1940–1943	Swedish-German Transit Agreement
1945	Raoul Wallenberg disappears into the Soviet Union
1946	Per Albin Hansson dies
1948	Folke Bernadotte murdered in Jerusalem
1952	Nordic Council established
1960	European Free Trade Association established
1961	Dag Hammarkjöld, UN secretary general, dies in plane crash in the Congo
1976	Thorbjörn Fälldin forms first non–Social Democratic government since 1936
1980	Nuclear Power Referendum
1982	Olof Palme forms new minority Social Democratic government
1986	Assassination of Olof Palme (28 February)
1991	Carl Bildt forms a four-party non-socialist coalition
1994	Göran Persson forms new minority Social Democratic government
	EU membership referendum
1995	Sweden joins the European Union
1999	Ford buys Volvo's Automotive Division
2000	GM completes the buyout of SAAB
2001	Prime Minister Carlsson serves as president of the European Union
	Göteborg Protest Riots

1

An Introduction to Sweden

Sweden has a long, rich, and varied history. Although people have lived there for at least the last 11,000 years, much of the story pre-dates what we can truly call history and is obscured from us behind the veils of uncertain sources and myth. Reasonably reliable written records date only from about A.D. 1000. As a political unit, Sweden emerged from the broad struggles among organizational options and internal power disputes during the Middle Ages. In the Early Modern Period (1500–1800) it was one in a group of successful European dynastic states or "new monarchies," which also included France, England, Spain, and Denmark; for a brief period it also enjoyed status as a European great power. In little more than a century following 1815 Sweden underwent a series of rapid and extensive changes to become democratic, industrial, and urban; today it is recognized as one of the world's most advanced nations in terms of politics, social welfare, gender equality, standard of living, technology, the arts, and participation in regional and global developments.

Sweden is part of two larger and sometimes confusingly defined regions of Europe: Scandinavia and Norden (the North). Scandinavia is a linguistic, historical, and cultural area that includes Denmark, the Faeroe Islands, Iceland, Norway, and Sweden. Norden is a broader term that allows the inclusion of Finland, a country with a history linked to Sweden's from at least

the Viking Age, but where a majority of the people speak a language unre-
lated to those of the other Nordic countries.

The country is located in the far north quarter of Europe, between 55°
and 69° North Latitude. It measures about 980 miles from north to south,
and 310 miles from east to west. This location matches much of Alaska.
Stockholm, the capital, is on the same latitude as Juneau. Except in the
northern interior uplands, the climate is moderated by the waters that border the country on the east, south, and southwest and especially by the Gulf
Stream, which warms the ocean west of Norway. Average January temperatures range from −1 to −10 C (31 to 3 F), while summer temperatures average from +17 to 15 C (62 F–55 F) south to north. An important result of
location is the contrast between the darkness of winter and the light of summer. Swedes in the far north enjoy twenty-four hours of daylight for several
weeks each summer, but this is countered by several weeks of total darkness in midwinter. In southern Sweden daylight extends for about twenty
hours at midsummer versus four hours at midwinter. All these natural conditions have had impacts on the people of Sweden, including the realities
and rhythms of farming, pre-Christian cult beliefs, folk and high culture,
and identities.

Nineteen or more different landscape zones, each shaped by successive
periods of glacial advance and retreat, climate, and human activities, make
up Sweden. In the upper half of the country, the land falls from the mountains that form the border between Norway and Sweden ("the keel") toward the Gulf of Bothnia. In the far north, below the mountains the land is
uneven, boggy, and sparsely covered; farther south gently rolling highlands dotted with lakes and rivers and increasingly dense pine forests
gradually give way to the coastal flatlands near the Gulf of Bothnia. In the
northern regions settlement is densest near the coast and around Storsjön
in the west. Central Sweden, between Stockholm and Göteborg, is one of
the last land areas of the country to have emerged after the melting of the
last great glaciers. It is relatively low-lying and contains four of the country's largest lakes (Hjälmaren, Mälaren, Vänern, and Vättern). Separating
this area from the shallow hills and more open landscape of the far south
are the northern Småland highlands. It is easy to describe Sweden as a land
of water and woods—to which one might add rocks. Over 92,000 lakes dot
the country, and they cover some 9 percent of the land. Numerous rivers
flow down from highlands into the Gulf of Bothnia, the Baltic, and the
Kattegat. The coasts vary from broad sandy beaches to rocky crags, and
splendid island archipelagoes spread north from Göteborg in the west and
eastward from Stockholm.

Sweden is a country rich in natural resources, and this affluence has contributed to the development of a relatively diverse economy for a country with a relatively small population. For much of its history the land has been covered with forests, mixed deciduous in the south and pine or fir in the north. These have provided building materials, fuels, and the bases for boat and boat rigging, tar, lumber, charcoal, and paper pulp and paper industries. Mineral resources include silver, copper, and iron. The silver mines at Sala, northwest of Stockholm, helped to establish the financial bases for the early modern state, but the mines have since been depleted. Copper from the great mine at Falun was a source of wealth for nearly a millennium and the country's greatest export in the seventeenth century. Iron has been mined in Sweden since around 500 B.C., and has repeatedly been the country's most important natural resource. The oldest source of iron was in bogs. During the early modern times mining and production was concentrated in the so-called Bergslagen, which lay across the middle of the country. For much of the twentieth century mining has centered on the far north around Kiruna. Iron has been exported in raw and processed forms and also has been essential to Sweden's own iron, steel, weapons, and machinery industries. Only about 8 percent of Sweden's land is arable. The richest soils lie in the far south and in the areas surrounding Lake Mälaren. The growing season varies from 240 days in the south to half that in the north. Historically, grain crops, livestock, and dairy have been primary in what was for millennia a subsistence farming system. Butter and grains were important exports in the Early Modern Period. In the last 100 years or so, farming has become increasingly specialized and the number of farms and the percentage of the population engaged in farming has fallen dramatically—from around 80 percent in the 1850s to about 3 percent in 2000. Today Sweden's farmers focus on grains, fodder, sugar beets, potatoes, rape seed, hogs, beef, dairy, poultry, vegetables, fruits, and nursery and ornamental plant production. Finally, from time immemorial the people of Sweden have drawn upon the resources of the rivers, lakes, and seas of the region.

Today the economy is modern, diverse, and much changed from the predominately agrarian economy of little over a century ago. Industrial output accounts for about 25 percent of gross domestic product (GDP). Among the products of Swedish industry are high-grade steels, automobiles, trucks, tractors, construction machinery, commuter and military aircraft, sophisticated weapons systems, ships, electronics, telecommunications equipment, packaging, pharmaceuticals, housewares, furniture, and processed food products. Some familiar corporate names are SAAB, Volvo, L. M. Ericsson, Tetrapak, Nobel, Bofors, Orrefors, and IKEA. Agriculture is less important in the international context but provides a high percentage of the country's foodstuffs. The public and private-service sectors are also important. Sweden's extensive social programs and the public employees who deliver them account for about 28 percent of GDP. Important since prehistoric times, trade is now particularly vital to the health of the economy. Exports account for over two fifths of GDP. Although cautious about international commitments that might compromise its policy of nonalignment during the Cold War, Sweden has become increasingly involved in regional, European, and global developments. It was a charter member of the European Free Trade Association (EFTA), founded in 1960, and became a member of the European Union (EU) in 1995. Since the collapse of the Soviet Union, it has been active in building an economic region in the eastern Baltic and in linking southern Sweden and Denmark. The latter trend is symbolized by the bridge that opened across The Sound in 2000.

At the turn of the millennium the population of Sweden hovered around 8.8 million. This was considerably more than the 2.4 million of 1800, the 5.4 million of 1900, or even the 7 million of 1950. Sweden's population is the highest in the Nordic countries, but it is low compared with the major states of Europe. Population growth remained very slow until the middle of the eighteenth century, held in check by crop failures, disease, and wars. Rapid growth in the following century was propelled by better diets and food supplies, improved medical practices, and peace. In the twentieth century, growth slowed and nearly stopped in the mid-1930s and again in the 1990s. Since World War II an important contributor to the rising population has been immigration accompanied by relatively high birth rates among these newcomers. The population is unevenly distributed, with nearly two-thirds of Swedes living in a belt that runs from Stockholm across the country to Göteborg. There is another large concentration in the far southwest around Malmö. Eighty percent of Swedes live in urban areas. The north is only sparsely settled.

For much of the country's history, the population has been homogenous. The approximately 20,000 Sami of the far north are the oldest minority in the country; the Finns, who were often recruited to settle in Sweden and today number some 100,000, are the largest minority. Although Sweden seems homogenous, immigration has repeatedly brought an influx of new people to the country, such as Dutch merchants, Scottish mercenaries, or Swabian metal workers in the seventeenth century. Since World War II, migration to Sweden by refugees, political exiles, and workers has totaled more than half a million and made the population far more heterogenous, especially in urban areas. Among the new peoples in Sweden are Bosnians, Iraqis, Iranians, Turks, and Chileans. This infusion of new peoples has literally and figuratively changed the face of Sweden. Population aging is an important aspect of contemporary developments, particularly in terms of social expenses and tax income. Average life expectancies in Sweden are among the highest in the world: eighty-two for women and seventy-six for men.

Swedish, a Germanic language related closely to Danish, Faroese, Icelandic, and Norwegian, is the national language. Its development took an independent course mainly since the Viking Age, as did the development of other Scandinavian languages. Trade and cultural ties in the Middle Ages, printing and the Reformation in the sixteenth century, the growth of a vernacular literature from the eighteenth century, and the establishment of compulsory education in the nineteenth century were important moments in this process. Foreign influences, especially from Germany, France, England, and the United States have been important in shaping the language. Although not always encouraged, Sami and Finnish are important minority languages. Today government programs support the retention of native languages by immigrants, and Sweden is a nation of many tongues.

Contemporary Sweden is predominantly Lutheran, but this has not always been the case. Conversion from the pagan practices of the Vikings to Christianity began in the ninth century but was not accomplished until the twelfth. The Reformation reached into Sweden in the 1520s and led to the establishment of a state church and a gradual shift to Lutheranism that took much of the century. From the 1500s until the mid-1800s, religious conformity and uniformity were maintained by the state. Since that time a small percentage of Swedes have opted for other Protestant denominations or Catholicism. At the close of the twentieth century, about 85 percent of Swedes were officially Lutheran. Catholics make up the second largest denomination, and there is a thriving free church minority. In addition, immigrants have brought a new religious diversity to the country. For much of the Lutheran majority, religious life seems to be more personal than institutional, and few attend services regularly. However, many still opt for baptism, confirmation, marriage, and burial within the church. Jews first came to Sweden in the seventeenth century and now number around 16,000. Although well integrated into society, they have faced episodes of anti-Semitism and continue to do so from small groups on the radical right.

Politically, Sweden is a democratic constitutional monarchy. Its most recent constitution was adopted in 1974 and went into effect a year later. The system has five fundamental elements. The most important is "the people." All citizens over eighteen have the right to vote, and even some noncitizens may vote in local elections if they meet residency requirements. They go to the polls in September every four years (more often if necessary) to elect the 349 representatives to the parliament (*Riksdag*) and to local or communal assemblies. Elections are direct and based on a system of proportional representation. Of the parliament's 349 seats, 310 are linked to constituencies. The remaining thirty-nine are "at-large" and allocated on the basis of a national tally of the vote in order to make the distribution of seats as representative of the electorate's wishes as possible. Since 1998 Swedish voters have also been able to indicate their preference for specific candidates. The outcome of this affects who in each district gets into parliament from lists prepared by the political parties. Seven parties secured seats in the 1998 election: Moderate, Christian Democratic, Center, Liberal, Green, Social Democratic, and Left. The parliament, which is the second element in this system, meets for about eight months every year to review and study issues and problems, hear government proposals, and enact legislation that may be introduced either by members of parliament or the government. The third element, the government (or cabinet), is determined on the basis of election outcomes. Ideally, a government is formed by the party that wins a majority. In a system with seven parties, however, this is unlikely. In practice, the party receiving the highest percentage of votes or making the greatest gains in the election might form the government. Another option is that several parties agree to form a coalition. Both have happened in recent decades. In 1991, for example, the Moderate, Liberal, Center, and Christian Democratic parties formed a coalition. Three years later the Social Democrats won about 45 percent of the vote and formed a minority government. Governments normally have about twenty members. Ten or more members of a government head specific ministries, including foreign affairs, defense, finance, education, health and social affairs, culture, industry and trade, agriculture, labor, and transport. The rest serve as ministers "without portfolio" (without the responsibility of heading a government department). Parallel to the ministries are administrative departments charged with implementing legislation and running their respective areas. The head of the government is the prime minister. Currently over 40 percent of the members of the parliament and half of the government are women. The fourth element is a system of regional and local government based on governors, boards, and assemblies in the twenty-one counties and on councils in the 288 municipalities. Finally, there is the monarch, currently Carl XVI Gustaf. He is the titular head of state, but he serves only ceremonial and representative functions. In addition, there is a separate and independent judicial system and a set of fundamental laws governing individual rights such as freedom of speech, assembly, and the press.

This system is the result of historical developments that reach far back in the nation's history. The monarchy and fundamental assurances of people's rights and rule by law have medieval roots. The parliament traces its beginnings to the fifteenth century, while local and provincial assemblies are far older. Many documents make up the sources of Sweden's constitu- tional history, including accession oaths from medieval and early modern times and more extensive "forms of government" such as those from 1634, the 1720s, 1772, and 1809. Democracy came to Sweden slowly and often- times quite grudgingly. Many milestones mark this process: 1809, because in that year an unpopular king was deposed and a new constitution writ- ten; 1865, when the number of houses in the parliament was reduced from four to two and election rather than social status became the primary means of determining members; 1909, when all men finally received the vote; and 1918, when this right was extended to women. Additional re- forms in electoral laws made the system much more democratic in the 1920s and 1930s. The voting age was reduced to eighteen in 1974. In 1971 the parliament became unicameral. Until 1917 the king could ignore the re- sults of an election and appoint whatever government he wished. The right of a woman to succeed to the throne was recognized in 1980. One might be- lieve that democracy was the inevitable end of Sweden's political history, but the truth is more complicated, as we will see in later chapters.

Social democracy is as important in Sweden as political democracy, and this commitment is embodied in the welfare state that developed there, be- ginning in the early part of the twentieth century, expanded in the 1930s, and vastly extended in the three decades following World War II. Services and benefits include health and dental care, education, maternity and new- born leaves, child allowances, preschool care, pensions, senior citizen care, housing subsidies, public transportation facilities, and cultural sites and programs. Many benefits are free or nearly so, and access covers almost anyone residing in the country. Most Swedes see the elements of the system as rights and as essential aspects of a good, just, and humane society; until relatively recently they accepted the collective costs involved. The Swedish welfare state is enormously expensive. It accounts for nearly a third of GDP. One-half or more of one's annual earnings go to taxes on income, property, purchases, and services; businesses pay high taxes as well. The scale and costs of the system have been themes of political debates that intensified in the last decades of the twentieth century, when economic and demographic problems drove costs up and tax revenues down. These developments led to deficits at home, problems in the international economy, and serious ef- forts to trim the system. Attempts to make the welfare system affordable in the context of new economic realities continue and include benefit reduc- tions, increased fees for some services, privatization of some elements, and reform of the pension system.

Gender democracy has made great progress in Sweden, but this has cer- tainly not been the case for very long. As elsewhere in much of Europe and the world, women in Sweden were considered inferior, had few legal rights, and were exploited and mistreated by men. Through struggles that have spanned the last 150 years, women have secured a nearly equal place in Swedish society. In that time they have won legal, economic, educational, occupational, reproductive, and political rights to degrees that make Sweden a leader worldwide. Today over 60 percent of women work outside the home. Women are strongly represented at all levels of government and are present in all the professions. Still, gender bias remains prevalent in some fields, women continue to be tracked into certain jobs such as teaching, and they have not achieved equality in the upper strata of corporate management. In addition, although household and childrearing responsibilities may be better shared between men and women in Sweden than in many other Western countries, many women continue to carry the burden of two careers—job and home—and this situation is complicated by the growing number of single-parent families.

For much of its history, Sweden has been relatively insignificant in international relations and has had to pursue policies consistent with this status. The exception to this was in the seventeenth century, when Sweden was one of the great powers of Europe and controlled an empire that included Finland, much of the Baltic region (including parts of the present states of Estonia, Latvia, Lithuania, and Germany), posts on the Gold Coast of Africa, and even a colony in North America. This empire and rank were lost in the early 1700s, although many of the country's leaders failed to appreciate these facts for more than a century. Since 1815 Sweden has not participated directly in any of Europe's wars. Neutrality in war and nonalignment in times of peace have defined its modern foreign policy, especially in the twentieth century. This stance has not meant disengagement from international affairs, however. Sweden has been active in many international organizations, including the League of Nations and the United Nations (UN), and in peacekeeping, humanitarian, and development efforts. A national army and navy were built in the Early Modern Period and used for offensive and defensive purposes through the Napoleonic wars. Since then, Sweden's armed forces have been chiefly defensive in nature, and their size and costs have varied widely. During and since World War II Sweden has built and maintained forces intended to deter any potential attacker. This has meant proportionally very large defense expenditures, continuation of a universal service requirement, and domestic weapons development and manufacturing programs. For a time it even meant an atomic weapons development effort. Paradoxically, this nonaligned and peaceful nation is an important seller of weapons such as combat aircraft, explosives, anti-aircraft cannon, and small arms. Since the end of the Cold War in the early

1990s and Sweden's entrance into the European Union in 1995, foreign and security policies have remained largely the same, but there is new room for flexibility, and as a result, some positions have come under review.

In the arts, literature, and music, as well as in technology, the sciences, and other academic and intellectual areas, Sweden has a rich history and continues to make important contributions. Although Swedes have often been acted upon and shaped by outside developments, they have frequently adapted foreign ideas or styles in creative and important ways or made original contributions. A small number of Swedes in various fields are well known internationally, including the botanist Carl von Linné (Linneaus), chemist and inventor Alfred Nobel, engineer John Ericsson, playwright August Strindberg, sculptor Carl Miles, and filmmaker Ingmar Bergman. Today writers such as Kerstin Ekman and Marianne Fredriksson have had their novels translated into many languages and they have been world bestsellers. In addition, Swedish universities and research centers enjoy global reputations for their quality.

It is relatively easy to define some aspects of Sweden—geography, climate, economy, and politics, for instance. But what about the idea of a Swedish culture? Historically, there was a religious culture determined by the Church in the Middle Ages and defined by art, architecture, church artifacts, literature, and education. Similarly, there was the court culture of the Early Modern Period with its artistic, architectural, literary, fashion, and culinary aspects—a culture as much European as Swedish. In addiition, there have always been many regional folk cultures, exhibited in buildings, objects of everyday life, decorative traditions, music, festivals, and dialects. Is there a common Swedish culture? Certainly there are elements that many Swedes can and do agree on: language, a shared official history, a list of great people, a canon of great books, holidays, and symbols like the national flag and anthem. However, what makes someone Swedish? As in any country, nationality is an imagined identity that is consciously formed and changing. In a very real sense "Swedes" and the culture that defines them have existed for only about a century—since the coming of compulsory public education, universal literacy, inexpensive newspapers and books, good communication networks, industrialization and urbanization, and mass politics. These and other developments have made a Sweden of localities into one of far greater unity and uniformity. Yet, in the early twenty-first century what makes up Sweden and Swedishness is becoming more, and not less, complex. Particularly important here is that Sweden is now a multiethnic state. There are, as well, the trends that work against nations and nationalisms, including regional, European, and international organizations; economic globalization and corporate mergers; Americanization;

and world travel. Where all these trends will lead remains unclear, but some Swedes find them alarming, especially for a relatively small country like Sweden.

A century ago few observers would have predicted that Sweden would become one of the world's most modern, industrialized, affluent, democratic, egalitarian, or open nations by the end of the millennium. Poverty was widespread, most people still lived by farming, cities were crowded and unhealthy, life expectancy was little more than fifty years, government was still controlled by the king and a tiny elite, the parliament represented fewer than a fifth of the people, social classes rigidly divided society, education beyond a few years of basic schooling was largely for the upper classes, women had few rights but many duties, and tens of thousands of Swedes emigrated annually, driven away by dreams of better lives elsewhere.

Many factors have contributed to making that Sweden of the past and to transforming it to the Sweden of the present. Geography, geology, climate, and ecology have all played important roles. These are the givens of the environment or the context in which people have lived and acted. Then there are human factors such as individuals, groups, ideas, inventions, and the immigration of people and ideas or new ways of doing things into Sweden. There are also the accidents or, if you prefer, the chance convergence of factors leading to events. It should also be kept in mind that there is **history**, meaning everything that happened in the past, and *history*, meaning someone's account of the past. We can never know everything that happened, and anyone's account of the past is always incomplete, biased, and subject to change. Perspectives change, the questions change, views of causes change. Thus, for example, what I write differs from what Stewart Oakley wrote in 1966 in the Praeger series, and that differed from what came before. Finally, some words of caution. Nationalism has been one of the most important factors in modern history, for good and evil. Without nationalism we would probably not be concerned with histories such as this one. Remember, however, that the history of Sweden could have followed many paths. The story could have been vastly different, for given other twists and turns in history, Sweden might never have come into being, and at several points in the past it was altogether possible it would cease to be.

2

Before There Was Sweden

People have lived in what is now called Sweden for a very long time. Although forced to leave by successive glaciations, inhabitants lived there perhaps as long ago as 400,000 years. We know the most about only the last 13,000 years or so since the melting of the most recent glaciers. The record of all prehistory lies in archaeological materials gleaned from short-lived camp sites, garbage pits, villages, burials, hoard deposits, offerings, and sacred sites and includes skeletal remains, tools, weapons, pottery, jewelry, textiles, small and large grave types, housing remains, works of sacred and profane art, and landscape impacts. Taken together the material record reveals aspects of technology, material culture, economies, social and political organization, and religious practices. Nonetheless, many questions remain about the people of this ancient time. Written sources make no mention of the area until around A.D. 100, and no truly reliable written materials were extant until centuries later. Interpretation is very difficult, for this far-distant past has to be reconstructed in an imagining process based on limited sources and influenced by fundamental historical and philosophical viewpoints and ethnicity or nationality. How people actually lived and what they said and thought can only be supposed and thus remain matters of debate.

Sweden's prehistory follows a standard pattern of chronology, but the dates are unique to the Nordic region (see Table 2.1). Period labels are useful and based on central defining aspects of each era, but they can also limit one's perspectives or willingness to see exceptions.

In general, the people of prehistoric Sweden appear primitive by today's standards. Life was short and at times very hard. Yet, the pictures that emerge from across the entire prehistoric period show complexity, skill, sophistication, and at times considerable affluence. We meet people well adapted to survival in a world far removed from the present. Although highly variable across an enormous span of time, their weapons of hunting and warfare (axes, spears, arrows, fish and animal traps, swords, and daggers), implements for farming (plows, hoes, and rakes), tools, eating utensils, textiles, pottery, personal articles, houses, and boats were functional and skillfully crafted. Until the development of farming around 4,000 B.C., their garbage shows that their diets were quite healthy and included meat, fish, clams, grains, nuts, and berries; thereafter they added dairy products

Table 2.1
Sweden's Prehistory

Period	Time	Climate	Temperature*	Baltic
Paleolithic/Old Stone Age	11,000 to 8,300 B.C.	Subarctic	11	Ice Lake
Mesolithic/Middle Stone Age	8,300 to 4,000 B.C.			
	8,000 B.C.	Pre-Boreal	14	Salt Sea
				Fresh Water
	6,500 B.C.	Boreal	18	Lake
	6,200 B.C.	Atlantic	20	Salt Sea
Neolithic/New Stone Age	4,000 to 1,800 B.C.			
Early Neolithic	4,000–3,300 B.C.			
Middle Neolithic	3,300–2,300 B.C.	Subboreal	18	
Late Neolithic	2,300–1,800 B.C.			
Bronze Age	1,800 to 500 B.C.			
Older Bronze Age	1,800–1,100 B.C.			
Younger Bronze Age	1,100–500 B.C.			
Iron Age	500 B.C. to 1,050 A.D.	Subatlantic	16	
Pre-Roman or Celtic	500 B.C.–0			
Roman	A.D. 0–375			
Migration	A.D. 375–550 A.D.			
Vendel	A.D. 550–800 A.D.			
Viking	A.D. 800–1,050 A.D.			

*Average July temperature in centigrade.
Source: Birgitta Hårdh. *Grunddragen i Nordens Förhistoria*. University of Lund, 1993.

from goats, sheep, and cattle, as well as cereals and breads, peas, beans, and cabbage. Particularly remarkable is the artistic record they left in elaborately decorated weapons, pottery, jewelry, small statues, rock pictures, and decorated everyday objects. An important aspect of Sweden's prehistory is the repeated influence of external cultures. The peoples of prehistoric Sweden developed in a surprisingly rich, constantly changing, and interconnected cultural world. Many ideas, technologies, decorative traditions, and materials entered Sweden through immigration and commerce and were either rejected or merged with and modified by existing practices.

During the prehistoric period the lands of northern Europe were constantly changing, rising with the removal of the glaciers' pressure, carved by rushing melt waters, alternately flooded or revealed by changing water levels. The area we know as the Baltic was variously part of the last glacier, an ice lake, an extension of the Atlantic, a freshwater lake, and a salt sea. Its present configuration dates to around 4,500 B.C. Sweden took millennia to form. As the ice retreated 14,000 years ago, only the far south was exposed. It was connected to a landmass that included what is now Denmark and extended all the way to Ireland. Central Sweden, from Stockholm to Göteborg, was completely submerged. Not until around 4,500 B.C. did a map looking much like today's evolve. The climate was also in flux during these ancient times. The glacial melt began with only slight warming, and Sweden was part of a huge circumpolar subarctic region. Gradually the climate became warmer and dryer until around the middle of the fifth millennium B.C., when the average daytime high temperature in July was around 20 degrees centigrade— several degrees warmer than today. Since then the climate has cooled and become wetter in a series of stages. Geological and climatic forces worked together to shape the plant and animal ecologies of the region. The landscape evolved from arctic tundra to scrub woods to a changing variety of forests dominated by particular trees—birch, hassle nut, beech, and oak in the south and pine in the north. At the same time the highly limited wildlife of the earliest tundra gradually became increasingly diverse.

THE STONE AGES

The oldest evidence of human presence in Sweden dates to between 11,000 and 9,000 B.C., and has been found at several sites in the far south, including Stegebro, Ageröd, and Simrishamn. In northern Sweden the oldest evidence comes from Garaselet near the north coast of the Gulf of Bothnia and dates to about 7,000 B.C. The best evidence about the people of the north has only surfaced since around 1950. They seem to have remained locked in a Mesolithic culture acted upon but not acting in the changes occurring to the south, and they do not appear to have played any role in the development of Sweden as a geopolitical unit.

Paleolithic people were almost exclusively hunters—mainly of reindeer. Later, Mesolithic peoples in both the south and the north mixed hunting of elk, wild boar, bear, and small animals such as rabbit with more systematic gathering of their environments' increasingly diverse resources, including berries, nuts, roots, and seeds. Fish and mussels were also vital. This economy gave rise to relatively healthy diets and balanced gender roles. These early people were mobile, and the archaeological record lies mainly in their seasonal camp sites. The struggle for survival for Paleolithic peoples appears to have been hard, but the Mesolithic was an era of relative plenty and even leisure—perhaps reflected in the carved amber amulets and picture stones depicting the animals they hunted from this period. Relatively simple fired pottery appeared late in the Mesolithic, along with systematic burial practices that may indicate a belief in an afterlife or veneration of family members. Attempts to estimate the population of Sweden during this time are difficult and vary widely. One guess for the coastal regions of the south is no more than 2,500; another, for the entire country, is 10,000–25,000.

Adoption of agriculture, improved pottery, greater settlement permanence, eventual development of villages, more structured organization of work, a new social hierarchy, long-distance trade in goods valued as symbols of importance, new burial practices, changes in the roles and status of women, and an influx of new peoples and/or ideas toward the end of the period help define the Neolithic Age. It was also a time with a darker side that included warfare as a result of competition for land, want because of overpopulation or agricultural problems, increased susceptibility to disease because of the close living arrangements, and slavery. These transitions extended from the south into east-central Sweden around Lake Mälaren and occurred over hundreds of years. They may have been the result of the immigration of new peoples, or they may have influenced inhabitants through the importation of ideas only. Whichever is the case, some social and economic bases of Sweden's agricultural society that lasted into the twentieth century were laid by these developments.

Neolithic farming involved clearing forested land by slash-and-burn techniques, the raising of grain crops, and the domestication of cattle, sheep, and goats. Early farms appear to have been the domain of small family groups in which tasks were probably assigned along gender and age lines. The development of a simple plow drawn by oxen, for example, excluded women. The techniques quickly exhausted the poorly developed soils of an area and required frequent relocation. Hunting and gathering, by necessity, remained part of people's lives. Populations remained small, but grew nonetheless, which necessitated the expansion of settled areas. Grave evidence indicates the frequency of early death, especially among children and women.

It was during this time that the oldest monumental or Megalithic graves were built. The oldest were relatively simple dolmen graves and date from around 3,500 B.C. They were based on several large, vertically placed stones capped with a slab to form a small chamber. The more recent passage graves, from around 3,000 B.C., were larger and more complex and involved building an elongated chamber of vertical stones and ceiling slabs. The grave at Barsebäck, northwest of Lund, is a particularly important example. Both types were originally covered with turf to form mounds. The remains of the dead were usually deposited along with a few articles of everyday life such as a weapon or domestic goods. The Megalithic graves were used more than once and probably also served as cult sites. Given the extent of effort and resources required to build them, they are believed to have been the graves of an elite in an increasingly stratified society. Located in what appear to be five regional clusters in the south and west, they may be the graves of powerful local farmers, family or clan leaders, or chieftains.

Archaeologists generally distinguish between three cultures in southern Sweden during the Neolithic period, the Pitted-Ware Culture (*Gropkeramik kultur*), the Funnel-Cup Culture (*Trattbägarkultur*), and the Boat Axe or Battle Axe Culture (*Båtyxkultur*). The first of these was most common in parts of the east, south, and west and the Lake Mälaren region. The second dominated the south and extended into Denmark and eastern Norway. The third is at the center of considerable debate. Evidence of this culture first appeared in much of northern Europe around the middle of the third millennium B.C. and was strikingly different from that of older groups. Some researchers believe Sweden, along with much of the south Baltic, Denmark, and Finland, were invaded by nomads whose origins lay along the western slopes of the Ural Mountains. These invaders were taller than the established people and had longer and narrower skulls. They rode horses, and some archaeologists think they brought with them the prototype of the later Germanic languages, including Swedish, and a new set of gods. According to this interpretation, these invaders descended on the peasant farmers of the north, conquered them, became a new elite, and erased the old cultures. Good evidence supports these views: The beautifully crafted boat-shaped ceremonial axes, crudely decorated pottery, and simple individual chamber graves became common and were strikingly different from their counterparts in either of the older Neolithic cultures. Recently, however, it has been suggested that the cooler and damper climate that developed around this time resulted in environmental changes that forced the existing cultures to adapt. The result was a new culture with new defining traits. The truth probably lies somewhere between these two views. External and internal influences have been important throughout Sweden's history. Rarely, however, did imports go unmodified by local customs. At the same time it is difficult to imagine that such abrupt and thorough changes could have occurred driven solely by relatively small and probably very gradual changes in agricultural practices.

THE BRONZE AGE

The Bronze Age in Sweden grew directly out of the existing Neolithic farming culture of the south. The name of the period derives from the alloys of copper and tin used and metal working technologies imported into the area from the British Isles and south-central Europe via trade routes along the rivers and coastal waters of the continent. Sweden had no native sources of tin, and its copper deposits were not exploited for another two thousand years. In the long-distance trade that developed, amber was the most important commodity the people of Sweden had to offer; but hides, furs, tar products, and probably slaves also played a part. For at least a few, great affluence came from this trade, and this is demonstrated in the rich archaeological record of the period.

For most people, bronze had few far-reaching impacts. Everyday tools and weapons continued to be made of stone, bone, and wood. Peasant farming remained at the center of almost everyone's life. The area under cultivation increased, and late in the period more intensive practices including crop rotations and more conscious manuring of fields appear to have developed to compensate for the worsening climate. At the same time villages, which contained small clusters of families, became increasingly important as the primary group units and organizers of social life and work. People lived in elongated rectangular houses built around central-pole frameworks with walls of turf or interwoven sticks and dried mud or clay. In some cases their interiors were divided into living, storage, work, and animal areas. Throughout the Neolithic Age a measure of work specialization had evolved within the increasingly complex rural economy, and this certainly continued in the Bronze Age. Particularly notable was the development of a small group of artisans able to smelt, cast, and work with copper, tin, bronze, and gold. These people may have held particularly important places in the society.

One thing that did change was the status or prestige goods of the elite—what the few had to demonstrate their positions in the society. Bronze weapons and jewelry, some decorated with gold, are among the primary symbols of this period, and they were clearly used as means of reward, to display status, and in cult practices. The wealth of the few is clear from the objects left in graves and what were probably offering deposits, especially during the Older Bronze Age.

Among the best-known and most easily seen symbols of the period are the grave mounds. Literally thousands of these were built in southern and central Sweden, Denmark, and southern Norway between about 1800 and 1100 B.C. They varied in size, but averaged around 20 meters in diameter and 3 meters in height. They began as graves for one person, but were re-used for hundreds of years. Their construction was complex and required considerable material resources and the work of a great many people. Typically, the remains of the dead, along with personal goods, were placed at the core, often on a specially built bed of stones and in a wood or stone coffin. A ring of stones was frequently then laid around the center. The mound itself was built up from stone, timber, and turf. One of the larger mounds, it is estimated, would have required about 3,200 cubic meters of turf cut from about 7 hectares (17 acres). Located on land that then was usually near to and had a view of the sea or other waterway, the mounds developed in clusters which may reflect the centers of power of local chieftain families. Skåne and Halland have the most turf mounds; stone versions predominate in parts of Småland, Östergötland, Södermanland, Uppland, and the islands of Öland and Gotland. One of the most remarkable of the mounds is at Håga near Uppsala. It is 50 meters in diameter, 9 meters high, and contains the remains of four people—probably a local chieftain and three companions, including one woman. The building of the mounds declined after around 1100 B.C., and cremation and burial of the remains in urns accompanied by a few goods in simpler graves became common. At about the same time some dead were placed in graves marked by ship-shaped stone outlines. There are over 350 of these on the island of Gotland alone.

Other important artifacts of Bronze Age Sweden are the hundreds of inscribed and painted picture stones located in many places in the southern third of the country and especially along the west coast at sites such as Tanum. These differ from the Mesolithic picture stones that usually depict animals. By the Bronze Age the most common images are of ships, circles and wheels, men with weapons, men with exaggerated phalluses, plows, footprints, and occasionally women. The purposes and meanings of these pictures, usually cut into flat, low-lying stones located along or near waterways, are much debated. They may be secular images depicting the central elements of everyday Bronze Age life including farming, hunting, and maritime trade; or they may be sacred images, including the sun, the ships that carried the sun across the sky, and gods and goddesses of the hunt, the field, and fertility.

There is much evidence to argue for the presence of complex religious beliefs and ceremonies in the Bronze Age. The burial practices, especially the inclusion of items necessary in an ongoing existence (weapons, personal articles, and even food and drink), certainly point to a belief in an afterlife. Offering finds, the picture stones, objects such as a bronze sun-wheel tambor from Balkåkra, small metal statues of men and women, site finds that appear to be places of worship, and bronze lures—the oldest musical instruments in the region—point in these directions. Putting all of this together, one archaeologist has imagined a ceremony in which pairs of men in horned helmets played lures, while others beat on metal percussion instruments or drums and chanted. All this took place on a field of picture stones and led up to the casting of offerings into the sea.

THE IRON AGE

The final era in the long prehistory of Sweden and the north, the Iron Age, began as the new metal superceded bronze in importance. How knowledge of iron making reached Sweden is unclear, but it probably came either via the immigration of the first smiths or through the acquisition of the needed technologies by way of trade and external contacts. Whichever the case, the raw materials for iron production (ore and wood for charcoal) were plentiful in Sweden. The new metal had far broader impacts on the general population as a material for tools and weapons, and it has been at the center of the country's development for some 2,500 years.

The first of the Iron Age subperiods was named for the Celtic peoples who spread across Europe from Hungary to Ireland and severed old trade routes. Although they apparently never reached Sweden in any number, ideas and some artifacts of their material cultures did. At the same time the old power centers in the eastern Mediterranean and Aegean collapsed, and the climate became increasingly cool and damp. Based on the material record in the simple graves from this time, Sweden and its neighbors were in a kind of backwater in terms of the status goods that had been so important in earlier periods for nearly half a millennium. This did not mean, however, development ceased in the rural society. In fact, the negative aspects of the economic and environmental situations resulted in intensification and refinement of methods and the continued development of villages. Whereas everyday life may have been harder in the Celtic Iron Age, it was also better organized and probably no poorer. This can be seen in the material record and in evidence that population and areas under cultivation actually increased until around A.D. 400.

Trade in luxury goods and increasingly complex cultural influences returned during the Roman Iron Age. The Rhine and Danube were vital avenues of commerce on the continent, and Sweden clearly shared in that
trade. A rich array of goods found its way to Sweden, including glass, ceramics, metal work, textiles, and coins in exchange for furs, hides, horses,
and slaves. Swedish smiths and other artisans were influenced by the techniques and styles of the Romans. Activity centered around Lake Mälaren
and the islands of Öland and Gotland. At the same time a few men from the
region may have served in the legions of the empire and returned to their
homes filled with their powerful southern neighbors' ideas including those
of political power and centralization.

Another aspect of the Roman Iron Age and subsequent Migration Period
was mention of the region in written sources. The oldest of these, written in
the fourth century B.C. by a Greek, Pytheas of Marseilles, is no longer extant.
But it was nonetheless used by others, including Pliny the Elder, who described an island he called Scadinavia and what are probably the Danish islands and southern Sweden around A.D. 79. About A.D. 100 Tacitus described
many northern tribal peoples, and Ptolemy, an Egyptian, provided the first
map of the area. It showed an exaggerated Jutland peninsula and three
small islands (parts of today's Denmark), as well as larger island he called
Skandia, which is taken to be the bottom of Sweden and Norway. After a silence that lasted for several hundred years, new accounts appeared in the
mid-500s. Jordanes described at length a large island, Scandza, and its peoples, including the Screrefennae (Finns or Sami), Hallin (from Halland),
Gautigoths (from Västergötland), and Suetidi (Swedes). Although the clas-
sical sources provide us with little specific information, they do reveal an
awareness of the region and provide clues to how Sweden and its neighbors
were organized. For example, it is clear that central authority did not exist
and that tribes were the largest organizational units.

The Migration and Vendel Periods were times of great wealth, artistic
creativity, change in cult and burial practices, and violence. The graves,
hoards and treasure finds, remains of literally hundreds of fortifications,
and a record of abandoned villages and farming sites reflect these characteristics. Many aspects of art, society, and politics in these periods may also
be seen as direct antecedents to the Viking Age.

The collapse of the Roman Empire in the west did not mean the end of
trade or cultural development. The center of Roman power shifted east to
Byzantium and remained important until defeated by the Turks in 1453.
The development of the Frankish state and the cultural richness of Celtic
Ireland are just two aspects of ongoing vitality in the west. Trade in goods
and ideas was important, and parts of Sweden figured in this commerce,

especially in the Mälaren area and on the Baltic islands. An important indicator of this is the trade and production site on Helgö in Lake Mälaren. The settlement there dates from between 400 and 800, and excavations show it to have been a center for iron production, jewelry making, and commerce. Among the thousands of finds are casting molds, Roman gold coins, a Celtic bishop's staff, and a small bronze Buddha from northern India. People from Gotland established trade colonies in the eastern Baltic. Crucial to these developments was the progress being made in boat building, as is evident in the Nydam boat from fifth-century Denmark and ships specifically designed for sailing depicted in eighth-century picture stones on Gotland.

Important political developments occurred that were linked to those in commerce and production. Some believe it was in the seventh or eighth century that the first Swedish state, centered in Uppland and extending south into Östergötland and perhaps beyond, emerged. This view is based on references in written sources (*Beowulf* and *Ynglingasaga*) and interpretations of the monumental graves at Old Uppsala, Vendel, and Valsgärde.

> King Adils was at a Disa sacrifice; and as he rose around the Disa hall his horse Raven stumbled and fell, and the king was thrown forward upon his head, and his skull was split, and his brains dashed out against a stone. Adils died at Upsal, and was buried there in a mound. The Swedes called him a great king. (*Ynglingasaga* in *Heimskringla*, Everyman's Library, 30)

Other evidence of political change may lie in the several hundred circular forts from this period. They may have served as centers of power from which royal aspirants attempted to assert control or as centers of local defense against those efforts. Also, place-name evidence points to considerable concentration of wealth in the hands of a regional dynasty in Uppland and a system of vassal supporters in neighboring areas. Finally, there is some evidence that the power of an emerging monarchy may have been based on control of the region's iron production and trade. Conflicting interpretations are possible, but it does seem likely that regional power centers were developing in Sweden and in neighboring Denmark and Norway. The leaders in this process were probably men similar to the *godi* of medieval Iceland—powerful local chieftains who built up networks of influence based on land and other sources of wealth acquired through skill, luck, and the judicious bestowing of gifts and favors. These men served political, legal, and religious functions in a highly complex systems with distinct local variations.

In Nordic art history this period is aptly called "the age of gold." Swedish and other Nordic artisans produced gold rings, bracelets, bracteates (medallions), clasps, horse harness decorations, and decorated weapons. Among the most spectacular pieces are the five-tiered neck collar from Färjestad on Öland, and the swords, shields, and harness plates from the graves at Vendel and Valsgärde. Most of the gold probably came to Sweden from Byzantium through trade. In Sweden it was melted down and employed by local craftsmen who mastered casting and gold leaf application techniques. They mixed Byzantine, Frankish, Celtic, and native impulses to produce a unique series of Migration Period art styles depicting geometric, animal, and human forms.

Another important creative medium was stone carving. In this genre, the most important and informative are some 400 picture stones from Gotland. They date from between 400 to 800 and changed in content and style over time. Stones from the fifth and sixth century often were shaped like ax blades, and the carving on them depicted circles, spirals, pairs of horses, rowed ships, armed men, and serpents. Examples from the eighth century were far more elaborate. They show remarkably detailed sailing ships, costumes, processions, battles, sacrifices, and Norse gods such as Odin. In the following centuries this tradition merged with the carving of runestones and continued on to about 1200.

THE VIKINGS

The Viking Age, the last of the Iron Age subperiods, holds a special place in the histories of all the Scandinavian countries. It was a time of affluence, energy, adventure, and achievements at home and across a world of surprisingly great breadth. It was also one of the moments in the past when Scandinavians stood out among their European neighbors; when what they did had impacts beyond their borders. Such times are relatively rare in any of the Nordic countries' histories. As a result, the Viking Age tends to be seen through highly nationalistic prisms that make bias, exaggeration, and romanticizing particularly common. It is, therefore, a time that must be approached with great care.

Remember, too, this is still prehistory. Archaeological sources remain central, and all the problems of interpretation continue to plague any student of the period. There are three groups of written sources from the period, and all of them present serious problems for historians. First, there are many sources from outside Sweden that contain mention of Swedes or Swedish Vikings. These usually had other primary purposes and often were very biased. Among these Archbishop Rimbert's *Life of St. Ansgar* is important for the descriptions it contains of Ansgar's missionary visits to Birka in 829 and 850. Then there are several particularly interesting works by Arab emissaries to places reached by the Vikings. One of these, Ibn

Fadlan, an ambassador of the Abbasid Caliphate centered in Bagdad, encountered Swedish Vikings at Bulgar, a trade center on the Volga, around 920. His accounts of their habits of washing themselves from a common bowl of water, the dress of women, a burial, and a funeral are particularly colorful and often quoted because they say so much about the Swedish vikings as real people.

> Each woman wears on either breast a box of iron, silver, copper, or gold; the value of the box indicates the wealth of the husband. Each box has a ring from which depends a knife. The women wear neck-rings of gold and silver. . . . Their most prized possessions are green glass beads. (Jones, *A History of the Vikings*, 164)

Even a Byzantine emperor, Constantine Porpyrhogenitus, provided an extended description of the Vikings who came to his capital from the Dnieper. Finally, *The Russian Primary Chronicle* (sometimes called *Nestor's Chronicle*), which dates from 1112, is often cited when dealing with the parts the Swedes played in the development of an early Russian state.

Second, there are the poems and sagas from Iceland. It is tempting to see them as accurately detailed histories. After all, some are about events and people from the Viking Age. Unfortunately, in the case of the sagas, purpose, audience, lack of responsibility to detail accuracy, the length of time they were passed on orally, and the biases of the people who wrote most of them down in the thirteenth century make them unreliable. This is not, however, to disregard them entirely. The sagas probably tell us a great deal about traditions, beliefs, practices, customs, and values in early medieval Iceland, and, by extension, Sweden.

Finally, there are the hundreds of Swedish runestones, most of which are located in the Lake Mälaren area. They are the only written sources native to Sweden and actually from the period. Although very limited in what they say, they also are probably the most reliable. Written in a sixteen character alphabet, these stones usually commemorated individuals and their deeds or dealt with land ownership and the like. Obviously, they could not be extensive. Their brief messages name people, places, and accomplishments, and they say much about the spirit and ideals of this time.

> Like men they traveled for gold
> And in the east they fed the eagle
> In the south they died, in Serkland
> (Gripsholm stone, *Cultural Atlas of the Viking World*, 101)

Inga has these runes carved for Ragnfast, her husband.
He alone inherited this village from his father.
God help his soul.
(*National Atlas of Sweden*, vol. 13, 106)

Although people from all the Nordic countries were involved in the activities of the Vikings, they followed different paths through the period
and have unique histories. For Denmark, Norway, and parts of western
and southern Sweden the story lies to the west and south, to the British
Isles, the western shores of the continent, the islands of the north Atlantic,
and on to Iceland, Greenland, and North America. Sweden's history lies
east and south, to the shores of the Baltic and the great rivers emptying into
that sea, to Russia, the Byzantine Empire, the Abbasid Caliphate, and beyond. It was in these regions that peoples from east-central Sweden, the
Åland Islands, and Gotland played roles in commerce, settlement, and
early political developments.

At the center of the eastern Swedish Vikings' activities were complex networks of trade. They were ideally situated on a great arc of commerce that
reached from Asia in the east to Greenland in the west. Swedish Vikings
were, first and foremost, merchants. Some operated from small harbors
along the east coast of the mainland and the shores of the islands. On
Gotland, for example, Viking commerce and production went on at many
locations such as Paviken on the west. This was a relatively small town
where iron was produced, a dry dock for boat repairs was located, and trade
was conducted. It was active between about 800 and 1000, and finds from
there include Arabic, Anglo-Saxon, and German coins, amber, Italian glass
fragments, flint, soapstone, and iron. There were several much larger trade
centers in Scandinavia, including Hedeby and Ribe in Denmark,
Kaupang/Skiringssal in Norway, and Birka in Sweden. Birka, which replaced Helgö around 800 (see above), was an ideally situated and well-forti-
fied town located on Björkö in Lake Mälaren. Water routes connected it with
the interior, Åland, Finland, the Gulf of Finland, Gotland, and the south Baltic. Excavations show it was a market and place of production for about two
hundred years. It also appears to have been a religious cult and administrative center for the emerging central Swedish state. On-going excavations
have revealed the harbor, artisan shops, fortifications, burial grounds, and,
recently, a large house for warriors. Among the artifacts discovered at the
site are Arabic silver coins, fine jewelry, weapons, beadwork, a writing sty-
lus, and exotic objects from Byzantium, central Europe, and the East.

Swedish Vikings were particularly active along trade routes in the Baltic
and the Gulf of Finland, and on the Oder, Vistula, Nemen, Western Dvina,

Neva, Volkhov, Volga, and Dnieper rivers. These connected them to an enormously rich and varied trading world. Swedes were part of the diverse populations at Baltic trade centers such as Rostock, Truso, and Wolin. They were present at Staraja Ladoga, a center for trade via either the Volga or Dnieper just south of Lake Ladoga. From there they could move up the Volkhov to a site they called Holmgård near Novgorod, then on down the Dnieper past Smolensk and Kiev to the Black Sea, and from there to Byzantium, which they called Miklagård, "the great city." Their other option took them east via the Volga to Bulgar, to Itil on the northwestern shores of the Caspian and to Gurgan to the south. This route linked the Vikings with the Silk Road to China and to the Islamic Middle East.

In this commercial system, the Swedes served as middlemen and provided products that had been staples of trade with the north for millennia; furs, hides, wax, honey, walrus ivory, and slaves. In exchange they sought silver, the most important precious metal of the Viking Age, and luxury items. The tens of thousands of coins, most of them from the Abbasid Caliphate, reveal the volume of this exchange. At home silver was used as a medium of exchange, and artisans melted it down and used it to decorate jewelry, weapons, and other material goods in the complex animal motif styles of the period.

In the context of their trading activities, Swedish Vikings were involved in many aspects of life in the areas they touched. Evidence of their presence is clear in grave fields and town site excavations at Staraja Ladoga, Novgorod, Gnezdovo/Smolensk, and Kiev. Many finds reinforce the importance of trade; while the large numbers of weapons found at some sites tell us that either the merchants were always armed or that there were separate contingents of warriors. There is also evidence of the presence of women, which leads to the conclusion that at least some of these Swedes were settlers, not transient traders.

A fascinating and much-debated aspect of the Vikings' history in the east is the role they played in founding the earliest Russian state. *The Russian Primary Chronicle* describes how around 862 various tribes south of Lake Ladoga joined together and invited three brothers, supposedly Vikings, to rule over them:

> Discord thus ensued among them, and they began to war one against another. They said to themselves, "Let us seek a prince who may rule over us, and judge us according to the law." They accordingly went overseas to the Varangian Rus: these particular Varangians were known as Rus, just as some are called Swedes, and others Normans, Angles, and Goths. . . . The Chuds, the Slavs, and the Krivichians then

said to the people of Rus, "Our whole land is great and rich, but there is no order in it. Come to rule and reign over us." They thus selected three brothers, with their kinfolk, who took with them all the Rus, and migrated. The oldest, Rurik, located himself in Novgorod; the second, Sineus, in Beloozero; and the third, Truvor, in Ozborsk. On account of these Varangians, the district of Novgorod became known as Russian (Rus) land. (Jones, 245–46)

The chronicle goes on to say that Rurik came to rule all three centers after his brothers died, and his successor, Oleg, seized Kiev and established it as the new state's center. The discussions over the truth of this account are endless, and for Russians and Swedes alike they are unavoidably tied to national identity, pride, and the uses of history.

What can we say about this issue with any certainty? *Varangian* was a term used to identify Norse peoples, Vikings, and probably comes from the Old Norse *Váraring*, meaning men bound together by oath. The imperial guard in Byzantium was called the Varangian Guard. *Rus* has several possible meanings, one of them is "Swedes." In this debate, proponents of the Swedes' importance argue that *Rus* derives from the Finnish word for Swedes, *ruotsi*, which in turn comes from the east Uppland area called *Roslagen*. There is virtually nothing in other written sources to tell us who Rurik was. The archaeological evidence demonstrates a Norse presence in many locations in Russia, but in every instance it was limited in both scale and duration. The building of all medieval states was a long and complex process involving many actors. In the case of Russia various Slavic tribes, Scandinavians, Byzantines, and Islams played parts. If Swedes did help to found an early Russia state, they were very few in number and thoroughly assimilated within a few generations.

Important political developments occurred at home during the Viking Age, and by its close three medieval monarchies were emerging in Scandinavia—Denmark, Norway, and Sweden. Exactly when and how each came into being are matters of debate, and one must realize that this was only a very early stage in a complicated and lengthy process. One danger is reading the present back into the past. Having existed for a millennium, it is reasonable to think that Sweden has always been or that its borders are natural and inevitable. There have, however, been a number of Swedens, and there were certainly many ways in which the Scandinavian region might have been organized. In this early period there were many obstacles to creating a centralized monarchy. Sweden was a land divided into a number of autonomous political areas corresponding with some of its historic provinces. Dense forests separated regions. There were few roads. The easiest way to get around was by water, and coastal areas were far better connected than the interior, where travel was easiest during the winter, when lakes and rivers froze and became highways through the sparsely settled and difficult landscape. Also, the parallel development of monarchies in Denmark and Norway overlapped. Aspiring neighboring kings thought in terms of a Denmark or a Norway that included parts of Sweden. Finally, great men and commoners alike saw few reasons to support monarchy.

The core of the earliest Swedish state developed around Lake Mälaren, an area dominated by the Svear. (The Swedish *Sverige* means "land of the Svear.") In addition to being a prosperous farming region, it contained a pagan religious center at Old Uppsala, and the thriving towns of Birka (until about 975) and thereafter Sigtuna. Slowly other regions were added, including the lands controlled by the Gauts or Götar to the west. As we have seen, some believe this happened as early as the seventh century; others opt for the early eleventh century under a ruler named Olof Eriksson Skötkonung (the Attentive) (c. 995–1020). Others say there was no Sweden before the late twelfth century—or even later.

Regardless of exactly when this happened, the first Sweden probably came to be to serve the selfish interests in wealth and power of a dynastic family and its supporters. The royal hold on power was tenuous at best. The kings of this state were little more than traditional tribal chieftains attempting to extend their influence and often lacking both the means and the support to do so. Some have called them "pirate sea kings," whose sway over their people was enforced solely by armed (naval) strength. This label tells us something about the very limited nature of their authority. Almost nowhere in Europe was monarchy established peacefully or very firmly, and Sweden was no exception. Civil war was a common feature of this age. Great men opposed monarchy because of the threats it posed to their own power; peasants feared the burdens the state would impose in taxes and service.

The earliest Sweden was actually a federation, not a unitary state. Succession was usually hereditary, but each new king had to be recognized in a series of steps that began at the center of the kingdom and spread out to the periphery. This was ritualized in what was called the *Eriksgata*. A new king was first accepted and crowned at the Mora meadow in Uppland and then traveled through Södermanland, Östergötland, northern Småland, Västergötland, Närke, and Västmanland, stopping at traditional centers of power, where he was recognized by local assemblies and he promised to honor the rights and laws in each. This practice was more than mere ceremony, and room was left for dissension and even the rejection of a candidate. Not until the 1540s did Sweden became a hereditary monarchy, and the *Eriksgata* was carried out at least symbolically through the Early Modern Period. For example, Gustav III made such a tour in 1772.

Sweden remained a rural, agriculture-centered peasant society for nearly 6,000 years. From the Neolithic Age on most people lived in tiny worlds defined by their farm or village. Few engaged in crafts or trade. Few ever traveled very far beyond their homes. This does not mean, however, that this society was stagnant. During the Iron Age there were two very dynamic periods, 500 B.C.–A.D. 400 and then after A.D. 700, when population grew, land under cultivation expanded, village organization in much of the country was refined, and new agricultural techniques and implements were adopted. Villages were at the core of most of Sweden's farming. As in earlier times, they occupied relatively fixed land areas, although actual building sites might be moved small distances every few generations. They were based on extended family or clan units. There were exceptions to the village pattern, especially on Gotland, where there were about a thousand individual farms. Over long periods of time clusters of villages or farms de-

Map 2. *Eriksgata.*

veloped as larger ethnic enclaves or chiefdoms. Over hundreds of years these grew into the *landskap* (provinces) mentioned earlier.

Until late in the period complex land- use systems based on small rectangular fields and separated by hedgerows or walls that developed over time to form patchwork patterns were the norm. Field shape was determined in part by the simple plow (ard) used at the time, which cut a small, shallow furrow, and fields were often tilled in two directions. During the Viking Age the iron plow became more common. Because it was difficult to turn, plowing was done in a single direction for as long a distance as possible, and fields became long, narrow strips. Oats, barley, rye, wheat, peas, beans, and cabbage were the primary crops, and yields were pitifully low. Goats, sheep, cattle, horses, and some poultry, all much smaller than today's animals, were the primary livestock.

Houses remained the same for centuries. Most buildings continued to be based on post and beam frameworks, and walls were made of easily available local materials. The interiors of the typical elongated, rectangular houses were divided into specific function areas. Toward the end of the Viking Age greater regional variations developed using log or board building techniques.

The most common clothing material was wool. Style and color reflected social status. Most people wore garments made of natural shaded yarns. A typical male costume included long stockings, short pants, and a tunic; most women wore a simple, straight, full-length dress covered by an equally long apron. Fashion was the domain of the rich, and a few of the wealthy dressed in bright blue, purple, red, and yellow garments.

Seemingly endless agricultural work filled the lives of most people. For men this included plowing, planting, weeding, harvesting and storing crops, slaughtering, hunting, fishing, cutting wood, building and repairing, fencing, and a host of other farm tasks. Women were, first and foremost, responsible for the day-to-day management of the household. This meant food preparation, childcare, cleaning, washing, spinning, weaving, making all of the family's clothing, tending to the small animals, milking, making butter and cheese, and lighter farm tasks. Today we can hardly imagine the time all these tasks consumed.

Slowly increasing social complexity is a trend of the prehistory periods and was certainly true of the Iron Age. One story from Norse mythology, the *Rigsthula*, explained the presence of three groups, jarls, karls, and thralls (great men, farmers, and slaves). But this is far too simple a picture of Viking society. Of course, there was a class of great men, but that group was not uniform. Power and wealth varied widely. The same was true for the free farmers; even slaves' positions varied in the degrees to which they were bound to a master. In addition, the story says nothing about the artisans who became increasingly important and more and more numerous during the period. Iron makers, blacksmiths, silversmiths, glass makers, leather workers, comb makers, potters, coopers, wheelwrights, boat builders, and runestone carvers are just a few of the skilled trades that developed.

The 12,000-year prehistory of the region set the stage for Sweden's 1,000-year history. Patterns of human settlement were laid down that still exist. The core agricultural economy that evolved went basically unchanged in terms of practices and landholding patterns until the late eighteenth century. The importance of iron, crafts, and commerce was firmly established. Towns, markets, and religious sites developed that continued as such in the centuries that follow. Three groups in the early society—great men, farmers, and town dwellers—remained central in Swedish society until the nineteenth century. The fundamental local and regional divisions of the country were set. Oral traditions in law and custom were established. The outlines of the first state were laid down.

3

Creating Sweden, 1000–1800: The Medieval and Early Modern Eras

It is important to note the title of this chapter, "Creating Sweden." The nations of the world are all "imagined communities." They are the creations of individuals and groups, and their histories could have taken any number of paths. Most of the states of contemporary Europe are the result of a course set in the Middle Ages and the Early Modern Period. Among the organizational options available at the outset of this timeframe were a church-led empire encompassing all of western and northern Europe, a secular empire following the Roman or the Charlemagne model, an economic empire linked together by an association of trading towns such as the Hanseatic League, tribal or highly localized decentralization, or geopolitical regions based on weak kings, strong kings, the rule of great men, or some other political option. A betting person around 1300, or even as late as 1500 in Scandinavia, would probably not have placed money on the strong-monarchy dynastic states that evolved into the modern European nation-states of the nineteenth century—or on the idea that eventually the whole world would be divided along "national" lines.

In the case of Sweden, the outcome of this state-building process was certainly not always clear. History could have given us a very large Denmark or a Norway that included Sweden, a much larger Sweden that included all of its Nordic neighbors and more, a German northern Europe, a

Polish northern Europe, or a Russian northern Europe. Among the central political themes in this long process of development are the consolidation and centralization of the power of the monarchy, the emergence of a parliament with changing amounts of influence, the growth of an administrative system with its center in Stockholm, the creation of reasonably efficient financial systems for the state, and the centralization and standardization of law and legal procedures. In the same period Sweden went from being one of the several relatively weak states surrounding the Baltic to a major power in the region and then back to relative weakness packaged in a history of what seems to have been almost constant war. Also during this period the country's economy moved ever so slowly from its primarily agricultural character to a more diverse one with important internal raw material, production, and trade elements. A small group of towns became larger and more important places in the complex merchant economy of the country. Reflecting the political and economic developments was the evolution of a hierarchical society based on four "estates" or large social groups: the clergy, nobles, burghers, and farmers. Finally, Sweden joined Europe—the latter being a concept that did not really come to the fore until about 1500. Its people were slowly converted to Christianity in a process that began around 1000, and they subsequently became Lutheran during the Protestant Reformation of the sixteenth century. In terms of high culture, at least, the country adopted predominantly European cultural norms in thought, art, architecture, fashion, tastes, and the like.

A few words of caution, however. Sweden was throughout this very long period a very backward place by the standards of the twenty-first century. Although a few individuals enjoyed wealth and power, most people were unimaginably poor. Life expectancies averaged less than forty years. Disease, filth, malnutrition, war, violence, and endless work consumed them. The common people had little voice in the affairs of state and were exploited for their labor, for their tax potential, and as cannon fodder. Although highly important and valued in the domestic economies of rural and urban folk alike and as a vital commodity in the marriage practices of the time, women were considered inferior, were used and abused, and seem rarely to have had very much direct influence in the affairs of the elites.

BECOMING CHRISTIAN

The religious history of Sweden throughout this period has at least three key elements: conversion, reformation, and the survival of folk beliefs. The victory of Christianity and the Church of Rome over the polytheism of the Viking Age was a very drawn-out process. One author has called

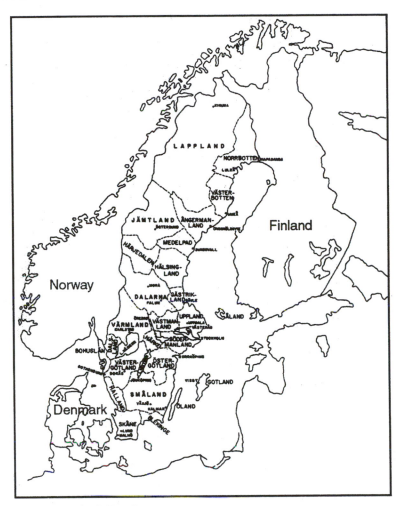

Map 3. Sweden's Provinces.

this the "300 Years' War" with some justification. The change of faith came as the result of Frankish, German, English, and Orthodox Church missionary activities as well as through the influence of Swedes converted abroad and by the decisions of political leaders. The earliest conversion efforts are symbolized by the largely unsuccessful work of (Saint) Ansgar, who was sent to the north by Louis the Pious and the bishop of Rheims. He visited the political center and Viking Age trade town of Birka twice, first around 825 and then again thirty years later. His work had little lasting impact, as the old pagan ways were firmly established and tenaciously adhered to. Real progress was made during the eleventh century, largely by German and English missionaries such as Osmund, Sigfrid, and Eskil. Many of the kings of the country were at least nominally Christian, starting with Olof Skötkonung around 1000, but they remained unsuccessful in efforts to force conversion. Total elimination of pagan beliefs was never fully accomplished. As elsewhere in Europe, the Church incorporated many of these old ideas and ways into its practices and calender. Even formerly sacred sites were annexed and churches built on them. The clearest measures of the Church's success came with the founding of the archbishopric in Uppsala in 1164 and the building of a system of bishoprics based on Linköping, Skara, Strängnäs, Västerås, Växjö, and Åbo and parishes in the twelfth and thirteenth centuries.

The conversion had great and far-reaching effects. Wood and stone churches replaced sacred groves and, perhaps, the ancient temple at Uppsala. Some of these buildings reflected traditional building techniques in wood, but many copied the Romanesque and then Gothic styles of the continent. The cathedral churches, such as that at Uppsala, rose as monuments to the development of medieval Christianity. Similar developments in art came, also. Images of the Trinity and the saints in wood, stone, and stained glass replaced those of Odin, Thor, Frey, and Freyja. Monasticism came first to the far south of the Sweden, with the establishing of Benedictine and Augustinian houses in the eleventh century. The Cistercians established a monastery at Alvastra in 1143. They were followed in the next century by the Franciscans or "grey friars" and the Dominicans or "black friars," which were primarily urban orders. Monasticism was important in the intellectual and educational life of the country, and the orders were providers of refuge, care, and protection. Women took part in this movement, and this is reflected in the founding of an order by (Saint) Birgitta Birgersdotter at Vadstena around 1370. Christianity brought the first books to Sweden, and the world became a much larger place for a few Swedes as a result of the knowledge they contained. New words from all the missionary churches involved in the conversion entered the language, and Swedish gradually developed a written form. The Church also gave birth to education in a formal sense. The monasteries were centers of learning, schools were established in the bishop towns, and a university was founded in Uppsala in 1477.

As an institution the Church acquired great power, influence, and resources. The leaders, and especially the archbishop, were important figures in state affairs. Until the early 16th century they advised, made, and unmade kings. Through donations of property, the Church became the owner of as much as a fifth of the land in the country.

MEDIEVAL POLITICS

The development of the Swedish state in the Middle Ages appears to have flowed seamlessly from the Viking Age and was closely tied to the conversion to Christianity. The one often served the other. The state offered protection, and in return its leaders demanded conversion; the Church offered support, sanction, rationale, a hierarchical model of organization, and a body of articulate and often literate spokespersons and supporters.

In constitutional terms Sweden's medieval monarchy was limited and elective. Kings were chosen by the powerful men of the country and secured recognition through the traditional *Eriksgata*, which means "king's way" or "king's path," for the *Eriksgata* followed a route from Uppsala to important centers in the provinces that made up medieval Sweden, including Strängnäs, Nyköping, Linköping, Jönköping, Skara, Örebro, and Västerås. The kings' positions were only as secure as their personalities, private resources, and supporters made them. Challenges to their authority and persons abounded. Few died natural deaths. Civil war involving multiple claimants to the throne, family squabbles, dissident great men, and foreign interference was endemic. Two families alternated in power between about 1150 and 1250. Temporary order was achieved by Birger Jarl. Through a complicated web of marriages and diplomacy, this remarkable person founded the Folkung dynasty, a line that ran from around 1240 to 1387. One dark and tangled story illustrates the unrest of these times. In the early 1300s the nominal king was Birger Magnusson, who had two brothers, Erik and Valdemar. In a move intended to prevent competition, Erik was made duke of Sweden and Valdemar duke of Finland. This quickly led to trouble. The brothers turned on Birger in revolt. He was captured and imprisoned for a time. Birger then plotted revenge. In a truly Byzantine move he invited his brothers to a banquet of reconciliation at the fortress in Nyköping in December 1317, fed them well, and then tossed them in the dungeon. The brothers' supporters laid siege to the fortress, and Birger, according to legend, threw the dungeon key into the moat. By the time the siege ended the brothers had starved to death.

In the context of this apparent chaos, a group of important governmental structures did develop. One was the emergence of the so-called great officers: the steward, chancellor, treasurer, marshal, and admiral. They often formed the core of an administration and were usually the men closest to the crown. A second was the council of state. From the early thirteenth century it developed as a body with important administrative and advisory powers. To us it might look a bit like a parliament, cabinet, and high court rolled into one body. It was composed of the highest lay and church officials, including the archbishop and bishops and the so-called law men of the provinces. It could have as many as forty members, but around a dozen was more common. Its functions and powers varied. At times it did little more than advise the king. At other times it might govern in the absence of the king or act as regent in the event of a minority. It also developed the accession charters, accepted by every monarch at the beginning of a reign, that served as important guarantors of the constitutional rights of the people. In this context the council was an important guarantor of a particular constitutional view that favored a decentralized monarchy in which power was shared by the crown and the great men. An important aspect of the growth of political institutions was the trend toward greater concentration of government activity in Stockholm, where the crown maintained Three Crown's Castle, built around 1250 on the site of an older fort guarding the entrance to Lake Mälaren. This seat of power and symbol of government was added to and remodeled over the next four centuries, until it was destroyed by fire in 1697. (The current Royal Palace is located on the same site.)

Two other important institutions were the *Herredag* and the *Riksdag*. They represented the area's long history of representative assemblies transferred to the national level. The former was an assembly of great men usually called by a king to deal with issues of war, taxation, or succession. The latter became Sweden's national parliament. Its roots lie in the fifteenth century, and the first meeting of this assembly is usually said to have occurred at Arboga in 1435. In structure the *Riksdag* evolved in a unique direction. Medieval European society was divided not into classes but into four so-called estates based on birth, wealth, and function: clergy, nobility, burghers, and landowning farmers; and there were, of course, other groups that did not fit into these, such as landless rural workers or urban laborers. Some medieval parliaments represented only one or two of these, but in Sweden all four estates gradually came to be included. The Estate of the Clergy included the archbishop, the country's bishops, and elected representatives of the parish clergy. In the seventeenth century this might mean a body of about sixty or seventy. Each noble family in Sweden was entitled to send a representative to the Estate of the Nobles. In 1540 this meant fewer than one hundred, the number had doubled by 1640 and rose to 550 by the end of the century. Obviously, this made for a potentially unruly assembly, but rarely did all those eligible attend. The Estate of the Burghers represented the elites of the country's towns, especially Stockholm, and usually included about seventy-five delegates. The Farmers' Estate was made up of elected representatives and numbered between 150 and 200. Stockholm increasingly became the usual site of meetings, but the parliament could and often did gather elsewhere, such as at Västerås in 1527,

Söderköping in 1595, Linköping in 1600, or Gävle in 1792. The four estate structure lasted until 1866.

The powers or prerogatives of this body were not clearly defined. For much of the period it was mostly a ratifier of royal decisions, not an initiator of policies or programs or a center of opposition to the crown. Its greatest utility was as an institution where opinion could be formed or as a forum for royal rhetoric. Still, it was important. The parliament helped to make Gustav I king, to carry through the Reformation, and to support the development of the empire. Its greatest power gradually became that over taxation. No new taxes could be imposed without its approval, and this compelled monarchs to consider actions and to justify them convincingly. It also gave the parliament important influence in the shaping of foreign policy and decisions of war.

In the countryside the state was represented during the Early Modern Period by the governors of the royal castles established at key locations across the country to secure the kingdom and stand as symbols of authority. In the sixteenth century there were three of these in Finland (Åbo, Viborg, and Olofsborg) and thirteen in Sweden (including those at Uppsala, Stockholm, Kalmar, and Älvsborg). At the local level the sheriffs and (following the Reformation) the clergy were the primary representatives of central authority and the idea of a national state.

The growth of the state also precipitated a change in the nature of society. For centuries Sweden and its neighbors had a social system based on two groups, the free and the unfree. Within the first of these especially there were great differences. An elite among the free, landowning group certainly existed, their positions based on land, material wealth, and carefully cultivated influence networks. The Conversion brought one new group, the clergy. The development of the monarchy, along with the changes in the nature of warfare, helped to create a second, an untitled nobility exempted from taxation in return for (military) service to the crown. This took place in the late thirteenth century.

In many ways this early Sweden was a very loose and often weak thing. The provinces or *landskap* continued to act autonomously in some ways, particularly concerning law, and the provincial assemblies (*tings*) continued to meet. For much of the medieval period, most law was oral and kept by the so-called lawmen, who carried the local codes around in their memories. It was made and modified through the hearing of cases. Written provincial codes generally date from the early 1300s, and it was not until the middle of that century that a relatively uniform national law code, for some aspects of the law, was developed. This came during the reign of Magnus Eriksson. Although tinkered with and revised, it served until a new uniform code was written in the 1720s. Towns and farming villages had their own laws, and for most people the state was an abstract, distant thing that had relatively little influence in their day-to-day lives unless the tax collector happened by.

The relative order in the state developed during the late thirteenth and early fourteenth century dissolved shortly after 1350. What happened over the next fifty years or so aptly reflects the potential chaos that lay just beneath the surface of virtually all medieval states. Magnus Eriksson represented a particular line of monarchy's development. He wanted to be king, to rule. He did not want to share power with either secular or church lords. His efforts to curb the powers of both led to opposition. The great men attacked him for his politics; the Church attacked him for his morals. Magnus´s own son, Erik, led a rebellion against him in 1356 that quickly escalated and became vastly complicated. Erik's death three years later forced the rebellious nobles to turn to the king's nephew, Albrekt of Mecklenburg, whom they believed would be pliable and submissive to their authority. They were wrong. Albrekt brought many of his supporters with him when he came to Sweden, and in a few short years a new civil war was raging. To make matters worse, these events took place in a very complex and troubled context. The bubonic plague or Black Death, as it was called in much of Europe, reached Sweden in 1349 and claimed as many as one-third of the people. The German merchants of the Hanseatic League controlled the international trade economy of the country and dominated the crafts and government of the major towns, including Stockholm. Denmark was in the midst of a resurgence of power and influence in the north under Valdemar IV Atterdag (1340–1375). He took advantage of the events in Sweden to launch a successful campaign to recover the historically Danish territories of Skåne, Halland, and Blekinge, lost to Sweden in the 1320s, and to acquire Gotland with its thriving trade center at Visby. The civil war continued on and off for three decades and merged with the development of a union or federation of the Nordic states.

Sweden and the rest of Scandinavia stood at a crossroad in the late fourteenth century. Was the region to become German—either through the political machinations of Mecklenburgs or the growing influence of the Lübeck and other German trade cities organized in the Hanseatic League? Were the medieval states in danger of being destroyed by squabbling over the rights of succession or of the great men for a share in power? An extraordinary person, Margrethe, daughter of Valdemar of Denmark and wife of Haakon VI (r. 1355–1380) of Norway, played a leading role in answering these questions and establishing a new period of stability. First, she secured the election of her son, Olov, as heir in Denmark and Norway. Then, following Olov´s unexpected death in 1387, she won the recognition of herself as queen in all but name and of her nephew, Erik of Pomerania, as heir in all three kingdoms. This was affirmed at Kalmar on the southeast Swedish coast, in June and July 1397, when leading men from all three states (but mainly from Denmark and Sweden) met, discussed, and produced two documents, known as the Coronation Letter and the Union Letter. These quite different sources were the written bases for what historians have come to call the Kalmar Union—it apparently had no name then. The deal struck was not to be the basis for a single state with a strong monarchy, although these ideas may have been in Margrethe's mind—and certainly were in the minds of several of her successors. Clearly the great men saw this as a step into a confederation, in which each of the kingdoms was to retain is own laws and its own governing elites. Unity was to exist in terms of foreign policy, security, and a shared monarch.

Many modern accounts of the history of the Kalmar Union have emphasized the confederation view because of the way events turned out and because of the role modern nationalism has played in shaping our views of the past. In 1397, however, no one could have predicted how the history of the union was to play out, much less that an independent Sweden would emerge from the conflicts that grew within that union.

The history of the Kalmar Union is, in many ways, the history of the conflict between the ideas of unity versus confederation. For fifteen years the idea of a unitary state prevailed under Margrethe and was carried on by her protégé, Erik. Erik, however, was far less able, and he soon found himself in very serious trouble. In the mid-1420s he imposed a tariff on all cargoes sailing into and out of the Baltic. These were called the "Sound Tolls," and they triggered a war with the Hanseatic League. This war had serious impacts on trade and taxation. In addition, Erik also went to war with Holstein, and his appointment of Germans and Danes in places of power in Sweden gave rise to a rebellion there in the 1430s. This was led by one of the heroes of Sweden's nationalist version of history, Engelbrekt Engelbrektsson, a wealthy landowner from Dalarna. It was not, however, so much a nationalists' revolt as one by powerful men who felt their interests threatened and by commoners burdened by taxes and economic problems. For the next ninety years a series of (civil) wars were fought over these and other issues. At times Sweden actually dropped out of the union; at other points the country was either forced or persuaded to rejoin by promises of autonomy.

EARLY MODERN POLITICS: 1500–1800

In the traditional chronology of European history, the year 1500 is the point at which the medieval ends and the early modern begins. Of course, this break and its accompanying labels are entirely artificial. Certainly no one in 1500 knew they had entered a new age, and there are many more aspects of Swedish history at this point that are old and linked to a distant past than there are new elements. Nonetheless, the chronology is useful for organizing what would otherwise be shapeless and chaotic.

Overall, government became larger and more pervasive during the Early Modern Period, 1500–1800. This may be seen in the growing number of administrators to deal with fiscal, tax, commercial, military, and diplomatic affairs, as well as in reforms and programs designed to bring the central government more and more into the lives of ordinary people and to extract resources for the "good" of the state. Whereas medieval government had been decentralized, amateur, often even mobile, and distant, early modern government was centralized, professional, fixed, and intrusive.

Rulers of the Early Modern

Gustav I Vasa	1523–1560
Erik XIV	1560–1568
Johan III	1568–1592
Sigismund I	1592–1599
Karl IX	1599/1607–11
Gustav II Adolf	1611–1632
Kristina	1632–1654
Regency	1632–1644
Karl X	1654–1660
Karl XI	1660–1697
Regency	1660–1672
Karl XII	1697–1718
Ulrika Eleonora	1719–1720
Fredrik I	1720–1751
Adolf Fredrik I	1751–1771
Gustav III	1771–1792
Gustav IV	1792–1809

The Kalmar Union ended so far as Sweden was concerned as a result of the last of the civil wars. This new round in the fighting was caused by the violent tactics of Kristian II, a mentally unbalanced and highly suggestible young man who succeeded to the throne in Denmark and Norway in 1513 and proceeded to reassert his control in Sweden. Kristian's mercenary forces successfully crushed a renewed rebellion in Sweden, and he was crowned king in Stockholm in the fall of 1520. Intent on silencing opposition and listening to the advice of Sweden's archbishop, Gustav Trolle, in November 1520 he had over eighty leading men executed in what has come to be known as The Stockholm Bloodbath. As part of this macabre show of power he even had the remains of the leader of the rebellion, Sten Sture the Younger, exhumed and burned. His return to Denmark through Sweden left a trail of blood. These actions unleashed a new revolt, this one led by Gustav Eriksson Vasa, a son of one of Kristian's victims. He managed to rally the support of commoners and great men, and he bought the support of the Hanseatic League in a campaign that drove the Danes from the country. In the process Gustav was first elected Protector of the Realm and then, on 6 June 1523, king. Although not a foregone conclusion at the time, especially for the Danes, this was the end of the union and the beginning of an unbroken history of state development that reaches to the present.

The history of the Swedish state for much of the next three centuries forms a coherent unit defined by the growth of state power, the centralization of government in Stockholm, and the continuation of the conflict between monarchy and the nobility for power. In this context the Swedish parliament, a body with generally growing importance and also a potential brake on both monarchy and aristocracy, was also a factor. Another theme was the building and then the loss of an empire, chiefly in the Baltic, but with short-lived pieces in West Africa and North America.

At the beginning of this period, two important processes again temporarily merged in Sweden's history: the political development of the state and the religion of the state. Martin Luther had begun the Protestant Reformation in Germany in 1517 when he posted his criticisms of Church practices for debate in Wittenberg. The religious ideas and the political implications of this movement reached Sweden quickly, carried there by German merchants and Swedish students. Reform-minded preachers were soon active in several of the country's larger towns; and although there was little popular discontent with the Catholic Church, they managed to establish a following. For example, Olaus Petri, one of the leading figures in the early stages of the Swedish Reformation, secured a following first in Strängnäs and then in Stockholm. Perhaps more important to the success of the new theology was Gustav I's interest in the wealth of the Church and in the role a church under the control of the crown and not the papacy could play in state affairs. Gustav was certainly aware of the potential gains to be made, and he tolerated the reformers' preaching. In 1527 he severed ties with Rome and confiscated the properties of the Church with the approval of the parliament. He replaced the Church of Rome with the Church of Sweden, asserted state control of the clergy, and used Church assets to stabilize state finances.

Gustav did not, however, firmly establish the Lutheran faith in Sweden. That happened by fits and starts over nearly eighty years. Lutheranism took hold slowly under Gustav and his eldest son, Erik XIV. A turn back toward Catholicism followed under John III and his Polish Catholic Queen, Katarina Jagellonica, and then with their son, Sigismund I. Threatened by the restoration of the Catholic faith and control from Poland (where Sigismund was also king), the Swedish clergy formally affirmed Lutheranism as the state's faith in 1593.

Gustav I has often been portrayed as the father of a modern Sweden, especially in the national romantic versions of the past written in the nineteenth century. This view is not without justification. From a certain perspective he was very successful. Gustav was presented with a unique opportunity to shape Swedish political life. Many of the most powerful members of the nobility were eliminated in Kristian II´s purges, and the development of gunpowder weapons significantly reduced the military independence of the nobility at large by making the tools of warfare too expensive for most of them. Gustav acquired important financial resources through the Reformation, and he was able to rally popular support at crucial moments. In addition, Gustav was personally very able, hardworking, and fortuitously long-lived. During his nearly forty years as king, he concentrated more and more of the machinery of state in the growing capital of Stockholm. He called in experts, including Georg Norman and Conrad von Pyhy, who were both Germans, and he placed men who supported him in positions of power across the country. He also personally meddled in the lives of farmers, miners, and merchants to improve the economy.

There is darker side to this history, however. Gustav was a suspicious, short-tempered, and violent person. He used intimidation as well as convincing rhetoric. Armed troops and loaded canon were often present at meetings of the parliament to encourage outcomes in the king's favor. He condemned a loyal advisor and ally, Olaus Petri, to death for daring to disagree with him. (The sentence was not carried out.) His reign was marred by a series of popular uprisings, including ones in Dalarna in 1527 and 1530 (the latter is called the Bell Revolt because it came in response to the king's demand for parish church bells to be melted down for canon), and the Nils Dacke Revolt in Småland in 1542. All were bloody and cruelly put down.

The half-century following Gustav I's death in 1560 was marred by internal disorder and costly foreign adventures. Gustav's eldest son, Erik XIV, was mentally unbalanced and adventuresome. He quickly alienated many of his nobles, squandered the treasury's surplus, and became involved in war with Denmark. His half-brother, John III, was more able but no more successful. His son, Sigismund, created a political crisis because of his ties to Poland, where he ruled as Sigismund III. The last of Gustav I's sons, Karl IX, orchestrated a rebellion in the late 1590s, seized the throne, and executed his opponents. His sudden death in 1611 brought on a succession and a constitutional crisis.

At this troubled moment in Sweden's history, two extraordinary men stepped onto the stage: Gustav II Adolf (Gustavus Adolphus) and Axel Oxenstierna. The former was just short of seventeen; intelligent and well educated, but with a questionable claim to the throne. The latter was a twenty-eight-year-old nobleman of extraordinary drive and talent. Together they contributed to one of the most remarkable chapters in Sweden's history. Politically, they established the legitimacy of Gustav II's claim to the throne, made peace with the nobility and then built a system in which crown and nobility worked togther, rationalized the organization of administrative power in a set of colleges or departments (chancery, treasury, justice, admiralty, and army) built around the council, redefined the system of provincial government, clarified judicial procedures and established a supreme court, and fostered the development of the parliament. Many of these steps were defined in a series of fundamental constitutional documents, including the Accession Charter of 1611, the Parliament Act of 1617, and the Form of Government Act of 1634.

Following Gustav II's death in 1632, the constitutional balance between the crown and the nobility broke down and tilted in the direction of the nobles for the next half-century. This trend was encouraged first by the fact that the king's successor, Kristina, was a minor. A regency, headed by Axel Oxenstierna, governed until 1644. Kristina's own record is difficult to assess. A very complex person who continues to fascinate and frustrate historians, she toyed with her nobles, hated the tedium of governing, and ultimately rejected both her Lutheran faith and Sweden. She abdicated and left the country in 1654. It is clear, however, that she favored the nobles with both crown lands and influence. Karl X , her cousin and successor, might have changed the balance, but his almost constant absence from the country worked to the nobles' benefit, and the regency interlude following his unexpected death in 1660 only worked to enhance their hold on power. The handful of very powerful nobles who controlled events abused their privileged position and alienated the young king, Karl XI, and much of the populace. In the late 1770s, with the support of the parliament, he turned on the nobility, and especially the old upper elite, depriving them of many of their lands and offices. In the process he carried through a kind of revolution. The parliament literally voted itself out of power, the council became purely advisory, and government became personal—to be conducted by the king without obligation to seek advice or heed any advice he received. Sweden thus joined France and neighboring Denmark as an "absolutist" state.

Under Karl XI absolutism worked well. The king proved surprisingly able at dealing with the tiresome business of running the state. He avoided war, encouraged economic development at home, and systematized paying for Sweden's army through the allotment of small plots of land to be worked by soldiers during peacetime, thereby minimizing cash expenses. His son, Karl XII, was less successful and discredited the system. By spending almost his entire reign (1697–1718) at war and absent from the country. He tried to govern by mail, and the country suffered horribly as a result. Absolutism ended with his death in 1718.

At no time during the Early Modern Period was Sweden's parliament more important than in the fifty-three years following the death of Karl XII. The period is called the Era of Liberty (*Frihetstiden*). It began, not as an experiment in rule by a representative assembly, but as an effort by the nobility to restore their previous place in the political life of the country and to prevent the abuses of absolutism they believed had occurred under Karl XII, who was seen as an obsessive and arbitrary monarch. For about forty years Sweden was a kind of aristocracy, led at times by an elite actually interested in governing well and quite able to do so. At the same time, however, there were plenty of others who were vain seekers of power and pleasure. One very able person dominated the political scene until 1738, Count Arvid Horn. He pursued policies of peace and restoration that helped the country to recover after two decades of war.

Toward the end of the 1730s, an unplanned and unexpected development occurred: Two opposing political factions emerged. These were called the Hats and the Caps, and over next three decades they came to resemble modern political parties in many ways. For example, in the capital they established social clubs where followers could gather to discuss policies, conducted election campaigns to secure majorities in the parliament, organized their members' actions in parliament, and founded newspapers to spread their views. The Hats orchestrated a peaceful seizure of power in 1738 that involved their gaining control of the council and the Estate of the Nobles. This group remained in power for almost thirty years and pursued aggressive foreign policies, encouraged economic development through subsidies and innovation, and minimized the importance of the crown. They were kept in power by their own efforts, the ineffectiveness of the opposition, and foreign meddling by the British, French, and Russians. The two monarchs during these decades, Fredrik I and Adolf Fredrik I, had either little interest in or capacity for governing. A low-point in royal importance was reached in the mid-1750s when, following the revelation of a plot to overthrow the system, government leaders created a bronze stamp of the king's signature to be brought out whenever Adolf Fredrik refused to sign measures approved by the parliament. In 1765 a new phase in the period's history began. A new generation of Caps captured a majority in the Estate of the Nobles, were supported by like-minded groups in the Burgher and Farmer Estates, and secured control of the key parliamentary committees and the council. These men had some truly revolutionary ideas. They were influenced by the ideals of the Enlightenment and believed the world could be made a better place by direct human action. They advocated laissez-faire economic principles, free speech, practical education, and the end of the special privileges of the nobility such as exclusion from taxation and a monopoly on government jobs and officer appointments. Between 1765 and 1771 a seesaw struggle between the factions ensued. Then, following another Cap victory that seemed to threaten the very foundations of historic Sweden, including the estate system of social organization, the monarchy, and the Lutheran faith, the new king, Gustav III, acted. In August 1772 he carried through a peaceful coup. The Era of Liberty ended quietly, without fanfare or disorder. Sweden was not ready for popular sovereignty, the end of the Old Regime, or the rule of the general will—and wouldn't be for another century or more.

Although the parliament remained, a new set of fundamental documents limited its powers, and it met infrequently. Gustav III, who belongs to a group of eighteenth century rulers historians call "Enlightened Absolutists" because of their apparent fondness for the cultural and intellectual ideas of the period and their attachment to the principles of strong monarchy, behaved increasingly arbitrarily. He would reform Sweden. By the end of the 1780s he had thoroughly alienated much of the nobility through his open neglect and mistrust of them. This rejection of the nobles was given form in the Act of Union and Security, a document Gustav pushed through a meeting of the parliament in early 1789. Under its terms the nobles were stripped of their privileges, including tax exemption, a monopoly on high government offices, and access to the crown. This was a revolution from above, and the nobles would not have it. A conspiracy of undetermined scope developed, and in March 1792 the king was shot by Jakob Anckarström, a young noble. Sweden entered the maelstrom of the French Revolutionary era with an underage monarch, an eccentric regent, and a badly divided society.

GREATNESS AND EMPIRE

For a little over a century and half (1560–1721) Sweden experienced an era of importance, influence, and expansion. It was then that its leaders were able to build and sustain an empire that may seem entirely out of proportion with the country's actual power and potential. This phase involved a series of wars with Sweden's Baltic neighbors and their allies, the acquisition of territory that nearly made the Baltic a Swedish lake, extension of Swedish interests and influence onto the broader stage of European affairs, brief forays into global empire building with a coastal fort in Africa and a colony in North America, and attempts to become a player in the European world trade economy. This happened for many reasons. Simplistically, Sweden's leaders built and maintained an empire because they could. The quality of government, army, navy, and leadership; economic assets and commercial demand; social pressures; personal desires; and security concerns were all factors at work At the same time, opportunities presented by external conditions and events were very important. The Europe of this period was vastly different from times before or after. The three most potentially powerful states were France, Spain, and the Holy Roman Empire. England and the Dutch Netherlands became important maritime powers during the seventeenth century. Russia was a regional player in the Baltic, but it did not become one of the leading European powers until after 1700. Poland (in union with Lithuania) had great potential, but it was in decline. Germany was not a unified state, and only Prussia was destined to become a great power before unification in the nineteenth century. Estonia and Latvia did not exist in a modern sense. In the Baltic region Denmark, Poland-Lithuania, Russia, and Sweden were the primary competitors for primacy. The Holy Roman Empire, Spain, France, the Netherlands, and England played secondary, but often supporting, roles.

No grand plan was involved in the building of Sweden's territorial empire. The first stage, in the last four decades of the sixteenth century, developed out of a convergence of circumstances. These included the personal ambitions of the unbalanced Erik XIV, his brother Johan, the impetuous Frederik II of Denmark, and his brother, Magnus. All were covetous of pieces of the southeastern Baltic (today's Estonia and Latvia), where a power vacuum was developing as the old ruling order declined. Conflict was triggered when, at the invitation of the burgher elite in Reval, Erik annexed the city and its surrounding territories (Estland) in 1561. Frederik II viewed this move as a threat to his country's seemingly dominant position in the Baltic and opted for war. The so-called Northern Seven Years' War was the first of eight Dano-Swedish conflicts in this period. It ended in a virtual draw in 1570, but it was very expensive for the Swedes, who had to pay the Danes an enormous sum for the return of the country's only port on the west coast at Älvsborg. Campaigns against the Russians were more successful, and Narva was added in 1581. Poland was a principal rival for several decades, and this was heightened because of the dynastic connection between the two countries arising out of the marriage of Johan III and the

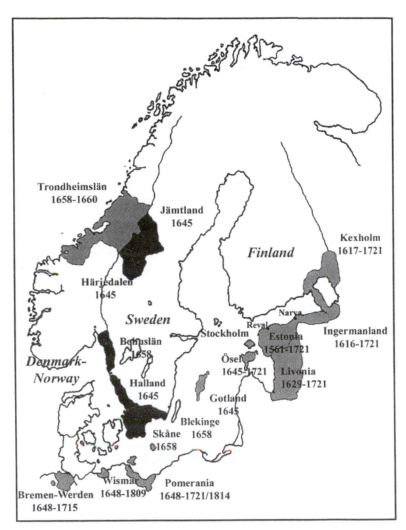

Map 4. Sweden's Baltic Empire.

Polish princess, Katarina Jagellonica. In 1587 their son, Sigismund, became king in Poland, and he succeeded his father in Sweden in 1592. Although deposed six years later, he refused to give up his claim to the throne. An on-again, off-again conflict followed that ended in a truce in 1629 (by which Livonia was acquired). In 1611 Denmark went to war with its neighbor again, and for the last time the Danes did quite well. Sweden was forced to return some territories and compromise on trade regulations, and again it was burdened with an enormous ransom for the return of Älvsborg. Major gains were made in Germany as a result of Sweden's involvement in the Thirty Years' War. Gustav II Adolf entered the war in 1630 for reasons of national security, religion, greed, pride, dynastic legitimacy, and image. Following his death at Lützen in 1632, Swedish forces remained engaged in what was an ongoing tragedy for the people of the German states. According to the terms of the Treaty of Westphalia (1648), Sweden received Pomerania, Wismar, and the bishoprics of Bremen and Verden. In a little sideshow war with the badly weakened Danes, the Swedes secured the islands of Ösel and Gotland, Halland, and the Norwegian territories of Jämtland and Härjedalen. The 1650s brought major gains as the result of two short wars with Denmark that involved Karl X, perhaps the most aggressive (and unrealistic) empire builder of this entire period. By the first of these (1657–1658) what might seem as the geographically logical "Sweden" was rounded out with the acquisition of Skåne, Blekinge, and Bohuslän, as well as the islands of Bornholm and (H)ven. At the same time a large chunk of central Norway, Trondheimslän, was annexed. This was the high point of the Swedish imperial experience. Karl X's second war, begun in 1660, may have been intended to put an end to Denmark entirely, but that was not to be. The Swedes had gone too far. They threatened the balance of power in the north. In one way or another, nearly all of Europe became involved in checking Sweden´s advance. In 1660 Karl suddenly and unexpectedly died, and international pressure forced the Swedes to return Bornholm and Trondheimslän. Another Danish-Swedish war was fought in the 1670s, but this ended in a draw. Sweden's time as a major player in European affairs was rapidly drawing to a close. Circumstances were changing. In 1699 a coalition of Denmark, Russia, and Poland formed, its leaders hoping to pluck pieces of the empire from the teenaged king, Karl XII. For the Danes and the Poles, it was a foolish gamble—and it was nearly so for the Russians under Peter I as well. A coalition did not mean a simultaneous and coordinated attack on Sweden; had that been the case, this would have been a short war. Each member fought its own campaigns, and this worked to Karl's advantage. Denmark was easily defeated. Russian forces were smashed at the famous Battle of Narva in November 1700. The armies of Poland's king, Augustus, held out in a kind of cat-and-mouse game for six years, but finally they accepted defeat.

Karl probably committed a serious strategic error in 1700 when he did not pursue the Russian forces at Narva and destroy them and their leader, Peter. By not doing so, he gave his most serious adversary the chance to rebuild and retrain his armies. When Karl turned again to the Russians in 1708, he met a far better prepared enemy. He also met the vastness of the Russian state and its weather. The march from Poland to the Ukraine, which covered nearly a thousand miles and took over seven months, gradually wore down Karl's army, and reinforcements and supplies never arrived. The Battle of Poltava (June 1709) was a terrible defeat for Sweden. There were 9,500 men lost or taken prisoner, and another 15,000 surrendered a few days later. Few of these men ever returned to Sweden. Karl fled with a small force into the Ottoman Empire, where he remained a guest and nuisance for five years! During this time the Russians occupied all of Sweden's eastern Baltic territories, including Finland. Denmark and Poland reentered the conflict, and Prussia and Hanover joined in for the kill. Karl never gave up the cause and was killed (possibly murdered by his own officers) while conducting a siege along the border with Norway in November 1718. After the fighting ended and the treaties were signed, Sweden's empire was gone. All Sweden's gains in the eastern Baltic along with a bit of Finland went to Russia. Prussia received a piece of Pomerania and Stettin. Hanover annexed Bremen and Verden. Denmark secured its claim to Slesvig and cash compensation. The Poles got nothing for their efforts, but by their participation they contributed to the wasting of Sweden's resources and power.

Sweden's days as the leading power in the Baltic were over, but that reality was slow to take hold. Over the next hundred years several Swedish leaders dreamed of reasserting the country's influence in the region and took the country to war to recapture territory or assert importance. A short war with Russia in the 1740s was a military embarrassment, increased Russian influence in Swedish affairs, and caused great suffering in Finland. About the only thing Sweden got out of participation in the Seven Years' War (1756–1763) was, according to legend, a taste for potatoes. Gustav III's campaign against Russia in 1788–1790 was frightfully expensive in many ways. Relatively few soldiers and sailors died in battle, but hundreds fell victim to disease. The military performed badly in part because many of the officers turned against the king and committed treason. For a time Denmark honored its commitments to Russia and joined the war, presenting Gustav with a three-front conflict. In the end, however, nothing was gained and a political crisis was created that led to the king's assassination in 1792. Gustav IV's alignment against Napoleon was even more expensive; it cost him Finland and his throne in 1809. In the century that followed the close of the Great Northern War in 1721, only Crown Prince Karl Johan's willingness to join the alliance against his former master, Napoleon, brought gain in the form of a dynastic union with Norway in 1814.

The costs of Sweden's empire were enormous in human and material terms. Estimates are that as many as half a million Swedes and Finns died in the wars of the empire, including about 50,000 in the 1620s, 80,000 during the time of the Thirty Years' War, and 200,000 in the Great Northern War. Virtually every generation of young men from 1560 to 1720 was bled by the conflicts. The country also had to build and maintain a navy, which, in the early eighteenth century numbered around forty-five capital ships stationed at the main base at Karlskrona. In addition, there was a system of fortresses to protect the country's coasts and borders. The costs of Sweden's military establishment, even in peacetime, were beyond the ordinary means of the state. Wars of the period were generally wars of attrition. They were neither won nor lost by the large battles so often described in history. Wars usually ended when one or both sides ran out of money or credit.

Sweden had several advantages in the wars of the imperial period—at least down to the last phase in the Great Northern War. First, at several times in this period the army was unique. This was especially true during the first few years or Sweden's involvement in the Thirty Years' War. Gustav II Adolf was an important innovator and contributor to the so-called military revolution of the seventeenth century. He was an advocate of firepower and mobility; and he adopted linear formations for his infantry over the traditional massed squares (*tercios*) that were vastly more cumbersome and less flexible, increased the number of artillery pieces and insisted on more mobile artillery, used sequential volleys of musket fire from his lined troops, and drilled his forces rigorously. He also tried to increase the proportion of Swedes in the army over the number of foreign mercenaries and then to generate patriotic nationalism in his troops to increase their fighting spirit. He used this new army with great success between summer 1630 and late fall 1632, scoring major victories of the imperial armies such as the one at Breitenfeld in September 1631. Once other armies adopted his methods, however, the advantage was gone. A second advantage Sweden had during much of this period was that the wars were fought away from Sweden. On home ground, wars were vastly more expensive. Armies were like hoards of locusts. They were not self-supporting. Food for troops and fodder for animals had to be obtained, peacefully or otherwise, from the local population. Pillaging was common. When armies went into "winter quarters," often they descended on a town or city and stayed for months. There was no end to the horrors facing the local populations. Parts of southern Sweden experienced some of this suffering early in the seventeenth century and again during the 1670s. The worst case was the Russian occupation of Finland (then still an integral part of the kingdom) between 1715 and 1721, an episode called the Great Wrath in Finnish history. A final advantage was that Sweden could draw on the resources of the empire to help pay for the wars. Men, material, and money were extracted. This lessened the burdens on Sweden and its people and helped to sustain a willingness among the population to continue involvement. When the human and material costs of the empire had to be borne by the Swedes alone, that willingness disappeared.

The history of the overseas empire is shorter and far less violent. The post in Africa at Cabo Corso, along the coast of present-day Ghana near Accra, lasted only thirteen years. Dreams of involvement in the triangle trade of European goods—African slaves—goods from the Americas drove the adventure. The Swedish African Company never made money, and the fort was taken over by the Dutch. The colony in America suffered from lack of consistent support and interest. The idea for a colony was first suggested to Gustav II in the 1620s, but resources were few and the war with Poland pressing. It was under the king's chancellor and regent, Axel Oxenstierna, that the idea moved forward. As a private, joint-stock venture with government participation, an expedition was dispatched in 1637 under the leadership of an experienced Dutch entrepreneur and colony builder, Peder Minuit. In spring 1638 the beginnings of a settlement that eventually included parts of today's Delaware, New Jersey, and Pennsylvania stretching out along the shores of the Delaware River was established. Over the next seventeen years a trickle of supplies and settlers followed. Land was purchased from the Native Americans, the Lenape, and farms and parishes were established. Small fortifications were erected. In all only a few hundred colonists came. In theory, New Sweden was to be a source of tobacco and furs. In fact, only a few shipments of American goods were ever sent back to Sweden, and the colony never provided a return on the investments of its owners. When the Dutch defeated the Swedes in 1655, they annexed the colony as part of New Netherlands. Eight years later the English took over all the Dutch territories in North America.

What is also interesting about the history of New Sweden is that many of the colonists chose to stay after 1655, and they and their descendants helped to shape colonial American history. For more than 150 years a little Sweden was maintained. The Church of Sweden sent out ministers, and the area was the target for visits by scholars from Sweden. The people in this history contributed to the extension of settlement, agriculture, cultural and intellectual life, and politics in colonial America.

THE ECONOMY

The economy that developed in this very long period was important to Sweden's emergence as a state and crucial during the Imperial Period. By today's standards, however, it was backward, undeveloped, and thin. Appropriate descriptive words are agricultural, preindustrial, protocapitalist, and conservative. This economy had four essential elements: agriculture, natural resource exploitation, production, and trade. Farming engaged an overwhelming majority of the people and was mainly subsistence in nature. The country's most important natural resources were forest products, iron, and copper. Most people lived outside of any sort of extensive exchange economy; they raised what they needed to eat and made what they needed for clothing, furnishings, tools, and housing. There were, however, agricultural surpluses, and some goods were produced. Both surpluses and goods were absolutely essential for the tax system, town development, and growth of internal and international trade. Overall, during medieval and early modern times, Sweden's economy experienced general growth between 900 and 1350, 1500 and 1620, and for much of the last three-quarters of the eighteenth century. Recessions occurred from around 1350 to 1450 and over the last half of the seventeenth century.

Farming

Land was owned by the crown, the Church (until the Reformation), the nobility, and a class of freehold farmers. The distribution of land ownership—that is, **who** owned the land—changed significantly over the centuries covered here. In the Early Medieval Period virtually all land was owned by freehold farmers, although the amounts each held varied widely and there were great differences in wealth and status. Gradually a four-part distribution evolved. Monarchs tended to amass considerable landholdings, and the development of the state brought with it the crown's theoretical claim that it "owned" all land. The creation of a military nobility exempt from taxes in the thirteenth century changed the status of the land owned by those freeholders who entered that nobility, for their land became tax exempt or "privileged." The same was true of the large properties donated to the Church. By the time of the Reformation, the distribution was around 20 percent Church, 20 percent nobility, 50 percent farmers, and 5 percent crown. The expropriation of Church lands in the Reformation obviously revolutionized this distribution, at least temporarily. Gradually, however, the crown alienated much of its land through sale, donations, or in return for services to the nobility; and many farmers, hard pressed by taxes, were forced to sell their land to nobles. By the early 1650s the nobility held almost three-fifths of all the agricultural land in the country and thereby contributed to a social, economic, and political crisis. This situation was partially addressed in the 1650s by a modest program of taking back donated lands; then it radically changed in the 1680s when through the "great reduction" the crown recovered much of the land it had lost since 1604. Thereafter, the shares were closer to one-third for each group. In the eighteenth century the crown's share fell to around 20 percent, whereas the farmers' increased to almost 50 percent.

In keeping with practices that had existed for centuries, as mentioned earlier, most farming was organized around villages, although this was less true in the north and in provinces such as Värmland where new land was being cleared for cultivation. The work was done by several groups of agricultural workers, including the freehold farmers, renters, and hired laborers. Arable land was allocated in long, thin strips, a form dictated by the implements used. Much of the actual farming was done collectively and strictly according to a traditional calender. Farmers had very little incentive to experiment with new crops or techniques, and the technology of farming remained largely unchanged. Wheat, oats, barley, rye, and fodder crops were central; livestock included cattle, horses, pigs, goats, sheep, and fowl. Yields were pitifully low, sometimes as little as two grains for each planted. Fallowing of a third of the available land was common. Because all Europe was in a period of colder, damper weather that stretched from around 1300 to 1850 and is sometimes called "the little ice age," these practices and conditions made for great vulnerability to disaster. Crop failures were common. Famine was hardly a stranger. In good years the system did produce some surplus for sale at local markets, transport to towns, and export. Grains, dairy products, including butter, livestock, and hides were regularly sold abroad.

The ideas and attitudes of the Enlightenment resulted in the introduction of important changes in farm practices in Sweden, and production rose. From the middle of the eighteenth century there was an effort to dissolve the old villages and consolidate the shares of individual farmers into rational, single-unit farms. This is usually called the enclosure movement, and it duplicated efforts made in many parts of Europe. Models were provided by large landowners like Rutger Maclean, who created seventy-three individual farms from the four villages that comprised his Skåne estates. Despite evidence that such reforms could lead to increased production, greater profits, and more freedom for the individual farmer, they were met with great resistance and took over a century to complete. A series of government enactments from between 1749 and 1783 provided for voluntary consolidations; new legislation in 1807 and 1827 made them compulsory. Other important trends included the introduction of new crops and better techniques. The potato was gradually accepted over the course of the century, more complicated crop rotations that took less of the land out of production were adopted, and livestock raising became more consciously a process of breeding for quality.

A parenthetical problem with Swedish farming was tied to the widespread use (and abuse) of alcohol. Valuable grain crops that could have been used to feed people or livestock were consumed in the distillation of hard liquor or *brännvin*. Virtually every parish, if not every farm, had its own still, and drinking habits were deeply ingrained. Gustav III considered this an economic problem, not a moral one, and he attempted to solve it by outlawing private stills and creating a state liquor monopoly. He was not successful, and his actions only served to alienate many of the farmers. The alcohol problem remained, to be taken up by temperance advocates in the nineteenth century and further state actions in the twentieth.

Production

The production of goods took place in three different settings during this period. Overwhelmingly, the things of everyday life were made domestically. Most people lived in a handcraft world. They made their own cloths, shoes, housewares, tools, and so on, and in small, regional markets they obtained those things they could not make, such as iron goods. In towns, production was in the hands of skilled craftsmen working in clearly defined trades. The number of these artisans and the specific trades varied with the size and purpose(s) of each town. For example, as Stockholm evolved into the country's capital, it also developed the most extensive craft population, with about thirty categories in the late sixteenth century serving government, church, military, noble, and merchant customers. Most common among the trades were tailors and shoemakers. In addition, there might be bakers, butchers, barrel makers, iron smiths, carpenters, apothecaries, printers, bookbinders, saddle makers, glass makers, glove makers, hat makers, and wig makers. During the fifteenth century artisans in the larger towns were gradually organized into guilds. These developed elaborate rules governing membership criteria and costs, education of new members of the trade, product quality and price, participation in religious events, and care of old and sick members. In the relatively constant economic setting that characterized much of this period, the craft system worked well. Growth and innovation were of little importance; stability and order were. From the late seventeenth century the guilds and the ideal of an unchanging economic order came under increasing criticism. Technological innovations, population growth, expanding demand, greater wealth, a changing international situation, and new trade opportunities worked in favor of change and growth. So, too, did the prevailing economic theories of the time, mercantilism and autarchy. Advocates of the former emphasized the primacy of exports over imports; those of that latter argued for economic self-sufficiency. Both supported the importance of thriving home economies. The economic liberals of the Enlightenment argued that the guilds' influence should be reduced on the grounds that they inhibited free economic development. Despite these criticisms, changing government policies, and the growth of many early "industrial" enterprises, the guilds survived until well into the nineteenth century.

The third mode was what some call protoindustrial or protocapitalist production. It involved the outlay of capital by entrepreneurs, some measure of concentration of workers and the tools of production, more organized marketing, and considerable government encouragement. Very little of this type existed before the seventeenth century. Copper, iron, and weapons (cannon) manufacture came under intensive development efforts after about 1630. In addition, textiles, paper, glass, sugar, and tobacco were among Sweden's early "industries." Their growth was encouraged by the state as well as by foreign and domestic entrepreneurs in order to strengthen Sweden's position in Europe and reduce its dependence on foreign sources. Government policies included granting subsidies and monopolies, and a few of these early capitalists earned wealth and noble status for their efforts.

One of the most important examples of this trend is the history of the copper mine at Falun, *Stora Kopparberg*, the great copper mountain. Copper was mined in this area for almost a thousand years, from the late ninth to the close of the twentieth century. The operation grew in scale during the Middle Ages, and from at least the late 1200s Sweden's kings took a direct interest in and sought to regulate what went on there, primarily because of the income potential for the state. Magnus Eriksson established a set of regulations in the 1340s. Gustav I and his sons all worked to increase production and to centralize the refining of the copper ore. Gustav II issued a number of decrees related to the mine, but the most important steps were taken under the leadership of Axel Oxenstierna during the regency and reign of Kristina. It was then that a central Royal Mine Board (1637) was established in Stockholm, a government-appointed Mine Master (Carl Bonde was the first) installed, and smelting consolidated at Avesta. The mine experienced a "golden age" in the first three-quarters of the seventeenth century. During this period other sources of copper in Europe were in decline, demand was high, and government involvement particularly intense. Output peaked around 1650 at about 3,000 tons per year. After about 1680, however, production gradually fell, as the quality of ore declined and operations became more and more costly.

A deeply interconnected society developed around *Stora Kopparberg* during the Early Modern Period. Throughout this time the actual mining was controlled by the "master miners," who never numbered more than a few hundred. They acted as semi-autonomous entrepreneurs working individual shares of the mine. Much of the actual mining was done by a contingent of men who moved from master to master. Many of these were the younger sons of area farmers; some were criminals who opted for work in the mine over prison. Connected to the operation of the mine was a network of smelters, wood suppliers, staple goods agents, farmers, transporters, and merchants. For a time Falun was Sweden's second largest town. Most of the refined copper was destined for export by way of Stockholm. The state was represented by a royal bailiff and, after 1637, by a Mine Master. In addition, the technical problems facing the mine's operation made it a magnet for technicians or mechanics, including Christopher Klem in the early seventeenth century and Christopher Polhem. As the mine's director of design from 1700 to 1716, Polhem was responsible for creating an ingenious but overly complicated system of pumps, lifts, hammers, and conveyors.

The actual mining work was miserable, dangerous, and backbreaking. Following the veins of ore turned the ground under the site into a honeycomb of chambers and tunnels. The raw copper was exposed and extracted using fire. Huge quantities of wood were consumed. Fires were set against the face of the rock, which caused cracking. Ore and rock could then be broken away from the face of the vein and hauled to the surface. This process was then repeated. Obviously, working conditions were horrible. Heat, smoke, dust, and water were constant irritants. Fire-setting had to be done according to a strict schedule because the mine became uninhabitable for a time. Water seeping into the shafts was a constant problem that challenged the most imaginative inventive minds of the day, who devised complex horse- or water-driven lifting devices to pump it to the surface. Cave-ins were common and could be deadly. Major collapses occurred in 1655 and 1687. Interestingly, life expectancies for miners were no shorter than for the general population at the time.

Similar developments also occurred in the iron industry, which was of greater overall importance during the Early Modern Period. Iron production was a highly decentralized operation located in a district called the *Bergslagen*, which extended across the middle of the country roughly from Uppsala to the Norwegian border, and in the southern provinces of Småland and Blekinge. Ore was extracted either from bogs, where it lay just beneath the surface, or from small open mines. Charcoal-fired ovens were used to process the raw ore. A product called *osmund* dominated until the early 1600s, when bar iron became primary. Both *osmund* and bar iron required further processing. The semiprocessed iron was gathered in area trade centers and then sent mainly to Stockholm for export. Some of it stayed in the country to be used in tool and weapon production. The mining and smelting operations, about 400 in number, were small in scale and scattered throughout these areas. Miners and smelters were conservative and resistant to change. As with copper, the state became more involved during the Early Modern Period. In the seventeenth century some concentration occurred, and new and more modern operations like those at Löfsta or Forsmark were opened—mostly by Dutch entrepreneurs, including Louis De Geer, Abraham and Jacob Momma, and the De Besche brothers. In the same period Walloon and German experts were consciously recruited for their new technologies and skills.

Another important early industrial sector was in textiles. Here a primary stimulus was the growth of the army and the standardization of uniforms. Centers of production included Jönköping, Norrköping, Göteborg, and Stockholm. The factory at Barnängens on the south Stockholm island of Söder is an example of this. Founded in the 1690s, it was a complex of buildings housing wool sorting, washing, carding, dyeing, spinning, plying, and weaving facilities. Men, women, children as young as eight, and even prisoners worked there. Entire families spent their lives within the walls of this "factory." They often slept and ate where they worked. These workers were near the very bottom of the social hierarchy. Although most of them developed skills important to the textile production, they were outside the estate-based social system. They had no guilds to protect them and no real bargaining power. Wages were pitifully small. In many ways they were trapped and were little better than slaves. Employers used the fear of further degradation or poverty to keep them on the job.

Trade

The third essential element in Sweden's medieval and Early Modern Period economies, trade had three basic aspects: localized rural community exchange, internal trade centered around regional market towns, and international trade. The first two of these were probably the most important in the lives of common people and the most extensive, but they had less obvious importance in the broader context of state development.

For much of this long period, Sweden's international trade was in the hands of foreigners. Following the close of the Viking Age, it fell under control of the Hanse or Hanseatic League. Established in the late thirteenth century, this organization developed as a powerful and fascinating alternative to the monarchies of the time. It had its own government, law, military, and foreign policy. For over 300 years the stoutly built, single-masted and square-sailed cogs of Hanseatic League carried the fish, grain, salt, wine, textiles, and other staple goods essential to medieval life, as well as luxury products. At the core of the organization was a group of German towns, including Bremen, Hamburg, Kiel, Rostock, and Lübeck, which served as its capital. Member merchants built up bases in almost every port city along the coasts of the Baltic and North Sea from which they organized and often monopolized trade and production. In Sweden, Visby was a member city, and Hanse "offices" were maintained in Stockholm, Kalmar, and Åbo. The importance of the German populations in these towns went beyond economic activities to include politics and culture. Architecture and language were two aspects of medieval Sweden strongly influenced by Hanse merchants. The Hanse frequently intervened in Swedish affairs. They were involved in the rebellion against Magnus Eriksson, in several of the wars of the Kalmar Union period, and in making Gustav I king. The organization and its influence declined throughout the sixteenth century, and by the mid-1600s it vanished.

The dominance of the Hanse did much to discourage the development of a native Swedish merchant class. Gustav Vasa discovered this to his dismay, and little progress was made during the sixteenth century. In the seventeenth century foreign interests, particularly Dutch, moved into leading positions in the country's international commerce. Their presence was encouraged by the government, which was open to immigration and rewarded foreign and domestic enterprise with privileges, subsidies, monopolies, and ennoblement. Stockholm and Göteborg were the most important international trade centers, but other towns, including Gävle, Kalmar, and Åbo played key roles, too. Gradually a group of great commercial families, who were or became Swedish, came to control trade, especially in Stockholm. They were called the Skeppsbron nobility, after the commercial dockside section of Stockholm's Old Town and still the site of many of the old trading houses. The leaders of these families were the men of "progress" and agents of change. They were merchants, capitalists, creditors, and investors in manufacturing. They operated in a "modern" world of paper money, credit, and investment. They carried on internal, Baltic, European, and global commerce; invested in manufacturing ventures; and contributed to the development of an early version of a consumer society through what they offered consumers and through their own international tastes. During the Era of Liberty many of these people also became involved in politics either through ennoblement and admission to the House of the Nobility or through the House of Burghers. Arfwidsson, Claesson, Hebbe, Pauli, Plomgren, Tottie, and Wahrendorff are some of the families.

Inseparable from the development of a merchant class were the trading companies. International trade, especially that at the fringes of the European world economy such as the Far East, was risky and required considerable capital outlays. Ships, crews, and cargoes were costly. Time was also a factor. All travel was slow, and expeditions to a place such as Canton in China could take a year or more. The companies were joint-stock ventures. Companies dealing with products such as tar, tobacco, and sugar were founded in the seventeenth century. Most were short lived and not very successful. The 1700s were more profitable times. They saw the founding of the West Indies Company, Levant Company, Greenland Company, and Swedish East Indies Company. The last enjoyed considerable success. Its owners, many of whom were Scots, dispatched 132 expeditions between 1731 and 1813, mainly to Canton. Tea was the principal return product of these, but silks and porcelain also were brought back to Göteborg. Some of these goods were sold for reexport; some stayed in the country and helped to foster consumer tastes.

During the 160-year period of the empire, Sweden's natural resources and their systematic exploitation and trade in highly favorable international markets were absolutely essential. Europe was a world of wooden buildings, wooden ships, iron tools, iron weapons, copper roofs, and copper coins, and Sweden's timber, naval supplies (masts, spars, and tar), iron, and copper were in high demand. Although the extraction of all these resources and the production of trade goods from them extends far back in Sweden's history, the extension of their exploitation in the Early Modern Period far exceeded any earlier efforts. Government policies were designed to these ends, and Sweden benefited from the abilities, resources, and interest of

Table 3.1

Imports (in % of total)

	1559	1649	1724
Salt	24.7	—	2.6
Grains	—	0.2	27.0
Finished textiles	35.8	38.1	13.6
Hops, malt	18.8	—	—
Metal goods	11.8	20.5	14.4
Wine, beer, liquor	3.9	14.0	7.9

Exports (in % of total)

	1559	1649	1724
Iron & Steel	28.8	46.7	73.0
Copper	5.5	33.3*	10.0
Tar	—	6.1	7.0
Timber products	11.6	5.2	6.1
Hides & Skins	22.3	1.5	—
Butter & Fats	24.7	—	—

*Copper was an important export during all of the seventeenth century, accounting for 43.6% in 1613, 33.8% in 1642, and 23.5% in 1685. Only in 1613, however, was it more important than iron.

Source: Eli F. Heckscher. *Sveriges Ekonomiska Historia, Från Gustav Vasa*, vol. I, Bilagor, 19–20.

many foreigners Individuals like Louis De Geer and Abraham and Jacob Momma were intensely involved in nearly every imaginable aspect of the economy, including mining, metal production, textiles, weapons, shipbuilding, transport, retail trade, finance, banking, export, and colonial adventures. Providing incentive, expertise, and capital, they were essential in bringing new ideas necessary for the country's growth and security. Many of these people settled permanently in Sweden and founded families who continued to serve economic development. After Göteborg was refounded in 1619, it became a Dutch city. This could be seen in its canals, architecture, population, and government. In a broader picture, immigrants from more common stock were also important. Finns were encouraged to migrate to the fringes of settlement. As the borders of the country moved north, their skills in forestry and slash-and-burn farming were important. Germans and Walloons brought mining and metal-refining techniques.

Overall, conflicting pictures of Sweden's economic development across this long period emerge. On the one hand, there was a great deal of stability, especially in agriculture, but also in production and internal trade. On the other hand, there was change. The scale of certain sectors such as mining and metals production and international commerce expanded significantly. New industries were established. Modern monetary, banking, credit, and investment practices were adopted. Government activities and policies became more extensive. Although certainly not as advanced as England by the close of the Early Modern Period, Sweden's economy developed many of the essential elements necessary for the great transformations of the next century.

EDUCATION, ARTS, AND CULTURE

It was in the context of these political, international, and economic developments that Sweden's cultural history occurred. This had two central aspects. One was the emergence of a culture of the Church, royal court, nobility, and merchant elites. Its characteristics were constantly in flux and determined increasingly by foreign influences. The other was the ongoing evolution of many folk cultures, locally determined, but also influenced by imported and upper-class tastes and styles.

The culture of the social elites was increasingly European. At first this was relatively limited in scope. The conversion to Christianity brought with it new Romanesque and then Gothic architectural styles and stone building methods. It also brought writing and medieval literary styles such as the chronicle, reflected in the fourteenth century *Erik's Chronicle*. As fashion in dress became increasingly important, styles migrated to Sweden. The colorful and puffy costumes of the Renaissance dominated much of the sixteenth century, but they were replaced by the somber black of the Spanish style, and subsequently by Dutch and then French styles. Urban architecture reflected the influence of Hanse during the Middle Ages, as is still evident in the older parts of Stockholm or Malmö. Dutch styles were transplanted to Göteborg. For much of this period the nobility lived little better than common folk. The growing wealth and power of the upper nobility in the Early Modern Period, however, allowed them to imitate their continental peers. Manor houses and urban palaces, along with their furnishings, art, and gardens, echoed Renaissance, Baroque, Rococo, and then Neoclassical styles. Diets and manners mirrored similar trends. As well, although a court or official Swedish developed, it was common to affect the use of a foreign language such as was the case with French in the eighteenth century.

Education was also an important aspect of this high culture. The country's first schools had been founded to produce new clergy. Slowly Sweden developed a broader educational system with close ties to the world of European ideas. Much of this occurred in the seventeenth and eighteenth centuries. Gustav II Adolf initiated the establishment of a system of secondary schools, and he is also credited with putting Uppsala University on a sound economic footing through land donations and by adding to its resources with gifts of books acquired in his wars. An academy was founded at Åbo in Finland in 1640, and a new university was opened at Lund in 1668. Although tiny by today's standards, they were dynamic places. In these institutions the ideas of the Early Modern Period were debated, and fights over intellectual systems were fought out. Their curricula gradually grew and became increasingly practical in the eighteenth century.

Although literacy rates were high, even among the common people, because of the Church's expectations for confirmation, very few people ever received a formal education. Private tutors and grand tours of the continent were the most common avenues of education for the nobility.

Many aspects of rural culture changed little in this period. This was especially true in terms of housing, basic dress, furniture, housewares, and tools. Iron plows and seed drills were among the only farm-implement improvements. For women, the far more efficient and faster spinning wheel replaced the drop spindle for making yarn and thread. The calender of rituals, celebrations, religious days, and farming activities was a constant. Superstitions were common, and elements of ancient folk beliefs persisted. Trolls, forest spirits, luck, and fate were very real parts of everyday life. Art was incorporated into the material culture and reflected in wood carving and weaving, for example. The relative isolation of most Swedes meant that language was localized, and dialects abounded. Toward the end of the period there is increasing evidence of efforts by the common people to imitate some aspects of upper-class culture. This may be seen in some elements of the skirts, blouses, aprons, vests, shirts, and pants of the distinctive and locally unique folk costumes worn on special occasions and today commonly worn by provincial folk dance groups. A second example is in the wall paintings of Dalarna, many of which depict biblical stories, but in eighteenth-century costumes.

4

Becoming Modern, 1800–1914

During the slightly elongated "nineteenth century" that lasted through 1914, Sweden experienced important, fundamental, and far-reaching changes. Politically, the country began the period as a semi-absolutist, constitutional monarchy with a parliament of very narrow representative scope and little power. By 1918 Sweden was well on the way to becoming truly democratic. The crown's authority was limited, most adult men and women had the vote, the parliament was broadly representative, and governing power was in the hands of a ministry responsible to that parliament. Socially, the medieval four estates structure, based on birth and function and already unable to make places for newly emerging social groups in 1800, was replaced by a class society based on economic position—although birth continued to be important. Economically, agriculture remained the largest sector, but important changes took place in old industries and new ones developed. Sweden was well on the way toward becoming an industrial nation at the close of this period. In the context of these changes, population distribution shifted from mainly rural to over half urban. This last change came with the vastly increased mobility of the Swedish people, which was also reflected in the emigration of about a million people during this period. Culturally, far greater homogeneity replaced the centuries-old social and regional heterogeneity. In a sense, the people of Sweden became Swedes, or were made into Swedes, as a more uniform national culture was created. In terms of gender history, women gained important rights and freedoms, but not real equality. For ordinary people, the last third of this period, at least, brought some improvement in their well-being. At the same time, the country's leaders and people became more aware of and better adapted to Sweden's status as a minor power in the European community of states.

POLITICAL DEVELOPMENTS

Although the transition from monarchy to democracy was gradual, five key events or developments illustrate this process. They include the relatively peaceful constitutional revolution of 1809, the impetus given to reform by the intense discussion of political ideals around midcentury and the revolutions of 1848, the sweeping structural reform of the parliament in 1865–1866, the achievement of universal male suffrage in 1909 and of women's suffrage in 1918, and the acceptance of parliamentarism by the crown in 1917.

Kings of the Nineteenth Century

Gustav IV Adolf	1792–1809
Karl XIII	1809–1818
Karl XIV Johan (Bernadotte line)	1818–1844
Oscar I	1844–1858
Karl XV	1858–1872
Oscar II	1872–1907
Gustav V	1907–1950

Sweden was a country in very serious trouble in the early nineteenth century. The young king, Gustav IV, was ill equipped to deal with the challenges of this period. The genie of political change had been unleashed in the revolutions of the late eighteenth century, most notably in France. Even in far-off Sweden the ideas of liberty, equality, and fraternity found adherents. Napoleon complicated matters, and Gustav regarded him as an anti-Christ. For that reason Gustav joined alliances against the French emperor and took an ill-prepared Sweden to war. The temporary alliance of Napoleon and the Russian tsar, Alexander I, in 1807 resulted in an impossible situation. Russia attacked Finland and pushed Swedish forces from the country and then raided the eastern coast of Sweden. Battle losses were compounded by miserable conditions and disease. Gustav's support evaporated, and a coup led by a handful of Stockholm nobles in March 1809 was virtually unopposed. Never popular, Gustav was now forced into exile as a new line of succession was established. At the same time, a new constitution was drafted, and although extensively amended, it served until 1974. Peace was made with Russia and France, but at the cost of the permanent loss of Finland.

A particularly difficult problem was the question of succession. Gustav's own children were rejected by all except a few members of the high nobility. For a time there was some thought of extending an offer to Frederik VI of Denmark as part of a conscious effort to build a new Scandinavian union. Frederik presented serious constitutional problems, however. He was an absolutist, no friend of constitutions or the men who wrote them, and unprepared to accept limits on his authority. The parliament settled first, therefore, on Gustav's aging uncle, Karl. Because Karl was without an heir, the issue of ongoing succession remained. Here the first offer went to Kristian August of Slesvig-Holstein-Sønderborg-Augustenborg, a relative of the Danish king, an experienced military leader, and the popular governor-general and military commander in Norway. During the March 1809 coup and throughout the following summer, he held off taking advantage of the weakened Swedish forces along the frontier, and he supported the idea of a new Nordic union under Frederik. When that option failed, he shifted his thinking to a dual monarchy of Norway and Sweden under his own leadership. The forty-one-year-old prince accepted the offer of the crown and came to Sweden as Karl August in 1810. Unfortunately, he was not a well man, and he died suddenly while attending a military review near Helsingborg in May 1810. Some suspected the supporters of the deposed king, the so-called Gustavians, of murdering the heir. At his funeral the marshal of the realm, Axel von Fersen, was dragged from his coach by an angry mob and beaten and stoned to death while the authorities watched. With fear of revolution in the air, troops were eventually used to subdue the demonstrators, several of whom were killed. The streets of the capital were carefully patrolled by soldiers.

Sweden's leaders first thought of offering the crown to Karl August's brother, but they turned instead to Napoleon's France and chose Jean Baptist Bernadotte, a talented military leader, marshal of the French Empire, and prince of Ponte Corvo. He was elected at a special meeting of the parliament intentionally held in Örebro, a quiet provincial town west of the capital and a long way from meddling foreign diplomats and a mob of potential revolutionaries. Bernadotte and his wife, Desiree, came to Sweden in October 1810. The new crown prince ruled in fact if not in title until 1818, when he succeeded to the throne as Karl XIV Johan. An interesting aside to the succession issue was that the new royal family was promptly reconnected with the old through the marriage of Karl XIV's son, Oscar (I), to Josefina of Leutchenburg, who descended from a sister of Karl X Gustav, and these ties were reinforced through the marriages of the later Bernadottes, Oscar II and Gustav V.

The 1809 political order was certainly not democratic. The constitution, which created a limited constitutional monarchy, was heavily influenced by Sweden's history. The king still governed, shared legislative initiative with the parliament, appointed his own council, took the advice of whomever he wished, and had an absolute veto over laws passed by the parliament. The parliament continued to be based on the ancient four estates and represented less than one-sixth of the population. What made this new system different, in theory at least, was that the king could not rule absolutely or arbitrarily. Parliament was to meet every five years, not solely at the king's call. It could review the advice given the king by his counselors and impeach those who broke the law. Very important was that it had power over taxation and budget decisions. Swedes were also guaranteed fundamental legal protections and free speech The latter was limited, however. Publications could be confiscated if they threatened national security or libeled individuals, and persons could be fined or imprisoned. As calls for reform developed in the following decades, these limits were frequently invoked to quiet opposition.

The political debates that developed, especially after 1830, created a constant pressure for change. Critics of the status quo became increasing vocal, particularly among the farmers and in the growing urban middle class. Public meetings and newspapers became important elements of a new political culture. Lars Johan Hierta was one of the most outspoken of the new liberals. He chronicled the parliament's activities through his *Riksdags-Tidningar* (Riksdag's News) and in the pages of *Aftonbladet*, a paper repeatedly confiscated for the opinions it contained. In this increasingly charged atmosphere, there were plenty of proposals from without and within the parliament for actual changes. Few of these got very far. In part this was because none of the early Bernadotte kings were actually friends of reform, and they clung tenaciously to their powers. This was made particularly clear in 1848, the year of revolution in Europe. Sweden, too, was visited by the specter of violent change, and in mid-March posters calling for the end of the monarchy and the creation of a republic appeared on buildings in the capital. A demonstration on the eighteenth resulted in armed clashes with the authorities, and several people were killed. In a pattern repeated by monarchs across much of Europe, the king, Oscar I, offered a liberal parliamentary reform package that included a two-house parliament based on a limited suffrage to the Riksdag for its consideration. He then retired from giving any support to the program, knowing it would die there for lack of consensus. The difficulty of getting any political reform package through the parliament was a second reason liberal changes did not come sooner. The clergy and nobles were effective obstacles of reform, and the very nature of the four-house parliament made it very difficult to build a body of supporters who could effectively move proposals through the archaic legislative labyrinth.

Despite the difficulties, there was some progress on the constitutional front. The nontheological faculty of the universities, rural entrepreneurs, farmers who had purchased lands formerly owned by nobles, and urban businessmen gained representation between 1840 and 1860. In 1840 the council of state, which until then might have contained as few as four members and rarely be consulted, was reorganized. Now it would be made up of the heads of at least seven ministries plus three or more other members "without portfolio." This body became the base from which the contemporary cabinet or government of Sweden evolved. The interval between sessions of the parliament was reduced to three years in 1845. The 1862 reform of county and municipal government was particularly important. Under this measure a system of elected assemblies at the parish, town or city, and county level was created. These assemblies were to be chosen by a complex electoral system that awarded one or more votes to individuals (including women!) on the basis of wealth. People who owned more property on which they paid taxes or those who earned larger incomes received more votes. This multiple-vote system was further skewed, for individuals with only one vote tended to avoid elections because their voices were easily canceled by those with many votes. Clearly, it was a system that assured a plutocracy.

The great change in the parliament's structure finally came in 1865–1866. It was designed by Louis De Geer, minister of justice in the council of Karl XV. De Geer's bill called for the end of the four estates and their replacement by a parliament based on two chambers of equal competence. This was not to be a step into immediate democracy, however. The suffrage and candidate eligibility aspects of this bill, which specified age and income or net worth as keys to both, assured continuity and stability. The First Chamber was to be chosen indirectly, by the county assemblies and communal councils: one-third of its 125 (later 150) members every three years. Candidates had to be at least forty years old and either earn a substantial annual income or possess a large financial or property estate. In a country of 4 million, about 6,000 were eligible. The Second Chamber with 190 (later 230) seats was more representative. A one-man, one-vote system that enfranchised about one-sixth of the population was installed. Candidates had to be thirty and earn or be worth much less than for the elite chamber. Most rural and urban common people were not enfranchised; nor were women. Essentially, the First Chamber represented the some of the old nobility, upper bureaucrats, military officers, and the urban rich. The landowning farmers dominated the Second Chamber until around 1900. Despite its limitations, the proposal served as a peaceful revolution. The representatives of the House of the Clergy withheld their support until after the nobles, who debated long and passionately in their chamber, finally approved the measure by a margin of about three to two on 7 December 1865. The last meeting of the old parliament took place in June 1866.

Initially participation in the new system remained limited. As few as one-fifth of the eligible voters bothered going to the polls. There were no true modern political parties, only organizations of like-minded representatives within each of the two chambers. Representative, parliamentary democracy evolved over the next sixty years only through specific laws, changing government practices, and the creation of a new political culture and context fostered by the development of clearly differing political ideologies, intense and constant public debate, a vocal and political press, street demonstrations, violence, and external events. Politics and society were gradually polarized or fractured along class and ideological lines drawn between the advocates of change and those of order, between left and right. Within each camp were wide variations in outlook and program. In addition, the kings of this period, Karl XV, Oscar II, and Gustav V, sided with the forces of order. They took a dim view of democracy, and none wanted to be known as the last real king of Sweden. Oscar and Gustav, however, grew to understand that they could do little to hold back the forces that worked toward democracy.

The growth of political parties was especially important to the democratization process, and by the early 1920s there were five positioned from left to right on the typical political spectrum of the time (socialist left–left/liberal–center–conservative/right). Three of these parties evolved from election organizations and parliamentary working groups that developed after 1867. Two had their origins in Marxist-Socialism and the growth of a politically organized working class. The largest group on the socialist left was the Social Democratic Workers' Party, founded in 1889 by August Palm, a fiery agitator and champion of working class interests. Some argue this was the first truly modern political party in Sweden because it had the earliest national organization. Ideologically, the Social Democrats were moderate or revisionist, and most of the party's leaders believed in the possibility of gradual change of the political, economic, and social orders through peaceful means. Rifts in the party developed in the years before World War I, and in 1917 a group with more radical ideals and inspired by the events in Russia left the party to establish the Communist Party. Discord soon developed, however, largely over the amount of influence Moscow had on policies and actions, and several few factions broke off during the inter-war years. The Liberals were the cornerstone of the non-socialist left. The party's origins reached back to 1868. Representing a diverse range of groups, including university faculty, intellectuals, farmers, the less wealthy elements of the middle class, workers, temperance advocates, and free church followers, they were advocates of political democracy and free market capitalism. In the political center was the Farmers' Party, which was the result of the merger of two national agricultural organizations in 1921–1922. This was the party of the small farmers, and it tended to be conservative on political, national, and economic issues; but its leaders developed an important flexibility that allowed them to play key roles in later political developments. The Conservatives (or Right/*Höger*), whose origins go back to 1867, occupied the right of the spectrum. This was the party of the old ruling elites and of order, stability, and legitimacy. In practice the Conservatives were not so much advocates of the status quo as of gradual change, and they frequently designed progressive legislation in order to prevent the left from pushing through more radical versions.

One of the primary goals of the Liberals and Social Democrats was electoral reform, at the core of which was universal suffrage. Pressure for reform in this area grew in the last decades of the nineteenth century, but repeated efforts in the 1890s and early years of the new century to craft a measure acceptable to both houses failed. The Liberals wanted to eliminate the power of the First Chamber, and the Conservatives wanted to prevent that. Tied to the question of extending the vote, however, was the issue of how those votes were applied. The left preferred a system based on single-member constituencies and election by majority (or plurality), which they believed would lead to sweeping election victories for themselves and their allies. The right supported one of multiple-member constituencies with the seats allocated on the basis of proportional representation, for they believed such a system would assure them continued election success and would slow or prevent the victory of the left. In 1906 Arvid Lindman's Conservative Government presented a proposal that included universal male suffrage for the Second Chamber, reducing to forty the number of multiple votes to the First Chamber, and, after amendment, proportional representation for both. The measure passed in both houses, but because some of the changes involved constitutional amendment, they had to be passed a second time. This took place in 1909, and they were first applied in 1911. As sweeping as these might sound, they increased the electorate only to about 20 percent of the population, and the elite nature of the First Chamber was preserved. Further reform came in 1918.

The other key element in the coming of democracy was unqualified acceptance by the crown of the principles that the Government (composed of the Council of State) was responsible to the parliament and not to the crown and should represent the will of the electorate through Second Chamber elections. This was a difficult goal to achieve and a hard threshold for the crown and the old ruling elite to cross.

There was nothing in the 1809 constitution about this concept of government. The king's ministers were just that, his ministers. He chose them, and they were expected to work with him to govern. During the nineteenth century, however, the Council of State had evolved into the cabinet or government. The body was often composed of men who were also sitting members of the Riksdag. It designed programs and policies for parliament's approval, and most of its members ran the various ministries of the state. Although they might pay some attention to the outcome of elections, until 1917 Sweden's kings appointed the Government as they chose. Oscar II and then Gustav V were reluctant to support parliamentarism because it meant yielding to a fundamental change in the nature of the system and, in the process, turning over power to the Liberals, whom they viewed as dangerous, and, worse, to the likes of Hjalmar Branting and his Social Democrats, whom they called threats to the entire old order and dangerous republicans. Repeatedly, kings tried to ignore the results of elections to the Second Chamber, even if they ran strongly against their Conservative allies. The right used the argument that government should be apolitical, not caught up in party politics; and they based the continued appointment of Conservatives on their ongoing control of the less democratic First Chamber.

In 1911 Gustav V was compelled to heed the message being sent by the people. The Conservatives had lost seats in the Second Chamber in the 1908 and 1911 elections. With the latter, the new voting laws had come into practice, and together the Liberals and Social Democrats had a two-to-one majority. To make matters worse, Lindman's Conservative Government had received a strong vote of no-confidence in the Second Chamber two years earlier. A governmental crisis developed. At first Gustav thought he might be able to put together a kind of moderate right-left coalition and avoid asking the Liberals' leader, Karl Staaff, whom he disliked intensely, to form a government. This tactic failed. However, although a Liberal cabinet under Staaff's leadership did come to into office, the king consistently avoided that first minister and his colleagues. Instead, Gustav quietly went about consulting his Conservative favorites and working to bring down the government.

The left and the right continued to disagree over suffrage, parliamentarism, and defense. Gustav used a crisis over the last issue to topple Staaff. The left favored economies in defense through reduced terms of army service and limited capital expenditures. The latter was symbolized by the

Government's canceling of plans to build a light battleship, the so-called F-boat *Sverige*, after it took office in 1911. The king and the right mounted an intense propaganda campaign against the left's defense policies. In the patriotic atmosphere of the time, and given the troubled atmosphere in international relations on the continent, some elements in the public responded enthusiastically. The *Sverige* and two other F-boats were built with funds, around 17 million crowns/*kroner*, raised in two public contribution campaigns! More dramatic was the march by some 30,000 farmers to the Royal Palace in Stockholm on 6 February 1914 to demonstrate their support of the right's pro-defense policies. Gustav addressed the protestors with what has come to be called the Palace Yard Speech—probably written by the famous explorer Sven Hedin. In it the king bitterly attacked the Government's policies and made it clear that they did not reflect his own views. In effect, he publically broke his ties with Staaff and his colleagues. The march and the king's words were all carefully planned to force a crisis, and they worked. Despite the support shown by some 50,000 workers in a counter-demonstration on 8 February, Staaff and his colleagues resigned and a "royal government," led by Hjalmar Hammarskjöld, took office. It had the backing of Gustav and the right in the First Chamber. For the moment Sweden was still governed by the king and the conservative elites that rallied behind him, including money and landed wealth, the nobility, and the officer corps. Old Sweden had triumphed for the time being.

World War I put constitutional questions on hold for about three years. Preserving neutrality was more important. Party politics and social tensions were set aside during the *borgfreden* or "holy truce" in the interests of national security. As the war dragged on, however, old issues resurfaced, fed by the economic problems and hardships brought on by the war. Increasingly it seemed the Government's tilt toward the Germans served only the interests of the few at the expense of the common people. The king and the old elites identified with the German monarchy and the limited (sham) democracy there, and they used the threat of Russia, the traditional enemy, to sustain wider public support. For the left, however, Germany represented all that was wrong with Sweden. The divide opened even wider following the February-March Revolution in Russia.

In early March 1917 the Second Chamber voted to cut by two-thirds a Government request for funding for the so-called neutrality watch. Hammarskjöld took this as a vote of no-confidence and tried to resign. After nearly a month of negotiations, a new Conservative government under Carl Swartz took office. The real challenge to the old order came six months later, following the September elections for the Second Chamber. The outcome of the vote was a crushing defeat for the right. The Conservatives managed to win only fifty-seven seats, down from the eighty-six they held since 1911. The Liberals won sixty-two. The big winners were the Social Democrats, who returned with eighty-six representatives. Clearly, the parties on the left, which had campaigned on the issues of parliamentarism and suffrage reform, had an overwhelming majority in the Second Chamber. What would Gustav do now?

The context in which his decision was made was also important. The United States had entered the war. The situation in Russia was deteriorating, and the Bolshevik Revolution was only weeks away. The Communists had won eleven seats in the election. The specter of revolution seemed to be everywhere. At first the king steered away from parliamentarism. Johan Widén, a moderate Liberal and speaker in the Second Chamber, was charged with the impossible task of forming a Conservative–Liberal–Social Democratic coalition. He and others advised the king to turn to Nils Edén, head of the Liberals, and to allow him to form a left coalition government that would include several Social Democrats, the party's leader Hjalmar Branting among them. They believed it would be safer to have the Social Democrats within a government than left outside it, for they would be moderated by being in power. Gustav relented, but with strings attached. He told Edén that there was to be no reorientation of Sweden's pro-German neutrality. Edén got from the king a verbal agreement to accept the principle of parliamentarism and an assurance that he would not in return create another shadow government on the right. In fact, a peaceful revolution had occurred.

The finale in this phase of Sweden's political development came during a special session of the Riksdag in late fall 1918. Again, the context was very important. Russia was under the leadership of Lenin, whose Bolsheviks advocated (and expected) revolution everywhere. The Finns had become independent in late 1917 and promptly gone to war with themselves. Left versus right, Red versus White battled for six months in a conflict that left scars for over half a century. Germany surrendered in early November, and a wave of revolutions, starting in Kiel, swept across the country. In Sweden old social animosities, labor-management conflicts, war shortages, as well as left and right agitation contributed to a tense atmosphere.

The Left's proposals for universal male-female suffrage in all elections and the elimination of the plural voting system for the First Chamber had been submitted the previous spring. The right had stalled passage because they knew these measures would mean the end of their hold on the First Chamber and their ability to slow the pace of change. Eventually the two houses would become largely identical and redundant. The special session returned to these proposals, and this time they were accepted by both houses. They went into effect in 1921.

By the close of World War I, then, Sweden had all the pieces usually expected of a modern political democracy: several political parties, an active political culture, universal and equal suffrage, and a monarch who had accepted parliamentarism in principle. Although largely peaceful, the transition from oligarchy to democracy had not been easy. It was resisted by the crown and the old ruling elites. What was achieved by 1918 was still rejected by some. Sweden remained socially and politically divided, and on the extremes of the right and left were groups who rejected the new order as either dangerous or not enough, respectively. The troubled decades that followed tested the Swedes' commitment to democracy and their abilities to make it work.

TOWARD A MODERN SOCIETY AND ECONOMY

Old Sweden, the Sweden of the four estates, agricultural Sweden, the Sweden of regional isolation, was dramatically transformed in the century following the Napoleonic Wars. Taken together demographic, social, economic, and technological changes created a new Sweden, a modern Sweden, an industrial Sweden.

Three of the most important and dynamic demographic aspects of this period were population growth, the decline of old social groups and the rise of entirely new ones, and increased mobility of the population. Between 1800 and World War I the number of Swedes rose from 2.35 to 5.5 million. At least three important factors lay behind this. For one, the country was not bled by any wars after 1815. Second, diets gradually improved because of better farming, the end of famines caused by sweeping crop failures, and increasingly diverse food imports. Finally, there was some progress in personal hygiene, public sanitation, and medical practices. Demographically, birth rates remained relatively constant or even fell among some social groups, and death rates, especially among children, declined. Life expectancy rose from about forty in 1800 to just over fifty in 1900, and more children lived to adulthood to marry and have children.

Along with these demographic changes came a striking increase in mobility. This involved movement within the countryside from farm to farm or from farm to rural industrial site, from the countryside to towns and cities, from city to city, and out of Sweden to destinations in Europe and beyond. Including in this was the emigration of over a million Swedes to North America between 1840 and World War I.

The new mobility had many causes, which varied from place to place and changed over time. Simply put, people moved because they wanted to and because they could. What made them want to move? Most important, rural population growth could not be absorbed by an agrarian system operating on a largely fixed land base and in a process of its own very gradual modernization. Simply put, there were too many people and not enough land or jobs in the agricultural sector. In addition, the working conditions of the rural poor were horrible, and farming in parts of Sweden at times was a futile endeavor, usually because of poor soil. A vital corollary to these negatives was the gradual development of rural and urban industrial employment opportunities for men and women, especially after around 1870. Although the pay and working conditions these jobs offered were often miserable, they seemed better than continued rural poverty. Then there was knowledge. This was the result of education, which became more or less universal in Sweden in 1842, and the easy availability of information in cheap newspapers, pamphlets, and books. People came to know more about Sweden, the world, and opportunities; and this heightened their expectations. Knowledge stimulated discontent, restlessness, and dreams. The other side of the explanation lies with the means—the development of better, faster, and more regular internal and international transportation. Mobility was limited in a world in which most people walked, and long-distance travel was by horse, wagon, or sailing ship. Canals, railroads, steamships, better roads, bicycles, and trams revolutionized travel in the nineteenth century and made migration possible.

There were other reasons, too, especially for those who chose to leave Sweden entirely. One of these was religious persecution. Until 1858 to dissent from the beliefs and practices of the State Lutheran church could mean violation of the terms of the Conventicle Act of 1726, which stipulated fines, imprisonment, and even exile for persons who conducted private religions services. Even after the law was repealed, subtle local persecution of people who opted to leave the Lutheran Church could be enough to trigger a decision to emigrate. The compulsory military service that had been introduced under Karl XIV Johan was unpopular, especially among the lower groups in the society, largely because the training periods, regardless of their length, involved physical and psychological abuse meted out mostly by upper-class officers. This appears to have pushed some young men into leaving to avoid what could be a very degrading and unpleasant experience. Other factors were the rigidity of the social hierarchy and lack of upward social mobility, the conservative political system, persecution of Socialists and trade unionists, and legal or financial problems.

Two twentieth-century Swedish novelists have captured some of the basic experiences of the migrants, Per Anders Fogelström and Vilhelm Moberg. In *City of My Dreams*, the first book in a five-volume series,

Fogelström follows Henning Nilsson to Stockholm around 1860 and then describes his life and the lives of his friends and family in the working-class district of Söder. Overcrowded housing, lack of sanitation, long hours of work in disgusting and dangerous conditions, lack of family planning, the fragility of life, the callousness of the upper classes, and the exploitation of women are among the negative themes presented. On the positive side, he also portrays the depth of human commitments and generosity that were present among the working class. Moberg's four-volume emigration novel series takes a company of emigrants from their farms in Småland to Minnesota in the mid-nineteenth century. Through these books he explains the causes of early emigration, the heartbreaking experience of leaving home and family forever, the experience of traveling across the Atlantic and on into the midwest, the process of building new lives, the gradual assimilation of successive generations into American life, and the shattering of dreams and the confronting of realities. Although both these series are fiction and given to exaggeration, they help one to understand two central aspects of nineteenth-century Swedish history.

In terms of social change, a dramatically new society was created in the course of the century. This was laid on top of the old "estate society" that had been used to define Sweden for centuries. The clergy, nobility, burgher elites, and farmers survived, but they lost much of their old importance. The new society was "class" based. It included entrepreneurs, commercial bankers and financiers, managers, civil servants, teachers, retailers, clerks, public and private service employees, and, perhaps most important, industrial workers. In 1870 there were around 80,000 workers classified as industrial. Forty years later the total was about 327,000. It also became a society in which, by 1920, over half the population lived in cities.

The economic transformation that was so crucial to these developments, Sweden's "industrial revolution," occurred between about 1850 and 1914, with many of the most important changes coming after 1870. One must be careful when using the term *industrial revolution*. The concept is often criticized because it implies a suddenness and completeness that ignores the gradual aspects of economic change. Sweden's industrialization began long before 1850 and continued long after 1914. As has been seen, the manufacture of many goods, including wool, iron, charcoal, porcelain, and weapons had taken on "modern" or "industrial" aspects in the late seventeenth-century. Also, over half of the population continued to be rural and engaged in agriculture until after World War I.

The essential elements of economic change included increased productivity across most sectors of the economy, significantly greater productivity in particular elements of the industrial sector, far-reaching organizational

changes in many branches of industry centering on concentration of production facilities, adoption of new technologies in the production processes, and increased demand for capital. A second "stage" in this occurred
from the 1890s and involved the adoption of mass production techniques.
The forest products, iron, textiles, machine goods, and food industries were
among those most involved in these changes.

Sweden's forest products industry had been closely tied with iron making for centuries. The principal commercial product of the sector was charcoal. The forests were generally owned as parts of the agricultural villages
and were exploited by hundreds of small operations close to the iron
foundries. Unlike Norway, Sweden was not a major exporter of sawed lumber. A new situation developed around the middle of the nineteenth century as new iron- and steel-making technologies changed foreign-market
demands. In short, the demand for Swedish bar iron fell, whereas the call
for the country's iron ore rose. At the same time domestic and European demand for sawed lumber expanded, providing a new outlets for Sweden's
forest resources. Here, too, new technologies were important. Steam engines made it possible to locate a sawmill virtually anywhere, and the circular saw speeded up cutting operations. Floating timber from forest to mill
aided in a process of production concentration. As a by-product of the
movement begun in the eighteenth century to consolidate individual
farmer's landholdings into single units and break up the old villages (enclosure), many farmers were left with forest properties that they were willing to sell to timber companies, and a forest ownership revolution occurred.
Some of these changes required large amounts of capital, especially the pre-
paring of rivers to be used for log floating and the building of large cutting
mills. Sweden became a producer of lumber, of sawed planks. The initial
growth took place in the 1850s, but the 1870s was a golden decade. Exports
then increased by some 40 percent.

A related and virtually new industry that also developed in the forest
products sector during this period centered on paper and paper pulp. It
was fed by an exploding world demand, especially for newsprint, and the
development of the sulfite and sulfate paper production processes. The
northern areas of Dalarna and especially Norrland became centers of this
new industry.

Two fundamental changes defined the development of the iron and steel
industry in this period. One occurred in the related, primary branch, and
that was the shift in the export sector from bar iron to ore. The other was a
fundamental change in the nature of the country's iron-making industry.
Precipitating these changes was a series of fundamental changes in iron-
and steel-producing techniques that began in the eighteenth century and

continued through the nineteenth, including the Lancashire method for pig iron manufacture and the Bessemer, Martin, and Thomas methods for making steel. Their adoption tended to start in England and then spread to the continent and Sweden. These developments made the country's bar iron less desirable and less competitive in the European market. Initially, however, Sweden's older methods prevailed, and efforts were made to find new markets. In the long run the industry experienced three basic changes: consolidation, technological adaptation, and product specialization.

The changes in the iron and steel industry of the last third of the nineteenth century are sometimes called *bruksdöden*, the "death of the foundry." In 1870 Sweden had nearly 400 relatively small iron-making foundries, most of them located in the historic *bergslagen* or iron district in the center of the country. By the time of World War I, the number of works had dropped to around 140, and most of the country's production was concentrated in a few large mills such as Domnarvet, Fagersta, and Sandviken.

In the manufacturing sector a number of branches and essential companies developed that have remained important to the present. These included telephone communications equipment from L. M. Ericsson, high intensity lamps from AGA, ball bearings from SKF, explosives from Nobel, cream separators and other dairy equipment from Separator, and a wide variety of power machines, including tractors and locomotives from Munktells. In the textiles branch the greatest changes came in cotton and wool production, whereas linen stagnated. Although this branch had been one of the early industries in Sweden, this had meant concentrating the workers in large factories. It had not meant, however, the introduction of new machines or new kinds of work. Gradually, however, machines like the spinning jenny replaced hand-spinners, and power looms replaced manual ones. Textile factories became textile mills. In the foods sector concentration also replaced localized, small-scale units in brewing, meat packing, flour milling, and dairy produce.

Supporting these changes were vastly improved transportation, banking, and finance systems. An extensive network of railroads was at the heart of the transportation changes. Beginning in the 1850s the state constructed a core of main lines, such as that between Göteborg and Stockholm. Connected to these were privately owned trunk railroads. Steam was also important to water travel, as it provided the means for regularly scheduled coastal, European, and international connections. The means to finance industrial development rested in a number of developments. In the past the venture capitalists of Sweden had been the commercial trading families. They had possessed the resources, and they did contribute to early industrial development. The capital requirements to build a private railroad spur, clear a river for log floating, or construct a steel or textile mill were beyond their means, however. Foreign investment filled some of the demands. Also important was domestic investment based on the rising profits of home industries, and capital accumulation was aided by the growth of commercial banks such as A. O. Wallenberg's *Stockholms Enskilda Bank* (1856), *Skandinavisk Kredit AB* (1864), and *Stockholms Handelsbank* (1871) and the increased popularity of joint-stock companies.

For the people of Sweden, the industrial revolution meant many things, including the creation of a working class, a consumer society, and a perpetually changing material world. It meant new jobs in vastly different settings, an unimagined variety of employment options, and a constantly growing array of manufactured goods that fundamentally altered daily life. Railroads, trolley cars, bicycles, sewing machines, telephones, electric lights, and ice boxes were symbols of that new world. In the long run, the lives of people improved, but at a price. There was a dark side to these changes. The early factories were unpleasant places in which to work, and there were no standards to regulate their operation. Heat, dirt, dangerous equipment, no regard for the environment, and long hours were just some of the evils of early industrialization. The working-class neighborhoods that grew up around the factories were no better. In the decades before World War I, tentative and limited steps were taken to alleviate these conditions. In 1881, for example, laws were passed to limit the hours of child labor and provide government contributions to health insurance funds set up by workers' organizations. A limited workers' safety law was instituted in 1889. Regulations covering women working in mines, in the first four months following a pregnancy, and at night were added between 1900 and 1910.

The workers could do little to improve either their wages or the working conditions. Government was the ally of the owners, managers, and entrepreneurs. To organize or join a union was dangerous. Employers were quick to dismiss union-minded employees, and the organization movement faced daunting legal obstacles such as the Åkarp Law from 1899 that prohibited union workers from blocking strike-breaking replacements hired by employers. Typically, owners responded to efforts by workers to organize or strike with lockouts and firings. Even peaceful protests or marches were often dispersed by sword-carrying mounted police.

Labor market relations are a key element in the social history of modern Sweden. The country's earliest labor organizations were not formed by industrial workers; rather, they appeared first among artisans. The first to organize were the typesetters of Stockholm in 1846. These associations had no strong ideological aspects and were not dedicated to labor-management issues. Their concerns were with identity, social solidarity, and the welfare of the members. More modern craft unions were established from the late 1860s.

The next stage in this process was the founding of national unions, first in the trades and then in specific industries. This occurred in the 1880s and after, by which time the economy had advanced enough to produce a critical mass of workers and the ideologies of union organization had reached Sweden from the continent, especially from Germany and Denmark. Again, the typesetters led the way in 1886, and they were followed by postal workers (1886) painters (1887), and bricklayers (1889). Metal industry workers were the first industrial branch to organize in 1888. Other branch unions included clothing (1889), building construction and woodworking (1889), unskilled and factory workers (1891), sawmills and transport (1897), and railroad (1899). Eventually there were some forty-five skilled trade or industrial unions in Sweden. Membership rose from around 8,000 in 1890 to 66,000 in 1900, to 614,000 in 1930. In 2000 it was over 2 million.

No universally accepted ideological affiliation has ever dominated the country's labor movement, nor have all unions' activities been coordinated by any single central group. Some unions were strong; others were weak. Some were Liberal in their political identification, others were Social Democrat. Over time syndicalism and communism entered as ideological alternatives. In August 1898, at a meeting of union representatives held at the Victoria Theater in Stockholm, a national federation of industrial unions was founded, *Landsorganisationen i Sverige (LO)*. There were close links between the leaders of *LO* and the Social Democratic Party, but it proved impossible to force unions and their members to support the party. Gradually *LO* gained primary importance among the industrial unions, especially during the interwar years.

Essential to the evolution of the labor market in Sweden was the creation in 1902 of *LO*'s counterorganization, the Swedish Employers' Federation or *Svenska Arbetsgivareföreningen (SAF)*. It was a collective of other industrial employers' groups. Both *SAF* and *LO* established their headquarters in Stockholm, and gradually the two developed as the most important units in labor-management relations in Sweden. In 1906 they concluded a basic agreement by which labor recognized management's right to hire, dismiss, and define job expectations, whereas management recognized the unions' right to represent the workers. This deal was an important step toward establishing the legitimacy of the unions and a relatively peaceful labor-management environment in which grievances could be settled without outside interference. It would be years, however, before this was achieved. The owners were part of the establishment in Sweden. They were among the elite that controlled the government, and they jealously guarded what they believed were their rights in the workplace. Labor was ideologically divided and until the 1930s relatively powerless in the political arena.

The strike was the most important action available to the unions. The lockout was the standard employer response, often linked with the hiring of replacement workers. Violence was more common than often admitted, and both sides in the labor market had their important historical moments and martyrs. For labor, a strike among the sawmill workers of Sundsvall in 1879 has always been taken as a key definer of issues, tactics, and responses. The workers were being asked to take reduced pay because of a downturn in demand. Their wages were already marginal, and they were unwilling to comply with the employers' demands. Without any formal organization, some 5,000 workers went on strike. The owners replied with a lockout, and the authorities backed the bosses. In a march on the town center, the workers were met by military forces. Many were evicted from their homes and replaced by new workers brought in by management. Without a strike fund, the workers' situation was hopeless. The lessons of Sundsvall were clear: Build strong organizations with sufficient resources to hold out and force the employers to negotiate, and do not expect help from the government.

A second key event involved dock workers in the port city of Malmö on the southwest coast. In 1908 workers struck for better pay, terms of work, and job security. The shippers responded by importing new workers from abroad through a well-established system that drew willing replacement labor from all over northwestern Europe, including Germany, the United Kingdom, and the other Scandinavian countries. A small group of angry and frustrated young people, members of the local socialist youth organization, hatched a plot over coffee in a local shop. They would scare the strikebreakers with a bomb. On the night of 11–12 July 1908, three of the conspirators rowed out to the *Amalthea*, a Swedish ship housing English replacement workers, and threw a bomb into an open ventilation hatch. The explosion did far more damage than expected. One man was killed and seven injured. The trail to the perpetrators was easily followed by the authorities. Following a trial, the two leading figures, Anton Nilsson and Algot Rosberg, were sentenced to die. A third man was given life in prison. Several others received fines or lesser sentences. Public outcries against the death sentences led to their later reversal, however. The darkest sides of the labor market were revealed by this event and the subsequent trials.

A third key event was the General Strike of 1909. The general strike was viewed as the single most powerful action the union movement could take. In theory, it probably was. Seven years earlier, *LO* had organized a three-day strike to demonstrate its support of suffrage reform. The 1909 action had more pressing and immediate issues behind it. Because of an economic slowdown, the employers were putting forth their usual list of crisis actions: They asked workers to postpone raise requests, accept freezes on wages, and even cut back work schedules. When talks stalled, *SAF* replied with a national lockout of workers on 2 August. Two days later *LO* called for a general strike in response. What followed was a debacle for labor. The *LO* leadership was indecisive, many unions' strike reserves were limited, and a number of major unions, including the Railroad Workers, did not support the action. Within a month most workers were back on the job; a few groups held out until Christmas. In the aftermath *LO* union membership fell from around 180,000 to under 90,000, and the leadership was badly discredited. In the long run valuable lessons in planning and public relations were learned, and the movement was able to recover over the following decade or so. (In 1920 *LO* had 280,000 members; in 1930 that number was around 553,000, and in 1940 it was 971,000.)

Certainly as important as the development of an industrial working class and its organizations were the changes that came about or were at least initiated in the lives of women. During this period new work situations developed, new occupation options opened up, legal rights were secured, direct political participation began, and attitudes altered. At the outset of the nineteenth century, women had few legal rights or options in life. They were considered physically, intellectually, and morally inferior; and they were always under the legal domination of a male, be it a father, husband, brother, or other guardian. Their lives, property, and income, and even their children, were not their own. They did not have equal inheritance rights. The only truly independent women were widows; yet they were expected not to remain widows for long. Of course, these generalizations omit the many exceptions. Not all women experienced lives of male-dominated misery.

An important aspect of the changes that did occur was the development of an understanding of women's lives. This came through the voices of articulate women writers and speakers. One of the most important was Fredrika Bremer (1801–1865). Although she was born in Åbo, Finland, Bremer grew up near Stockholm in a comfortable but unpleasant upper-middle-class home. Her father was a tyrant; her mother a self-centered socialite. What formal education she received was through governesses and tutors, and it focused on the social graces expected of someone of her class. Through her own travels in Sweden, Europe, and the New World she rose far above this limited background. During the 1830s and 1840s she published several novels that described in vivid detail the world in which she was raised. These novels established her as a founder of the realistic school in Sweden. She entered the public debate over the rights of women with the novel *Hertha*, published in 1856, in which she attacked the situation women of spirit and energy faced in a world that legally and socially restricted their freedoms. This work probably contributed to the passage of a law in 1858 that gave legal independence to women over twenty-five.

Ellen Key (1849–1926) belonged to the next generation of women's rights champions. She, too, grew up in a privileged home, but with a father who was a political liberal and shared her ideals. She became a teacher, lecturer, and writer. Her interests were as broad as those of Fredrika Bremer, but her medium was nonfiction, mainly short studies of particular issues. As a feminist she was controversial, and she was scorned by some because she argued that women should not try to imitate or compete with men but, rather, should pursue lives and careers that reflected their natural, nurturing traits.

The struggles for women's rights took two tracks during this period, one middle class, the other working class. The former focused on legal questions, the latter on work issues. The former worked through organizations of like-minded bourgeois women with the time to write, publish, and campaign, groups including the Fredrika Bremer Association or the Association for Women's Suffrage. The latter was the domain of women without leisure time. They worked through unions and political parties, especially the Social Democratic Party, in which they had their own organization. The former track was the more successful in this period, as important changes were passed by parliament, including equality in inheritance (1845), legal independence (1858), suffrage (1862 and 1918), access to the universities through the right to take the admissions tests (1870), right to their own incomes (1874), and independence for married women (c.1890).

The tangible changes in their lives form another important aspect of women's history in this period. For all women this meant greater access to education, through the 1842 reforms, the gradual opening of the universities after 1870, and the founding of teaching colleges. Linked to these developments were new career options, including medicine and teaching at all educational levels. Ellen Fries was the first woman to receive a doctorate in 1883. Middle-class women were not expected to work and may have been in the most frustrating position of all. The societal ideal was portrayed by the Norwegian author Henrik Ibsen in *A Doll's House*. Bourgeois wives were showpieces. They were responsible for running the household, but the actual duties were taken over by domestics. Perhaps the greatest changes came for working-class women. Job opportunities were many in manufacturing, retail, and domestic service. Whole new jobs appeared such as that of telephone operator, whereas others vanished, such as that of hand spinner. Gaining jobs and rights, however, did not mean gaining equality with men. Women were still expected to raise children and maintain households. Working women, regardless of their social class, had two-careers—one on the job, one at home. Further, women's work was not equally valued with men's work, and they were paid less even for doing the same job. Much changed and much was accomplished during the nineteenth century, but much remained to be achieved.

The introduction of comprehensive, compulsory education was an important aspect of this period, too. It reflected social needs and state interest in shaping society. Literacy rates had been relatively high in Sweden for centuries primarily because of the Church's concern with the people's ability to read the basic literature of the faith, including the Scriptures, psalms, and catechism. The requirements for confirmation in the Church also included basic literacy. The parish clerk was usually expected to also act as the parish teacher. The Early Modern Period is filled with steps toward increased educational opportunities for various groups in the society, but none of these were universal. By the 1830s, without central planning and with very little government action, about half of the country's parishes had schools and many others were served by itinerant teachers who would set up classes in private homes.

The 1842 school law came after decades of study by parliamentary committees and was designed to create a national system. It followed similar moves in Denmark (1814) and Norway (1827). Under the terms of the new law, every rural and urban parish was to have at least one permanent school (*folkskola*) for boys and girls staffed by a trained teacher; unless home-schooled, children were to start school no later than their ninth year; teacher seminaries were to be established in each of the bishop towns; teacher pay was set; school governance was to be under the control of a council headed by the local rector; costs were to be met by a combination of taxes and fees; and these steps were to be taken within five years. Although progress was slower than the law mandated, a national system, with wide local variations, did gradually develop. From the parliament poured revisions affecting every aspect of the system, among them the division of the basic school into two units where possible, one for younger children, the other for older pupils (1858). Other revisions included the establishment of a seven-year term for compulsory schooling in 1882 and the extension of teacher training from three years to four in 1863. Curricula in the lower schools focused on Christianity, Swedish, arithmetic, local history, work skills, singing, crafts, and games. The upper schools emphasized traditional subjects such as geometry, geography, natural science, history, art, and physical education; but they also might offer courses in specific crafts or occupations. It was in these schools that young people learned what it meant to be "Swedish." A strongly nationalistic version of history was taught, along with respect for national symbols. Much of what students read, saw, heard, and did was strongly nationalistic.

A second important educational development for the lower classes was the folk high school movement. This movement originated in Denmark and spread throughout Scandinavia in the second half of the nineteenth century. It grew from the ideas of N.F.S. Grundtvig. He believed schools should provide young people with a "living" education rather than the old-fashioned education in stale and often useless material through rote learning. History, mythology, poetry, and language were central to the curriculum, which was supposed to nurture a love of the nation and a sense of community. The first folk high school was established in Rødding in northern Slesvig in 1844. The earliest Swedish folk high schools were founded in the late 1860s in Skåne. By the end of the century there were over two dozen. (Today there are about 150.) Initially the folk high schools were rural, and their curricula often included agricultural subjects alongside the original core studies. Over time schools were founded with different emphases, among them labor organization, temperance, folk crafts, or a particular church denomination.

The basic state schools and folk high schools were primarily for the lower classes, and they did little to bring the varied layers of Swedish society together. The parish organization of the national system virtually guaranteed social segregation. Besides, the upper classes had other options including private schools and tutors. Also, the state school system did not provide for ongoing, secondary education. Students were allowed to leave school after the compulsory seven years, and most did. Secondary schools and universities remained largely for the elites. This dualism lasted until well into the twentieth century.

Higher education in Sweden experienced considerable growth in scale and diversity during the nineteenth century. Naturally, the universities in Uppsala and Lund experienced these changes. A college, referred to as a "high school," was established in Stockholm in 1878. It became Stockholm University in 1960. A college established in Göteborg in 1891 evolved into a degree-granting institution in 1907 and became Göteborg University in 1954. The Royal Technical High School in Stockholm, established in 1827, and Chalmers Institute, founded in Göteborg in 1829, were the premier schools for students pursuing technical careers. The Karolinska Institute in Stockholm, whose roots go back into the eighteenth century, became a center for medical studies. In addition, a system of teaching seminaries or colleges developed.

Another important theme of this period is the creation of what might be called organization Sweden. This involved the founding of a wide range of secular and religious organizations, the expansion of their membership, and the development of their varied and important roles within society. Some of these groups, such as the political parties, labor market organizations, and women's rights groups, have already been considered. There were, however, many more groups, including those dedicated to the preservation of historic handcrafts, the welfare of children or the poor, the spread of religious ideas, continuing education, and the use of leisure time. Among the most important (or the most visible) were the free churches or denominations and the temperance societies.

The religious freedom guaranteed under the 1809 constitution and the repeal of the Conventicle Act in 1857 opened the way for religious diversity in Sweden. Tentative steps in this direction were taken prior to about 1860, and a powerful and vital religious revivalist movement developed thereafter. In part, it included offshoots of the State Lutheran Church such as the Evangelical Patriotic Society and the Mission Society, but it also was defined by the growth of thriving Baptist, Methodist, and Salvation Army elements.

Temperance was an old issue in Sweden, and for good reason. In 1850 annual alcohol consumption was nearly eleven liters of hard liquor, plus small amounts of beer and wine, per person. Redistribute this figure to the primary consumers, adult males, and the potential problems are obvious. Gustav III, as we have seen, tried to eliminate private stills in the late eighteenth century in part because of the social evils they produced. Eighteenth-century Lutheran pietists and nineteenth-century Lutheran revivalists objected to alcohol use. During the early nineteenth-century, groups such as the Swedish Temperance Society developed a movement to abolish hard liquor. They partially achieved their goal in 1855, when private stills were banned. A new phase in temperance history took shape in Sweden from the 1870s. It was represented by a number of diverse organizations including the free churches, the International Order of Good Templars (IOGT), *Sveriges Blåbandsföreningen* (Sweden's Blue Ribbon Society), the National Templar Order, *Vita bandet* (the White Ribbon, a women's group), and *Verdandi*. By 1900 the IOGT and Blue Ribbon Society had a combined membership of about 230,000. In addition, many of the trade unions favored temperance, in part because it was believed that the liquor producers and retailers were among those responsible for perpetuating the misery of the working class. Also, many Liberals and Social Democrats were pro-temperance.

Although never fully unified on ideals or goals, the movement generally favored the total prohibition of all alcoholic beverages. As far-reaching as

86   The History of Sweden

this was, a national referendum, organized by the temperance societies in 1909, showed that over half of the country's adults agreed with the goal. By this time, however, a measure of political realism had made its way into the primary organizations of the movement, and in the years just before to World War I they pushed for a local option system that served as the basis for 1917 legislation making it possible for individual communities to ban alcoholic beverages. The same year also saw the introduction of the Bratt system, under which adults were issued a ration book used to control liquor purchases. Devised by Ivan Bratt, a Stockholm physician, the system remained in place until 1955.

In addition to serving the special interests of their members, almost all these organizations fulfilled other functions and needs as well. They were important as social and cultural centers, as focal points around which like-minded friends gathered. In a rapidly changing and highly mobile society, they often replaced the family. In addition, they acted as schools in participatory democracy. Organizational meetings were places where arguments could be made, debate conducted, resolutions designed and passed, and compromise effected. A high number of the country's leading political figures were also members of one or more of these organizations. In 1914, for example, seventy-four of the Social Democratic representatives in the Second Chamber of the parliament were also members of temperance groups.

All the political, economic, and social developments outlined here were pieces in the larger process of creating a modern Sweden. In the context of this process, the people of Sweden also became "Swedes." Through a complex blending of self-identification and national identity creation, they were nationalized. Of course, there had been earlier forms of nationalism. Gustav II Adolf had, for example, used the Church to encourage a sense of national identity. The clergy were his public relations agents. But until the second half of the nineteenth century, most Swedes built their identities on a scale that ran from farm to parish to county to country. The change came for many reasons, some personal and others political. First, old localisms dissolved as a result of population mobility and better communications. Second, people uprooted from their local communities needed and sought new bases for their identities. Third, a far more informed national awareness (patriotism) could be created through public schools and the media than had ever been possible before, and this was desired by some political leaders. Finally, the nation was considered an ideal and, by some, as the *end* of history.

Important to the process of creating national identity were many reinforcing elements. The blue and yellow flag became increasingly important.

An old provincial folk song, *"Du gamla, du fria"* (You old, you free), rewritten in the 1840s, became accepted as the national anthem by the 1890s. Popular national histories that focused on the development of the state and the achievements of a small circle of heroes (the Vikings, Engelbrekt Engelbrektsson, Gustav I Vasa, Gustavus Adolphus, and Charles XII) were written and made available in inexpensive editions, such as *Berättelser ur Svenska Historien* (Tales from Swedish History) by C. G. Starbäck and P. O. Bäckström from 1885. Nearly vanished folk arts were revived, and common folk learned to carve medieval runes. The Nordic Museum in Stockholm was founded in 1880 to preserve the country's material past. Popular art and literature emphasized the past, and mythology and folklore enjoyed great popularity.

INTERNATIONAL RELATIONS

Despite any and all pretensions to the contrary, Sweden has been a minor player, a country acted upon rather than acting, in most diplomatic situations since 1721. As has been seen, several eighteenth-century leaders refused to recognize this. Gustav IV also ignored realities when he took the country to war against Napoleon in 1805. Two years later he was at war with Russia as well. The disaster that followed cost him his throne and Finland. The Swedes fought their last wars in 1813–1814, against Napoleon, Denmark, and Norway. Thereafter, they stood aloof from or managed to stay out of every European war, including World War I and II. This does not mean, however, that Sweden does not have a diplomatic history in the modern period. Virtually all the nineteenth century monarchs had dreams of becoming engaged in one foreign adventure or another. At the same time Sweden was a factor, albeit a minor one in most cases, in the European state system of the period, playing parts in episodes that involved Denmark, Russia, Great Britain, France, and Germany.

In general Sweden's leaders worked to maintain peace in the Baltic region. Until midcentury they generally pursued a policy of rapprochement with Russia, despite the loss of Finland and easily aroused anti-Russian feelings in Sweden. This line was strained, however, in the 1830s, when the Russians began to build fortifications on the Åland Islands. Barely thirty miles from the Swedish mainland and less than a hundred miles from Stockholm was too close for comfort. A visit by Tsar Nicholas I eased concerns but did not erase them. The Swedes also sought to strengthen relations with Britain and France during the same period. However, when the Great Powers clashed, as in the case of British and Russian interests in the eastern Mediterranean in the 1830s, they remained neutral.

The Crimean War (1853–1856) pitted Russia against Britain, France, and Italy and triggered a dramatic change in Sweden's foreign policy. The pro-Russian line was dropped. In part this was because Oscar I had a tendency to go his own way on foreign policy. It was also because the British and French dangled recovering the Ålands and even Finland before the Swedes as bait, trying to entice them into entering the war. Oscar was tempted, but he remained cautious. Sweden declared its neutrality in the conflict, though tilted in favor of the Western powers. Swedish territorial waters and ports were open to their warships, and French forces even razed the new fortifications at Bomarsund on the Åland Islands. The potential of Swedish involvement may have encouraged the Russians to seek peace. Hoping for spoils, Swedish representatives attended the peace conference in Paris. They came away only with the guaranteed demilitarization of the Ålands.

Oscar I and then Karl XV very nearly committed Sweden to direct involvement in two wars between Denmark and various German states over control of the duchies of Slesvig and Holstein. These two territories were tied to Denmark through a web of historic links with the royal family. Ethnically, Holstein was German, and Slesvig was partially so. German nationalism in the duchies clashed with Danish nationalism, however. The duchies were caught up in the revolutionary fever of 1848 and declared their independence. The Danes went to war to keep them, and Oscar I offered aid, sending some 15,000 Swedish-Norwegian troops. They did not see combat and were recalled after only a few months. Oscar also helped arrange a ceasefire in the summer of 1848; although Sweden was part of the multinational agreements that ended the war in 1852, it failed to solve the nationality problems in the duchies. Eleven years later, in 1863, Sweden nearly became involved in the second Slesvig-Holstein War. In this instance Karl XV, who also dreamed of establishing a new Nordic union under his leadership, met with Frederik VII in July 1863 and promised support. Karl's advisors were divided when they learned of his personal diplomacy, and neither the public nor the parliament in either Norway and Sweden favored war. In this instance no troops were sent, and Karl's dreams were dashed. Denmark's forces were mauled, and both duchies were lost.

During the last decades of the century, Sweden's foreign policy was curiously multifaceted. In part this was because Oscar II took a personal interest in foreign affairs, which he regarded as a prerogative not yet entirely the domain of his ministers and parliament. He knew Sweden needed friends to parry any threat from the east (Russia) and to support Sweden in the event of troubles with Norway. As a result, Sweden pursued friendly relations with Germany after its unification in 1871 and with Britain. Sweden viewed Bismarck's Germany as a natural friend and ally against a Russia that seemed more and more unpredictable and aggressive. Also important in the pro-German shift were close dynastic, cultural, intellectual, economic, and political ties. At the same time relations with France became more distant after the founding of the Second Republic.

Despite its largely peaceful foreign policy, Sweden did not abandon maintaining significant military forces during this period for at least three reasons; fear of attack, to give the country options in foreign policy, and to maintain internal order. Calls for a sweeping reform of how the army was recruited went unfulfilled for nearly a century after 1814. Karl XI's allotment system remained in place. To supplement this, however, Karl XIV Johan succeeding in winning the approval of a compulsory service law at a special meeting of the parliament in 1812, despite strong opposition from the House of the Farmers in the Riksdag. Under this act all men between twenty and twenty-five were eligible, except for certain officials, and inductees could avoid service by sending an alternate. The law was intended to provide additional forces in an emergency, and the length of service was not specified. In 1841 the training term was set at twelve days. This subsequently rose in a series of changes in the final decades of the century, finally reaching 240 days in 1901. Along with the gradual growth of the army came the building of new fortifications. Karlsborg, on the west coast of Lake Vättern, was begun in the 1820s, but modifications on the site continued into the twentieth century. Boden, in the far north, became the center of defense preparations around 1900. The locations of these two centers reflect how the perceived dangers changed over the course of the century. Karlsborg was to defend Sweden from an attack from the west; Boden would protect the country from a Russian attack from the north through Finland.

Until late in the century the navy received less attention than the army. The coastal and high seas units merged following the Napoleonic Wars; in general, though ships and facilities were neglected and reliance was placed on England's support in the Baltic. After 1880 new attention was given to naval strength, triggered by Russia's increasingly expansionist foreign policy and then by its moves to "russify" the Finns. Between 1883 and 1903 twelve new ironclad ships were built.

As new weapons such as breech-loading rifles, smokeless gunpowder (developed by Alfred Nobel), a more modern cannon, and steam-powered ironclad ships were developed, Sweden took steps to adopt them. The growing size of continental armies in the late nineteenth century alarmed security-minded Swedes. Compounding the concern were increasingly troubled relations with the Norwegians. Defense became a major political issue of the time and exposed important fractures in the society. Bureaucrats and military officers found willing supporters of greater defense expenditures especially among the farmers. On the other side of the debate, the Liberals and Social Democrats were highly critical of increased military expenditures when there were other serious social and economic problems. They often used the term "the fortified poor house" to describe the Sweden their opponents seemed to favor. Nonetheless, the decision to build the new fortress in the far north at Boden in 1900, the extension of the universal service term to 240 days in 1901, the appropriation of funds to build the F-boat in 1911, and the scale of the Farmers' March in 1914 demonstrate the strength of the pro-defense forces.

On an entirely different diplomatic level, Sweden became involved in many Scandinavian and European cross-national programs. Sweden and Norway cooperated in joint railroad projects connecting the two countries. A Nordic postal union was established in 1869, and a Danish-Swedish currency union in 1873 that Norway joined two years later. There was even agreement on spelling standards across the languages. In a broader context, Sweden adopted the metric system in 1855, participated in the Hague International Peace Conferences of 1899 and 1907, and supported the agreements reached at the latter covering the rights of neutrals and neutral shipping.

An issue that was not just diplomatic but also economic, political, and cultural haunted the Swedes for much of the century and especially between about 1880 and 1905, and that was the union with Norway. This poisoned relations between the two peoples and distorted the political arena in both countries, drawing needed attention away from serious domestic problems. It was an issue often driven by emotions and not by reason. For both peoples it was a matter of national pride.

The Swedes had lost Finland to Russia in 1809, and Norway became a target, seen as compensation for that loss. In 1813 Sweden was a member of the coalition fighting to defeat Napoleon. Following the emperor's defeat at Leipzig in October 1813, Karl XIV Johan turned his army toward Denmark. A flurry of negotiations led to the Treaty of Kiel, signed in January 1814, by which Norway was to be awarded to the Swedish king—not annexed, but attached to Sweden by a dynastic union. Within the cauldron of these events, a politically active elite in Norway opted to try to establish their country's independence. A constitution was written at Eidsvoll and a popular Danish prince, Christian Frederik, chosen to be king. Independence was declared on 17 May 1814. Karl Johan's response was to move troops and naval units against Norway. Some 45,000 Swedish troops faced off against about 33,000 Norwegians in "The Cats' War," a two-week series of border clashes and posturing that began at the end of July. Almost simultaneously talks were initiated, and on 14 August a diplomatic solution was reached at Moss. In the end the Norwegians accepted the union, bitterly, but on relatively favorable terms. Most important, they kept their constitution without significant amendment and preserved their autonomy.

Many accounts of the history of this union emphasize the differences that divided Swedes and Norwegians, thereby making the union's dissolution appear inevitable. Perhaps this view is true. Nationalism shaped much of the history of Europe in the nineteenth century, and Scandinavia was certainly not immune to or divorced from its influences. In general, uniqueness was emphasized over similarities in art, literature, and history; and after midcentury the trend was toward separation. In an increasingly charged atmosphere a number of basic issues were used to heighten tensions. One of these was the position of governor general or *ståthållare*, a royal appointee who resided in the Norwegian capital of Christiania/Oslo and symbolized the union. Karl XV created a noisy political crisis in the late 1850s when he personally proposed to eliminate the position. Conservative opinion in Sweden was outraged, and the king's council refused to support him; as a result, Karl was forced to withdraw his offer. The "great Sweden" faction had won the day, but at the cost of inflaming anti-union opinion in Norway. Ironically, the office went unfilled for nearly twenty years and was eliminated by Oscar II in 1873. A second base for contention involved fundamental constitutional differences between the two realms. Norway's constitution provided for a more modern, two-chamber parliament and gave the king only a delaying veto. A crisis over the latter issue led to its reaffirmation and the adoption, in practice, of the principle of ministerial responsibility to the Norwegian parliament (parliamentarism) in the early 1880s. A seemingly trivial dispute raged over flags. Some of the flags of each country contained the colors of the other in an upper quadrant, symbolizing the union in a very public way. Many Norwegians wanted a "pure" flag for their merchant fleet. They got their way in 1898. The issue used to break the union was Norway's right to have its own consular service, that is, its own network of diplomatic offices to represent Norwegian interests abroad short of a separate foreign office and diplomatic service. The failure of negotiations over this and other questions in 1895 led to a war scare in the late spring, but the Norwegians backed away from confrontation because of their military unpreparedness and diplomatic isolation. Unresolved, the union issue dragged on into the new century.

The truth of the matter is that compromise was impossible. Swedish officials could not simply negotiate an end to the union, which is what the Norwegians really wanted. How deeply ordinary people in either country were engaged in the union controversies is unclear. On a day-to-day basis Norwegians and Swedes seemed to get along well. The border was virtually transparent, as the languages merged and people and products flowed freely across it. Only a series of aging fortresses such as the one at Halden stood to symbolize the historical differences. Yet, school curricula were designed to instill national pride in the people of both countries, and public opinion was manipulated by the press. Politically, the left in Sweden was generally opposed to continuing the union. Democracy, suffrage, and workers' rights were more important than clinging to some remnant of Sweden's heroic past. A few ardent nationalists on the right, including Sven Hedin, supported the union, but even among Conservatives the costs were being questioned. Following the failure of the last union committee to reach a consensus on the consular question in 1904, Norwegian government leaders chose to act. A bill to establish a consular service was passed, Oscar II vetoed it, and the Norwegian government resigned. When the king was unable to form a new government in Norway—because the Norwegians had planned it that way—the union was declared dissolved on 7 June 1905. Sabers rattled amidst a frenzy of diplomacy, but there was no real danger of a war, and no real support for one, especially in Sweden. The Riksdag accepted in principle the Norwegians' actions in late June, and negotiations at Karlstad led to the signing of a formal settlement in October.

5

Troubles and Achievements, 1914–1945

The thirty-one years between the onset of World War I in August 1914 and the close of World War II in Europe in May 1945 was an oddly paradoxical time, a time that seemed to be beset by unresolvable problems and frightening new developments on the one hand and filled with promise and creativity on the other. The era began and ended with a world war, each of which offered opportunities and created very serious tensions and problems for a Sweden. The 1920s and 1930s were deeply troubled by some of the worst economic crises of the twentieth century, social and political polarization, the rise of fascism, the destruction of democracy in much of Europe, and the gradual unraveling of peace. They were also decades of political cooperation and the successful working of the country's new democracy, creative and long-lasting social and economic programs, economic and social progress, and remarkable culture achievements.

WORLD WAR I

The outbreak of war in the summer of 1914 surprised few observers. The length, intensity, and impacts of the war surprised many. Expectations did not match realities. Both the Entente (Britain, France, and Russia) and the Allied powers (Germany and Austria-Hungary) planned for quick victories. Sweden and its Nordic neighbors hoped to avoid involvement. Denmark, Norway, and Sweden had announced their intention in 1912 to remain neutral in any Great Power conflict, and this stance was jointly reaffirmed on 3 August 1914. The Hammarskjöld Government, with Knut Wallenberg as foreign minister, charted a course that alleged compliance with the rules of neutrality but actually favored Germany for the next three years. This pro-German tilt was not surprising. Sweden's foreign policy had leaned toward Germany for over forty years. The royal family, as well as many members of the old nobility, had strong ties to Germany. Gustav V's wife was Victoria of Baden, a cousin of the Kaiser, Wilhelm II. Germany's political system, an autocratic monarchy disguised as a parliamentary democracy, was popular among Swedish conservatives. Economically, Germany was a vital source of raw materials and finished goods as well as a key buyer of Sweden's iron ore and manufactured products. Intellectual and academic links with Germany were close. Even some of Sweden's socialists sympathized with Germany because of the ideological and historical importance of the movement there. Also, there were those in Sweden who saw the war in France as a tragic mistake that would soon end and who supported Germany's war against Sweden's historical enemy, Russia. That was the war that mattered.

Until spring 1916 public opinion supported the Government's conduct of foreign affairs with little criticism, and a political truce, the so-called *borgfreden*, held. Constitutional and social problems were laid aside. Only a small radical fringe on the right, including the explorer Sven Hedin, voiced discontent and called upon Sweden to join Germany in a crusade to save civilization. In effect, the country's neutrality tilted benevolently toward Germany, especially in economic terms. A prewar bias toward Britain in trade was reversed. Germany received the bulk of the country's iron ore production, for example. In return, the Germans provided much-needed coal and other essential goods through the Baltic. Trade with the Entente Powers dwindled because of their trade policies and the effectiveness of both sides' blockades. Particularly concerned that potential war materiel reaching Sweden would be reexported to Germany or be used in the manufacture of war-related products, the British imposed very strict limits on shipping for all the neutrals. At the same time mining operations by the belligerents and Sweden effectively closed the Baltic to most outside traffic. Overall, Sweden's export-import trade fell precipitously, and this led to serious problems, especially in the last two years of the war. Shortages of fuel and raw materials forced cutbacks and closures in industry, and layoffs of workers followed. In order to deal with the economic troubles, a number of special government commissions were created to regulate prices, supply, use of commodities, and distribution. Rationing began in 1916 and grew to include sugar, coffee, milk, bread, and eventually even potatoes. The food situation was made worse by poor crops, government restrictions on the uses of domestically grown grains, and the lack of imported fodder. Animal populations fell, dairy production declined, and meat virtually disappeared from stores. Despite the Government's efforts distribution was uneven, a thriving black market developed, and prices rose by as much as 300 percent over the course of the war. Whereas a few entrepreneurs got rich on the war, many people suffered.

The worsening economic and supply situations led to heightened social tensions, demonstrations, food riots, shop looting, and growing criticism of the Government, especially from the socialist left. The situation became acute in spring 1917. Hammarskjöld, who was being called "Hungerskjöld" by critics, and his colleagues came under attack in the streets, press, and parliament. The country's leaders were accused of putting favoritism toward Germany ahead of the interests of the people, especially in their stalling on negotiations with the British on trade. (Britain and the United States after entering the war in April 1917, wanted Sweden to alter the bias of its neutrality toward them.) The Government did not represent the will of the voters for the Second Chamber and was seen as a royal ministry, not a democratic one. In this charged atmosphere the revolution in Russia in March 1917 was especially important. It must have terrified the right. The tsarist regime dissolved, and the Provisional Government took steps toward installing a genuine democracy in Russia. These developments weakened any argument about how the Germans were protecting Sweden from the tyranny of Russian barbarism. Following the defeat of a national defense appropriation measure in the Second Chamber, Hammarskjöld stepped down and was replaced by the Carl Swartz at the head of a moderate conservative government. Policy did not change, however, and the real clash of constitutional options was postponed until after the fall election.

The summer of 1917, leading up to the September Second Chamber election, was a lively one. Criticism of the Government grew. A demonstration outside the Parliament Building in June was dispersed by mounted police wielding drawn swords. The Germans, fearing they might lose Sweden's trade and believing they were going to win the war, courted Swedish favor. They used the return of the Åland Islands, lost to Sweden in 1809, as bait. At the same time the situation in Russia worsened. The summer offensive was a disaster. Lenin had been smuggled back into the country through Finland in April and was at work encouraging a more far-reaching revolution. Making matters worse for the Swartz Government was the well-timed revelation by the United States and Britain that the German minister in Argentina, Count Karl von Luxburg, had been routing coded dispatches to Berlin through the Swedish embassy in Buenos Aires. Some of these dispatches provided shipping information; others ridiculed members of the Argentine government. Whichever the case, Sweden's assistance was a flagrant violation of the rules of neutrality. Taking place in this highly charged atmosphere, the election was a disaster for the Conservatives, who lost twenty-nine seats. As we have seen, the outcome of the election and the volatile context convinced Gustav V to turn to Liberal leader Nils Edén to build a coalition with the Social Democrats and to accept the principle of parliamentary responsibility.

Outside events played important roles in developments in Sweden right down to the end of the war and beyond. During the winter of 1917–1918, it was the Germans who seemed to have the upper hand in the war. The Communists seized power in Russia in November 1917, took the country out of the war, and signed a peace treaty with Germany the following March. This freed the Germans to focus on the Western Front. In this context they continued to use the possible recovery of the Åland Islands as a bargaining chip in trade negotiations. Following the failure of the Germans' major spring offensive on the western front, however, Sweden moved away from supporting them and turned more to Britain and the United States. An important trade deal reached with them in May 1918 involved guarantees of shipments to Sweden, the transfer of Swedish merchant vessels to the British or Americans, and reductions in ore exports to Germany. In Sweden a long-brewing split in of the Social Democratic Party finally occurred, resulting in the formation of the Left Socialist Party. The political environment in Finland was radicalized by the developments in Russia, and moderates declared Finland's independence in early December 1917. A little over a month later a civil war began in which socialist (Red) and nonsocialist (White) Finns fought each other with Russian-Soviet support on the one side and Germany support on the other. Whereas the public in Sweden generally favored the White forces, the government took a noninterventionist position and volunteers for both sides left to join the fighting.

World War I was costly for Sweden. Some 290,000 tons of shipping were lost, along with about 800 lives. Social and economic problems were aggravated by the disruptions of trade and production. Hunger, unemployment, high prices, and degradation haunted the poor of the country, and postwar developments were destined to make these problems worse. Swedish authorities had repeatedly used force against the lower classes during the last two years of the war. The political environment was fragmented by the founding of the Left Socialists. Making matters worse, the winter of 1917–1918 was especially harsh, and in fall 1918 the Spanish influenza epidemic took about 35,000 lives. That Sweden escaped the revolutionary wave of 1917–1920 is to a large degree remarkable.

INTER-WAR POLITICS

Political life was defined by fragmentation, hostility, and instability in much of Western Europe after World War I, and Sweden's new political democracy was put to the test during the interwar years. There were certainly moments when it appeared it might fail. In the end, however, Sweden was one of the democracies in Europe to work effectively and survive those very troubled times. Why and how are important questions to explore.

It is important to remember that Sweden was still a country deeply divided along social class lines. On the one side was the relatively new industrial working class; on the other, the bourgeois and upper class elites. The workers' ideologies (Communist, Social Democratic, and Syndicalist) rejected the bourgeois, capitalist society and all that went with it. Owners, management, nobility, and monarchy were the enemy. This was made perfectly clear by the frequency of labor-management disputes, the dualism and elitism of the educational system, the perpetuation of social and behavioral norms, and even language and dress. The middle and upper classes feared the workers and still believed in a world of clear, understandable social ranks. Alongside these differences was another divide, that between the past and the present, between historic Sweden and the new, modern, industrial Sweden. In this case traditional groups, including the farmers and the old nobility, confronted the new industrial classes. In this complex mix of differences, revolution confronted order, change confronted stability, socialism confronted conservatism, secularism confronted Lutheranism, and the present confronted the past.

Political democracy had been achieved, at least in an institutional sense, but it had yet to become firmly accepted by the old order or established in practice. The lower classes wanted social and economic democracy as well. The political campaigns of the 1920s were filled with the rhetoric of difference. During the crises years of the 1930s, however, the tone became less shrill and some compromise and cooperation occurred that helped to carry Sweden through the Depression and World War II.

Seven political parties, each based on class and ideology, vied for power in this polarized society during all or part of this period. The two communist parties, one independent and the other closely allied with Moscow, talked of revolution and advocated sweeping social and economic reforms in parliament. Although the Social Democrats became increasingly reformist through the 1920s, their rhetoric continued to attack the status quo even as a new generation of leaders worked to build a position in the parliament

that would allow them to carry programs designed to address issues of social and economic justice. The Liberals, who had been so important in the
achievement of political democracy, were split into two parties between
1923 and 1934 over the issue of prohibition. A single Farmers Party was established in 1921–1922. It sided mainly with the Conservatives and was
preoccupied with the chronic economic problems that faced agriculture in
this period. In 1933 the party shifted its support to the Social Democrats in
the most important political realignment of the period. The Conservatives
held fast to their worldview of social order and legitimacy; some members
of their youth organization even drifted toward the extreme right. Sweden
also had two Nazi parties and a number of other fringe groups to compli-
cate the scene in the 1930s.

At no point during the interwar period did a single party command a
majority in the parliament (see Table 5.1.) The Social Democrats came closest to this in 1936, when they won 112 of the 230 seats in the Second Chamber. The years 1917–1932 were characterized by what some have called
"minority parliamentarism," "committee parliamentarism," and "issue
parliamentarism." Governments were always based on a coalition or built
by a single party. In the latter case, the governing party had to find
short-term partners in the parliament in order to pass anything The average life of a government was about sixteen months, and none was able to
pursue an extensive, planned program of legislation. This situation
changed in 1933, when the Social Democrats' leaders arranged a "Red-
Green" coalition with the Farmers' Party that gave them a stable, working
majority in both chambers of the parliament. Although this cooperation
broke down over the issue of defense in 1936, it was rebuilt following the
election that fall and lasted until the formation of a wartime coalition cabinet in December 1939.

Despite the frequency of government change in the 1920s and the absence of majority parliamentarism, important issues were addressed, including membership in the League of Nations, control of the Åland Islands,
defense appropriations, labor market relations, unemployment, agricultural problems, prohibition, and school reform. In the case of most of these,
compromise solutions were developed and passed through the parliament,
often in ways that engaged the political parties in important dialogue and
demonstrated the flexibility of the new system.

In the area of foreign affairs, Sweden joined the League of Nations in
1920, despite opposition from the Communists, who viewed the organization as an agent of bourgeois capitalism, and from the Conservatives and
some farmers, who put little faith in the League's idealism and believed it
would be controlled by the Great Powers. Once membership was ap-

Table 5.1
Inter-War Governments

Nils Edén	October 1917–March 1920	Liberal-Social Democrat
Hjalmar Branting	March 1920–October 1920	Social Democrat
Louis De Geer/Oscar von Sydow	October 1920–October 1921	Non-Party
Hjalmar Branting	October 1921–April 1923	Social Democrat
Ernst Trygger	April 1923–October 1924	Conservative
Hjalmar Branting*/Rickard Sandler	October 1924–June 1926	Social Democrat
C. G. Ekman	June 1926–October 1928	Liberal coalition
Arvid Lindman	October 1928–June 1930	Conservative
C. G. Ekman**/Felix Hamrin	June 1930–September 1932	Liberal
Per Albin Hansson	September 1932–June 1936	Social Democrat
Axel Pehrsson	June 1936–September 1936	Farmer
Per Albin Hansson	September 1936–December 1939	Social Democrat-Farmer
Per Albin Hansson	December 1939–July 1945	Social Democrat-Farmer-Liberal-Conservative Wartime Coalition

*died
**resigned

Source: SNS. Studieförbundet Näringsliv och Samhälle. www.const.sns.se/swedish politics/govts.htm

proved, participation in the League became a core element of the country's foreign policy for almost two decades. Sweden turned to the organization to solve the Åland Islands' crisis with Finland, and worked to find compromise on issues such as sanctions and selection of council members following Germany's inclusion in 1925. Until his death Hjalmar Branting served as Sweden's chief delegate, and he became known as a staunch advocate of the rights of the small states.

One foreign affairs issue created a crisis, and that was over who should control the Åland Islands. As has been seen, Germany's policy in the last year of the war had aroused Sweden's interest in recovering the islands, and the civil war in Finland seemed to present a situation in which their status could be reexamined. During winter and early spring 1918 Red and White Finnish soldiers, as well as Soviet Russian, Swedish, and German troops, were stationed there for various periods of time. No solution came with either the end of the fighting in Finland or the close of World War I. At Paris, Sweden argued for transfer of the Åland Islands, and used as evidence the outcome of a January 1919 referendum on the islands, in which 96 percent voted to belong to Sweden. Unmoved, the new Finnish government insisted the islands belonged to Finland. In June 1920 Sweden submitted the question to the League, which decided in favor of Finland the following April. A special multinational Åland Convention was then negotiated under which sovereignty of the islands remained with Finland, self-government and the use of Swedish were assured, and "no fortification or other military constructions, no garrisoning of armed forces, no landing of warships" was to occur. Sweden, Finland, Denmark, Estonia, Latvia, Germany, Italy, France, and Great Britain signed this agreement, which went into effect in April 1922. The Soviets protested their exclusion.

Defense policy was, of course, tied to foreign policy. On this issue the old, prewar divisions between left and right continued. Postwar optimism about peace in Europe, faith in the "collective security" promised by the League, the horrors of the war, and the increased influence of pacifism influenced the Social Democrats and some Liberals; pessimism, fear of domestic unrest, and deeply ingrained self-interests or direct involvement with defense influenced the right. Even the latter were willing to accept cutbacks, but they could not support stripping Sweden of an independent security capacity. In 1919 the Riksdag passed a defense bill that reduced the compulsory training period for the infantry to 165 days, adjusted other service terms, and cut spending. The bill was too much for some, not enough for others, and the issue continued to simmer. A Conservative proposal to reorganize the army, establish an independent airforce, and impose some economies failed in 1924. The following year, however, parliament passed a bill from the Branting-Sandler Government cutting spending, shortening the training period to 140 days, reorganizing the army, and consolidating army and naval air units into a separate airforce. Overall, this was the low point for defense in the interwar years, and it aroused scathing criticism. In 1927 new spending on the navy and coastal defenses was approved, and from the mid-1930s even the Social Democrats were willing to consider more spending for security in the context of the worsening European situation.

In economic affairs the decade began with a postwar boom that quickly faded. By 1921 productivity and supply exceeded demand in many sectors, and this situation led to cutbacks in production, soaring unemployment, wage reductions, and labor disputes. In early 1922 some 163,000 union workers were unemployed. This translated into 34 percent of the unions' members and was the second highest level attained during the whole interwar period. Recovery set in quickly, however, and the years from the middle of the decade to 1930 were relatively good—except in agriculture.

From the political perspective the central economic questions were how to maintain peace in the labor market, the extent to which labor-management general agreements were binding, how much the state should be involved in the labor market, the nature of unemployment insurance, and how to solve the farm crisis. Concerning the first three of these, the right favored establishing a state-based system that would enforce labor-management agreements and adjudicate disputes. The unions favored government noninterference in the labor market, whereas some Social Democrats were open to compromise. C. G. Ekman had the support of the Conservatives, Farmers, and both liberal parties when in spring 1927 he put forward a proposal affirming the binding nature of collective agreements and the establishing of a "labor court" to settle labor-management disputes. Despite a three-hour work stoppage protest involving some 365,000 workers, the so-called labor peace law passed. In the long run this measure was probably most important in pushing *LO* and *SAF* into working out the Saltsjöbaden Agreement in 1938, which defined and helped to maintain labor-market peace, free of government intervention, until the 1970s.

State assistance for unemployed workers was at the center of the political debate during the early 1920s and again in the early 1930s. On this question, the right advocated a minimalist approach consistent with their belief that deflationary policies, including government economies, were the ways to reverse downturns in the economy. Regarding unemployment, this meant providing relief through emergency jobs that paid below the established market rate. Until the early 1930s the left did not have a fundamentally different approach to dealing with recessions, and on the matter of unemployment only argued for more extensive help. During the severe crisis of 1921–1922, the right's restrictive approach prevailed. Some relief jobs were established, mainly in road building, and many workers were forced to turn to various sources of poverty relief.

In 1930 the Social Democrats and their union allies adopted the ideas of the English economist John Maynard Keynes. Articulated by the Social Democratic economist Ernst Wigforss, these included extensive public works projects that created jobs, paid market-level wages, and would be financed by government-incurred debt. The argument behind this approach was that purchasing power would be restored and the economy would recover more quickly. The debt would be repaid through increased tax revenues during good economic times. These policies were set forth in a 1932 proposal to the parliament and were important in the Social Democrats' election campaign that year. They were applied as unemployment soared in 1932–1933 and contributed to the country's relatively rapid recovery.

Sweden's farmers faced many problems during this period, including low prices for their products, competition from cheap imports, rising costs of operation, debt, and falling real incomes. In addition, the number of farm operators fell, and there was a flight from the land by the children of farmers. In 1920 17 percent of the country's labor force was in the agricultural sector. Twenty years later the figure was only 9 percent. Two issues were central: the place of farming as a valued and historically important occupation and the economy. The former was addressed by new organizations, some of them ultraconservative, that promoted farming and farm interests. The latter repeatedly occupied the attention of governments and the parliament. In 1930 and again in 1931, for example, proposals were passed that set minimum prices for some grains, imposed quotas that restricted the amount of foreign grain that could be ground or foreign flour mixed in Swedish mills, and provided a subsidy to sugar beet growers. Attempts to raise tariffs on imported grains and sugar, which were opposed by free-trade-minded Conservatives and Social Democrats who wanted to keep food prices low, failed. None of the measures taken solved the farmers' problems, and they remained to be taken up again, this time by the new Social Democratic Government, in 1933.

Sweden was not the only country in which a powerful temperance movement forced the issue of prohibition to the fore in the decade or so following World War I. Norway was dry from 1919 to 1926, and the United States from 1920 to 1933. In 1922, responding to pressure from the Liberals, Hjalmar Branting's second government held a national referendum. The outcome was a defeat for the anti-alcohol forces. Over 1.8 million votes were cast, 51 percent of which opposed prohibition. The Government accepted the vote and backed away from the issue, leaving the Bratt rationing system in place. Never a homogeneous group or one unified on the temperance issue, the Liberals were subsequently torn apart by ongoing disagreement. In May 1923 a more moderate minority group led by Eliel Löfgren left the party to form the Swedish Liberal Party.

Education was also a major issue of the interwar years, one closely tied to class and ideological position. For the Conservatives and others on the right, schools were a means to preserve the social order and tools for creating citizens. For the left, they were agents of enlightenment, progress, change, and social mobility. By the early 1920s Sweden had a seven-year compulsory system and then a complex web of schools, including the elite gymnasia, practical schools, girls' schools, community middle schools, and folk high schools. The secondary system was elitist and sexist. Social class limited one's access to most of the secondary schools, from which girls were excluded. In 1927 Liberal prime minister C. G. Ekman, nicknamed "the weigh master" for his ability to put together voting majorities in the parliament, successfully orchestrated the passage of a compromise reform package by the Riksdag with the support of the Farmers and the Social

Democrats. It provided for a nine- or ten-year compulsory education based on primary (*folkskola*) and middle (*realskola*) schools. At the same time secondary programs were made more open and included women. The secondary options took three or four years and followed two tracks, one practical and the other academic. Both left and right gained by these reforms. The former extended the scope of compulsory schooling and made it more accessible. The right preserved elitism through admissions examinations and curriculum options.

POLITICS IN THE 1930S

A new era in Swedish political history characterized by the dominance of the Social Democrats and majority parliamentarism opened with the September 1932 elections and continued until 1976. This resulted from several factors. Some of these were external and included, on the one hand, fear of fascism and Hitler's rise to power in January 1933 and, on the other, fear of Stalin's Soviet Union. This alarm tended to push Swedish politics toward the center and toward compromise. Among the internal causes of this change were the Great Depression's impact on Sweden, the violence that erupted in a labor dispute in northern Sweden in May 1931, the collapse of Ivar Kreuger's financial empire in the spring 1932, a scandal involving Liberal leader C. G. Ekman, the Social Democrats' new program and campaign strategies, and the willingness of Social Democrats and Farmers to cooperate.

The world economic crisis reached Sweden by 1930. International and domestic market demand fell, financial markets were squeezed, and unemployment soared. The latter reached the highest levels in the country's history in early 1933, when about 187,000 union workers were without jobs. Some industries posted 30–40 percent unemployment rates. Farmers were also hard hit by the crisis. When employers tried to increase competitiveness by cutting labor costs, tensions rose and tempers flared in the labor market. The paper pulp industry was particularly hard hit, and conflicts were common. A strike at the Långfors pulp plant in the Ådalen area of northern Sweden near Sollefteå in 1930 led to the employers' calling in strikebreakers. Workers in other companies joined sympathy strikes, and increasingly heated rhetoric aroused emotions. As the local authorities grew more and more nervous, they asked for troops. Sixty soldiers, wholly unprepared to deal with civil unrest, were sent. On 14 May 1931, a protest meeting in Fårnö was followed by a march by over 3,000 workers to Lunde to face the strikebreakers. The marchers were met by a jittery contingent of well-armed soldiers. Accounts of what then happened vary largely by social class. The army and local officials claimed that some workers had guns, shots were fired, and the army responded. The workers argued that the troops opened fire without provocation. Whichever the case, no soldiers were injured, but four marchers and a bystander were killed and five were injured. The labor movement was outraged, and 80,000 demonstrated in Stockholm the next day. The principal newspaper of the left, *Social-Demokraten*, called the national government "bumbling," the local government "wholly without good judgment," the military action "senseless," and the employers' policies "conscienceless and provocative." On 21 May 12,000 attended the funerals of the victims, and work throughout Sweden stopped for five minutes of silence at noon. A government investigation and subsequent court actions did little to abate the workers' anger. Whereas the county governor and local sheriff were absolved of responsibility, the commander of the troops was placed under arrest for eight days. In contrast, Axel Nordström, an Ådalen area Communist, was sentenced to two and one-half years in prison, and other labor activists received lesser sentences. Swedes killing Swedes was unusual and intolerable to many on both the left and the right. In the context of the growing success of authoritarian movements across Europe, maintaining social peace and making democracy work seemed more and more important to more and more people.

A second important development—or pair of developments—that helped to shape the political environment involved the phenomenally successful engineer, businessman, and financier Ivar Kreuger (1880–1932). Trained as an engineer, he was a cofounder of Kreuger & Toll, a construction firm that became the largest in Sweden and developed global contacts. Kreuger also made his fortune in safety matches. He created a virtual monopoly in Sweden through *Svenska Tändsticks AB* and by the early 1920s had established control of about three-quarters of the world's match production. This may seem trivial to readers in the early twenty-first century, but in a world that still used candles and lanterns, in which stoves and furnaces and fireplaces were lighted manually, and in which many more people smoked, matches were important indeed. More significant than these business ventures, however, was the paper financial empire Kreuger created based on them. By drawing on his good credit or issuing new shares in his companies, he arranged huge loans in return for contracts or influence. By the end of the 1920s, these loans amounted to some 1.25 billion crowns. Kreuger saw himself as a financial wizard who would single-handedly create world prosperity. Because the success of his enterprises rested on that prosperity, the Great Depression ruined him. Debtors defaulted, banks called in their loans, and shareholders panicked and sold. On 12 March 1932 Kreuger committed suicide in his Paris hotel room. In Sweden chaos ensued, and the media feasted on Kreuger and the evils of the system.

Swedish banks faced losses of over 800 million crowns, not counting what they might have held in shares in his companies. Private losses were enormous, and the stock market was closed to prevent a total collapse. Prime Minister C. K. Ekman was also a victim of the Kreuger affair. He was forced to resign when it was revealed that he had taken money from Kreuger Although stability and recovery came relatively quickly, the system and those who represented it were discredited again.

In the early 1930s several important conditions or issues colored the political environment. For one thing society remained polarized, a polarity enhanced by a new economic crisis. Within the trade union movement there was growing anger over employer tactics in labor disputes and a feeling that the system was rigged in favor of the old elites. At the same time recent history seemed to show that the political system was capable only of passing a series of half-measures to deal with pressing social and economic issues. The context was made more volatile by the increasingly damaged and discredited capitalist financial system and the ongoing crisis for farmers, who had not shared in the prosperity of the late 1920s and continued to face ongoing economic distress. Elsewhere in Europe democracy was on the wane and totalitarian regimes, apparently able to solve all of society's ills, were on the rise.

The Social Democrats capitalized successfully on this environment to create governmental stability and a parliamentary majority. Between 1933 and late 1939, a package of legislation was pushed through that established Sweden as a leader in economic and social planning. This was accomplished under the leadership of a group of highly motivated and committed individuals in the Social Democratic Party and with the support of the Farmers' Party.

Earlier legislation had established a basis from which these reformers could work. It included a small pensions program adopted before World War I, the eight-hour work day and forty-eight-hour work week for industrial laborers (1920), and limited emergency unemployment insurance. The new legislative program was far more extensive and had different ideological foundations. Some of the earlier steps had been enacted by the Conservatives, which copied the German model and saw the steps as parts of an effort to prevent revolution and hold on to power. The right saw none of these steps as rights to which all were entitled. The Swedish Social Democrats, despite their frequent use of revolutionary Marxist rhetoric, had never really been committed to the violent overthrow of the existing system. They were revisionists who believed the system could be changed from within through peaceful parliamentary means. The radicals in the party, such as Hinke Berggren, Karl Kilbom, and Zeth Höglund, broke with the party and became leaders of the left socialist and communist parties.

The new vision of the Social Democrats was defined by Per Albin Hansson (1885–1946), who became chairman of the party following Hjalmar Branting's death in 1925. Unlike many of the early leaders of the party, Hansson came from humble origins. He was the son of a painter. His education went no farther than the compulsory folk school, and he started work as an errand boy at age twelve. He became active in the Malmö socialist movement in 1902 and helped to found a Social Democratic youth organization there a year later. In 1909 he moved to Stockholm, where he became a reporter and eventually editor of the party's daily newspaper, *Social-Demokraten*. In 1918 he was elected to the Riksdag, and he held posts in Branting's three governments during the 1920s. In September 1932 Hansson was invited to form a government. The following spring he succeeded in working out a "crisis agreement" with a faction of the Farmers' Party led by Axel Pehrsson i Bramstorp. Sometimes called the "cow deal," this involved a promise of government support for farmer relief legislation that ran against labor's interest in low food prices in exchange for Farmer support of the Social Democrats' program. With the exception of summer 1936, he continued as Sweden's prime minister until his sudden and unexpected death in 1946.

P. A. Hansson believed democracy was the best form of government, and he thought it was possible to build a just and democratic society. He was convinced that solving the issues of the interwar years was a crucial test for democratic institutions, and one of his central goals was to make democracy work in Sweden. In addition, Hansson also had a programmatic vision of the kind of society a working democracy could build. In 1928, he used the term *folkhemmet* (the people's home) as a label for his ideas, among them social, political, and economic democracy; economic security; fairness; and justice. It would also involve a redistribution of wealth and the sacrifice of some individual freedom for the common good. The specific pieces of this ideal were designed by a group of very remarkable people, most of whom served in Social Democratic governments for over twenty years. Ernst Wigforss was minister of finance in every Social Democratic government from 1925 to 1949. An advocate of deficit financing, he designed the national budgets and created the finance and tax systems that were to pay for social programs. During World War II he also headed the committee that designed the labor movement's twenty-seven-point postwar program. Arthur Engberg was a brilliant advocate and spokesperson for the Government's programs and also served as minister of education. He was responsible for many of the school reforms of the 1930s, including adding a seventh year to the mandatory folk school system and redesigning the secondary curricula. Gustav Möller, who served as minister of social affairs under Branting and then under Hansson, was responsible for many of the human services programs introduced in the 1930s and after. Also important were the contributions of researchers like Alva and Gunnar Myrdal, who provided information and rationale for government's policies.

Specific legislative elements of the program included more generous unemployment benefits, government works projects to relieve unemployment that paid workers at a market rate, extensive public housing projects to alleviate shortages and raise living standards, housing loans to facilitate apartment and private home purchases, two weeks' paid vacation for workers, an eight-hour work day for agricultural laborers, child-dependent allowances, a national health insurance scheme, and a limited national pension program, all paid for through loans and a graduated income tax, inheritance taxes, and taxes on liquor and luxuries.

The record the Hansson governments established before World War II was remarkable. So, too, was the degree of political peace that characterized that period. Sweden was set on a political path defined by cooperation and consensus building. The right was put in a position of opposing what was defined as truly national, truly for the good of *all* the people.

SOCIAL AND ECONOMIC DEVELOPMENTS

One must be careful not to overemphasize the positives of this period. Not all was instantly perfect. Far from it! Inequality, elitism, social and political tension, and vastly different socio-economic philosophies remained. Change was in degree only. At the same time there existed real or potentially real dark sides to this history—sides carried to extremes by groups like the German Nazis and even advocated by a few in Sweden. Seen in a larger perspective the ideals of the Social Democrats grew from a worldview that held that all aspects of society could be engineered for a common good. This view was applied in mainly positive ways to physical fitness, public health, education, notions about women as ideal mothers and homemakers, housing, and the like. In the matter of public health and reproduction, however, Sweden either came dangerously close to or embraced, depending on one's perspective, racial policies not far from those of the Nazis.

"Social engineering" was a popular concept during the interwar years in Europe and the United States, and was part of the public and political conversations of the period. It involved relatively benign issues such as population size and growth rates and the importance of demographic vitality in maintaining economic and cultural growth. In 1934 Alva and Gunnar Myrdal published a very important study of Sweden's population, *Kris i befolkningsfrågan* (Crisis in the Population Question), triggered by the alarming fact that the country's population was actually declining. In part the subsequent legislation designed to provide better care for pregnant women and make children less a financial burden through tax incentives came as a result of this book.

The dark side of social engineering involved controlling who had children, with the end goal being genetic manipulation (eugenics) of a population in order to improve it. In Nazi Germany this meant genocidal attacks on Jews and others. In Sweden, Canada, the United States, Great Britain, and elsewhere it meant discouraging marriages by people with certain physical or mental problems and a campaign of sterilization. Advocacy of eugenics in Sweden stretched back to before World War I and may be seen in organizations like the Society for Racial Hygiene, founded in Stockholm in 1909. After the war a small institute for the study of eugenics was established at Uppsala University. It was supported by state funds and headed by a long-time advocate Dr. Herman Lundborg. In 1926, it published *The Racial Character of the Swedish Nation,* in which the attempt was made to *define* the Swedish people physically on the basis of measurements and photographs of about 100,000 volunteers. Although the institute got a new director in the early 1930s, Gunnar Dahlberg, and the focus of population worries in Sweden shifted from quality to quantity, concern about reproduction by certain groups in the society remained that clearly involved ideas of racial or folk purity. Laws passed in 1935 and 1941 provided for the sterilization of mentally retarded individuals or those with certain illnesses (mental or physical) or genetic deformities, or those unable to care for a child. Normally, sterilization was to be done only with the approval of the patient, but provision was made for exceptions. Between 1935 and 1975, 62,888 people, including about 2,000 before World War II began and just over 7,000 during the war, were sterilized. Ninety percent of those affected were women.

Women continued to make political, economic, and social progress during the interwar years. They voted for the first time in a national election in 1921, and that election returned five women to the Second Chamber of the parliament. Women's status in the family improved through a number of changes: They were recognized as equals in marriages in 1921, access to and information about birth control increased, and government programs in the 1930s included pregnancy and childcare clinics and child-support payments.

In education women were given equal access to secondary schools through the major school reform legislation of 1927. This was a vital step in putting women on the same level as men in admissions to the universities and many of the professions. In terms of employment, women were given equal opportunities to government bureaucratic positions in 1923 and equal pay in such jobs in 1937. A year later a new law stipulated equality for married women in work opportunities and prohibited dismissing women who married after employment. Legal changes were only slowly followed by changes in attitude and actual practice. In many sectors women were paid less than men for the same work. During the hard economic times of this period, women were criticized for taking jobs away from men. Working women were still expected to perform their usual household responsibilities. Women were still barred from the ministry, and few were found in law, in management, or on university faculties.

There was, however, no lack of remarkable women who set lasting role models or led the way in advocating changes for their sex, including the social researcher Alva Myrdal and the poet Karin Boye. Another was Elise Ottesen-Jensen, a Norwegian who moved to Sweden after the war. Called "the family apostle," she crisscrossed the country speaking to women about sexuality and birth control—even though public advocacy, discussion, and sale of condoms and diaphragms was illegal under a 1911 law. Ottesen-Jensen saw how family size tended to be strongly class-determined. Middle- and upper-class families were small. Lower- or working-class families were large. She agonized over the hardships of pregnancy, child raising, and toil to which women of the lower classes seemed to be doomed. Ottesen-Jensen wanted to change all that. Sex, she argued, was natural and good; children need not be a byproduct. In 1933 she helped to found the National Association for Sexual Enlightenment (*Riksförbundet för sexuell upplysning—RFSU*) that went on to play a leading role in spreading information, providing clinics, and pressing for change. Five years later the law against birth control was repealed, and abortion in certain cases was legalized around World War II. Optional sex education programs were introduced into the schools in 1942 and made compulsory in 1956. A result of the work of Ottesen-Jensen and others was an increasing trend toward two-children families across social class lines.

It is easy to paint a dark picture of the economic developments of this period, but such a picture is inaccurate and incomplete. Despite the crises the overall trends were positive. It is really in this period that Sweden became an urban, industrial nation. Productivity increased. The complexity and diversity of Sweden's industrial sector grew, as reflected in the founding of domestic aircraft (SAAB, since 1937) and automobile (VOLVO, since 1926) industries. Housing construction boomed. Real incomes and living standards rose. World War II interrupted these patterns, but they were resumed after 1945.

An interesting component of this economic growth was that Sweden became more and more a nation of consumers during the interwar years. This trend had begun around the turn of the century, but it accelerated in the interwar years and was very much a part of Sweden's becoming a modern country. Shopping replaced self-sufficiency, and many of the old needed skills were forgotten or became part of the home craft movement. Consumer goods in an ever-widening variety became available, including the latest clothing fashions, gas and electric kitchen ranges, refrigerators, vacuum cleaners, radios and phonographs, and packaged foods. At the same time Swedes were deluged with advertising. For rural people the products were available in town shops, often clustered around the local railroad station, or from mail order firms like the one founded by Johan Peter Åhlén and Erik Holm in 1899. In the cities specialty shops virtually replaced the open air markets, and a whole new urban architecture developed in the process, defined by large windows and electric lights. Competing with the shops were the variety and department stores. The two leaders in this were *Pariser-Bazar*, founded by Josef Leja in Stockholm in 1852 and taken over by J. Sachs in 1895, and Karl M. Lundberg's elegant store, also in Stockholm, opened in 1895. Seven years later Leja and Lundberg created *NK* (*Nordiska kompaniet*), and their anchor store in the heart of downtown Stockholm opened its doors in 1915. *NK* set the standard in opulence, customer service, and class for the shopper, but there were large stores for every social level. Middle market options were represented by PUB, named after its founder, Paul U. Bergström, who began his career as a clerk in a Stockholm linens shop in 1882. An aggressive and imaginative entrepreneur, he moved into men´s clothing and acquired a number of shops around the city's old main market, Hötorget. He was also one of the first to adopt a policy of fixed prices for his merchandise. In December 1925 he opened the seven-floor store that dominated the west side of Hötorget. Although men's wear was the largest department in the store, his motto, "Everything under one roof," reflected the range of merchandise available. When Bergström died in 1934, PUB was purchased by the consumer cooperative organization *Kooperativ Förbundet* (*KF*), which continued to operate it until 1994. Least expensive were the stores that copied Woolworths, the American five-and-dime chain. In the ideal they sold everything for one price, 25 *öre*. In this group were the *Epa* stores (the name is a contraction of *Enhetsprisab* or Single-price company) established by Herman G. Turitz of Göteborg and *NK* in 1930 and Åhlens' TEMPO chain.

Connected with this shift toward consumerism but also forming a vitally important element in Sweden's twentieth century economic development was the cooperative movement. Its roots lay in the late nineteenth century, and it grew to encompass farming, the manufacture of food products and industrial goods, fuel refining and retail, housing construction and finance, insurance, and retail trade during the first third of the twentieth century. On the consumer side a central organization, *Kooperativ Förbundet* (*KF*), was founded in 1899. In addition to providing retail outlets and organizing wholesale efforts to minimize costs, one of the most important roles *KF* played was in breaking the market hold that monopolies and cartels had on certain product sectors of the economy. This struggle began around 1910 and achieved important victories during the interwar years. In 1921, when the organization's own plant in Norrköping began production, the price of margarine fell from 2.70 SEK to 1.90 SEK per kilo. The following year *KF* acquired a major flour mill in Stockholm, broke the dominance of a cartel, and brought down the price of flour. They had a similar impact on the price of rubber boots when they entered into a deal with *Gislaved* in 1926 and when they began to manufacture electric light bulbs in 1930. (The last began as *Hammarbylampan* and became *LUMA* in 1942.) These successes were symbolic of the larger victory, which was creating a more competitive and less expensive retail market. The leader of *KF* from 1924 to 1957, Albin Johansson, helped to give the movement its diversity, which included a horticulture school and an architectural office, and had the foresight to begin stockpiling essential goods in the last two years before World War II.

INTERWAR CULTURAL DEVELOPMENTS

The 1920s and 1930s were rich and varied decades. In literature several trends predominated. One was deeply intellectual, psychologically probing, and reflective of the leading themes in much of Western literature at the time. The novels and plays of authors like 1951 Nobel Prize–winner, Pär Lagerkvist are representative here. A second was more personal and spoke to a younger generation. Karin Boye, a troubled and intense young poet who took her own life in 1941, is representative of this trend. A third was the social realism and often semiautobiographical writing of working-class authors like Eyvind Johnson, Ivar Lo-Johansson, Vilhelm Moberg, and Harry Martinson. (Johnson and Martinson shared the 1974 Nobel Prize in Literature.) Theater experienced a renaissance, especially in Stockholm and Göteborg. Set designers experimented with incorporating modern art styles, normally traditional theaters like *Dramaten* in Stockholm staged daring productions of Strindberg's psychological dramas, and the delightful eighteenth century theater at Drottningholm outside Stockholm was restored and used for productions of period opera and ballet. Radio drama also became important.

Motion pictures enjoyed great popularity in this period. The earliest films came to Sweden in the 1890s, and a thriving cinema business developed around 1910 based on foreign and domestically produced silent movies. The production company *Svenska Bio* was formed at this time and merged with another company to form *Svensk Filmindustri* (*SF*) in 1919. This company remains the center of Sweden's independent filmmaking industry. Until the mid-1920s Swedish film production was relatively successful, particularly in making feature films based on Scandinavian literature and directed by Mauritz Stiller or Victor Sjöström. Hollywood presented a growing challenge, however, and this increased with the advent of sound films at the end of the 1920s. It was difficult to compete with the flood of westerns, romances, thrillers, and comedies coming from the United States. *SF* survived, however, and during World War II, when imported films were difficult to obtain, the company enjoyed a renaissance, especially with serious films such as *"Rid i natt"* (Ride Tonight).

Two of the most important areas of cultural development, from both domestic and international perspectives, were architecture and design. Sweden and its Nordic neighbors became leaders in both fields during the interwar period, establishing a style known as Swedish or Scandinavian modern. In architecture, the break from the neoclassical and national romantic schools that had dominated the early decades of the century was striking. Ragnar Östberg's Stockholm City Hall (1909–1923) has clear ties with the Doge's Palace in Venice with its arched walkways, open courtyards and interior halls, and massive corner tower. It was intended as a symbol of the city. Its interior was furnished with the work of local craftsmen, and mosaics depicting Stockholm's history covered the walls of the so-called Golden Hall. In contrast, the power station at Hammarforsen by Osvald Almqvist reflects all the basic elements of the new school: simplicity, functionalism, integration with the environment, and exploitation of new building materials—especially concrete, steel, and glass. A figure who bridges the shift was Gunnar Asplund. Echoes of the past and elements of the future are combined in the Stockholm City Library from 1929, and he helped to define the new style with the main building at the 1930 Stockholm Exposition. During the decade before the war, hospitals, apartment and office complexes, factories, churches, railroad stations, bridges, and private homes were designed and built in the new style. Design followed a similar path and, in fact, was often incorporated into the new buildings. In textiles, glass, ceramics, metals, and wood, Swedish designers created a style defined by its grace, simplicity, functionalism, and, not infrequently, a hint of the Swedish past.

A rich and varied popular culture, often heavily influenced by trends in Europe and the United States, flourished between the world wars. In fashion this translated into ever-changing styles for women and men. Young women, at least in the cities, adopted the flapper styles of the 1920s, cut their hair short, and took up smoking in public. Young men donned knee-length knickers, patterned socks, wide-lapel jackets, and spats. In the 1930s the sophisticated followed the lead of Hollywood; young people opted for the wide skirts, blouses, white shirts, and baggy slacks of the "Swing Kids." Bicycles, trams, buses, and cars gave people much greater mobility; and entertainment options became more varied and more afford-able. Filling the leisure time of the working classes became one of the great growth industries of this period and later times. The traditional high-cul-ture opportunities (theater, ballet, and opera), of course, remained, as did the older dance and show halls for the lower classes. Independent theaters, the cinema, restaurants, jazz clubs, swing clubs, and coffee shops were pop-ular, especially for young people, who were afforded greater freedom in the new urban, industrial society. Also popular were the amusement parks. *Liseberg,* which today claims to be the largest in Europe, opened in Göteborg in 1923. *Gröna Lund Tivoli,* in Stockholm, was founded in 1883 by a German, Jakob Schultheis, and it enjoyed growth and success under the leadership of Gustaf Nilsson during the interwar years. There Nilsson opened one of the city's most popular restaurants, the Tyrol, in 1933; the park was the cite of many concerts—including a 1934 debut performance by Jussi Björling, Sweden's great operatic tenor. Just across the road from Tivoli was another amusement park, *Nöjesfältet* (literally, the pleasure field).

Sweden also joined the rest of the West in becoming a country of tourists, hikers, campers, and automobile drivers. The Swedish Tourist Association, founded in 1885 by a group of students at Uppsala University, helped to spread the popularity of hiking and bicycling; it also provided information and a network of shelters for travelers. Sweden was not overwhelmed by the automobile in this period. Although in 1939 Sweden there were only about 200,000 cars (one for every thirty-two people), the popularity and affordability of the automobile was growing. A few could afford to tour in cars. The Royal Automobile Club, established in 1903, became a source of information for travelers, but it also worked to improve roads and fuel sup-plies in the country. Air travel came to Sweden in the 1920s, and a Swedish airline, *Aktiebolaget Aerotransport*, was started up by Carl and Adrian Florman in 1923.

WORLD WAR II

The worsening international environment of the 1930s pushed Swe-den's leaders away from their faith in the League of Nations as a source of security and basis for the country's foreign and security policies. Gradually and in concert with their Nordic neighbors, they returned to neutrality. This was affirmed in a series of meetings of foreign ministers, prime ministers, and monarchs that began in 1930 and led to a joint declaration of their intent to remain neutral in the event of war in May 1938. In order to strengthen the position of the region's neutrals, Rickard Sandler, Sweden's foreign minister from 1932 to 1939 (except during summer 1936), floated the idea of a Scandinavian defensive pact at several of these meetings. The idea lacked support in Sweden, the Danes were reluctant to do anything that might attract German suspicions, and the Norwegians seemed convinced that neutrality would work again for them. The Finns were more interested, but a bilateral agreement was less appealing. Negotiations between Sweden and Finland that began in April 1938 led to a proposal to remilitarize the Åland Islands, called the Stockholm Plan. Approval of the signers of the 1922 agreement on the islands was sought and obtained, but the plan was dropped in early summer 1939 when the Soviets voiced their opposition. Ignoring the Russians, the Finns went ahead to install new fortifications independently.

At the same time as Sweden's foreign policy direction swung back toward neutrality, steps were taken to enhance the country's military preparedness. In summer 1936 the compulsory service term was extended to 180 days for the infantry and 200 for basic airforce and naval recruits. At the same time a system of centralized command during wartime was developed and appropriations modestly increased. The airforce received increased funding for planes, could now recruit on its own, and was given jurisdiction in training of its own officers. The actual growth of defense forces was slow, however. By fall 1939, for example, the airforce was flying a motley array of mostly outdated airplanes, some purchased from Britain, Germany, Italy, and the United States; some built by the country's own company, SAAB, under license from abroad. The navy received even less attention, but it was able to add over eighty ships to the fleet during the war. None of these steps actually prepared Sweden for what was to come, and the lack of real preparedness influenced policy decisions during the war.

To avoid direct involvement in World War II, Sweden (along with Ireland, Portugal, Spain, and Switzerland) was one of the five self-declared neutral European nations, but this does not mean Sweden was able to carry on as usual. The war affected almost every facet of life in the country.

In concert with its Nordic neighbors, the Swedish Government declared neutrality in early September 1939. All hoped they could avoid being drawn into the European conflict. To facilitate these efforts, the government was reshuffled in December 1939. Foreign Minister Rickard Sandler, who favored aid to Finland and was considered too idealistic, was replaced with

Christian Günther, a career diplomat who was uninterested in ideals and ideologies, had no political party ties, and acted on the basis of cold political realities. At the same time all political parties except the Communists were given seats in the government. This coalition lasted until August 1945. Parliamentary life almost ceased for most of the war.

Sweden was the only Nordic country to remain outside direct involvement in the war. The Soviet Union attacked Finland at the end of November 1939, and the ensuing "Winter War" lasted until the following March. In 1941 the Finns carried out their own campaign against the Soviets in cooperation with German actions. Public support for the Finns was strong in Sweden in both conflicts, but the Government avoided committing to full-scale assistance, although it did allow humanitarian aid and some war materiel to be delivered to the Finns. During the Winter War members of the armed forces were permitted to take leaves and serve as volunteers. Most of these opted to help the Finns, although some Swedish Communists sided with the Soviets. In the second or "Continuation War," the Government's position was more reserved, largely because of the critical situation Sweden found itself in at the time. However, humanitarian aid, including emergency medical supplies and ambulance units, was sent, and some volunteers joined Finnish units. Denmark and Norway were invaded by the Nazis on 9 April 1940. Denmark surrendered almost immediately, but Norway held out for over two months. Each case is different. Military realities gave good reason for caution. By the end of June 1940 Denmark, Norway, the Low Countries, and France were in German hands. The Nazis seemed invincible. Sweden's leaders feared the country would suffer the same fate, invasion and subjugation, if they gave the Germans reason to attack. As a result they offered little help to their neighbors and agreed to a number of Nazi demands that were clear violations of neutrality. These included allowing a fully equipped division to cross from northern Norway to Finland in July 1941, permitting the transport of men and equipment on Swedish railroads to and from Norway from July 1940 to August 1943, allowing German vessels to travel through Swedish territorial waters and aircraft to transit Swedish airspace, and continuing high levels of exports of products crucial to the war, including iron ore and ball bearings to Germany. The trade-off for these clearly unneutral actions was that Germany did not invade Sweden and agreed to allow some crucial imports through the blockade.

Public opinion ran strongly against the Nazis throughout the war; consequently, the Government was forced to restrict the freedom of expression guaranteed since 1810 and impose a new censorship measure in 1941 to pacify German anger over attacks on the regime. Many journalists openly criticized both the Germans and the Hansson Government's policy decisions. Best known is Torgny Segerstedt, a former professor of religious history and editor of *Göteborgs Handels-och Sjöfarts tidning*. He used his daily column, *"I dag"* (Today), to criticize individuals and decisions. Hitler's regime was a frequent target of his pen. Even Gustav V was not immune when he awarded a medal to Hermann Göring in 1939. Naturally, the Government came under repeated assaults for its compromises of neutrality. Segerstedt argued that the country had no real policy and that the Government had sold Sweden´s freedom to the Germans. Ture Nerman, a poet and left socialist leader for most of the interwar period, was another outspoken journalist. He used his wartime weekly *Trots Allt!* (Defy Everything!) as his platform. These men and others paid for their opposition with fines and / or imprisonment, and entire print-runs of individual newspapers editions were frequently confiscated.

In academic circles there were also many articulate critics of the Nazi regime, fascism, and Sweden's policies. A leading example was Herbert Tingsten, a political scientist who published scholarly studies and more popularly targeted newspapers articles on fascism, Nazism, and the dictators' regimes. Within the writers' community, critics included Pär Lagerkvist, Karen Boye, Vilhelm Moberg, and Eyvind Johnson. Moberg published *Rid i natt* (Ride Tonight) in 1941. Set in Småland around 1650, the story was a thinly veiled call for resistance to oppression regardless of the risks. In it a Småland free farmer opts to resist the efforts of the local noble, a German who has received his estate from the Queen Kristina, to turn the area's farmers into serfs. The queen, nobility, parliament, Church, authorities, and most of the farmers gradually side with the noble, which is to take the easy path. The book was highly successful and was staged as a play at the National Theater and made into a film. Eyvind Johnson's *Krilon* trilogy parodied the Government and also called for resistance. The war also produced a wonderful body of cutting political cartoons, a genre in which the Swedes are particularly good.

On the other side of the spectrum, the Swedish Nazis and Nazi sympathizers also attacked the Government. Many small but noisy radical right-wing groups had developed during the interwar years. Modeling themselves after the German Nazis, they were anti-Semitic, racist, nationalistic, anti-Communist, antimodern, and antidemocratic. There were two Nazi parties during most of the 1930s: the Swedish National Socialist Party, headed by Birger Furugård, a veterinarian from Deje in Värmland, and the National Socialist Workers' Party, under Sven Olof Lindholm. Neither ever had much success. The two parties together polled fewer than 20,000 votes in the September 1936 election, after which Furugård's party was dissolved. Lindholm's was renamed the Swedish Socialist Union Party; it was most outspoken 1941–1942, and then gradually declined. Nazi ideals were heatedly debated and found a base among some faculty and students at Sweden's universities, especially in Lund. In 1939 the student organization there and at Uppsala supported petitions to deny permission to ten Jewish doctors from Germany to immigrate to Sweden.

International trade was vital to Sweden. When the war began, the Government announced its hope to maintain prewar trade levels with both sides in the conflict. Major exports included iron ore, wood products, and finished goods; much-needed imports were coal, petroleum products, chemicals, metals, rubber, medical products, foods, and textiles. Trade was essential to keeping Sweden's economy running and to meeting basic domestic needs. The belligerents knew this. Germany and Britain imposed blockades that effectively made the Baltic a German lake and closed off access the North Sea. Sweden's position was terrible, and the Germans and the Allies exploited this dependence when circumstances allowed. From 1939 to mid-1943 the advantage went to Germany. Nearly 80 percent of Sweden's import-export trade was with Nazi-occupied Europe during this period. As the tide of the war shifted, Allied pressure on the Swedes to reduce and then to stop all trade with the Nazis increased. The balance slowly shifted, and by the close of 1944 most Allied demands had been met.

Between 1940 and 1943 the Swedes were under constant pressure from the Nazis to expand exports of goods crucial to Germany's war efforts (especially iron ore, cellulose, and ball bearings) and to extend trade credits. The Germans also manipulated prices, so their products became more expensive, whereas Sweden's were held constant in value. In return the Germans promised deliveries of essential goods, including coal, petroleum, and weapons. The Germans also cooperated with the Allies in reaching several trade agreements that specifically covered shipping in and out of Göteborg. Although not always honored and constantly subject to manipulation by both sides, these guaranteed the passage of only four (later five) ships per month for much of the war. The traffic was designed to keep Sweden's economy producing the products the belligerents needed.

Sweden has been criticized long and often for its obviously pro-Nazi actions, especially those taken between April 1940 and late 1943. From a purely ethical perspective this criticism is understandable. From the perspective of realistic politicians of the time, however, meeting most of the Germans' demands was an unpleasant necessity. Prime Minister Hansson and his colleagues did not like the Nazis, but they believed they had little choice if at least a pretense of independence was to be maintained. A German attack was thought to be a very real possibility. Sweden had begun a modest rearmament program in 1936, launched sweeping efforts once the war started, and eventually had as many as 600,000 men prepared to defend the country. The country became a kind of armed camp. Virtually every able-bodied man was trained in some aspect of defense. Women were called upon to serve as observers, drivers, mechanics, and other support personnel. Tens of thousands served in so-called Lotta corps, in which they cooked and delivered meals to field army units. Numbers and training did not make up for a lack of equipment and supply, however; and, at least until mid-1943, military leaders believed the country could not hold out long against a concerted attack. Nonetheless, they were sure they could make any attacker pay a high price and hoped this would act as a deterrent. A propaganda campaign to illustrate the extent of rearmament and preparedness was conducted.

The change of Germany's fortunes in the war, evidenced by the surrender at Stalingrad and the failure of the North African offensive, was not the only reason for Sweden's policy shift in 1943. A second concern was the growing power of the Soviet Union and the threat that posed to Sweden´s security. The great historical enemy gradually reemerged as the potentially dominant power in the Baltic. This concern was made particularly acute by the success of the major Soviet offensive in Finland in summer 1944, and Soviet occupation of the Baltic states. Finland was compelled to accept an armistice with the Russians and then to drive the remaining German troops from the country while the Russians stood by to watch. It was beginning to look as if the postwar world was going to include a Baltic arena in which the Soviet Union controlled Finland, Estonia, Latvia, Lithuania, and Poland; meanwhile Germany would be demilitarized, England would be weak, and the United States would be very far away. These developments influenced Sweden's leaders' decisions. They also contributed to the shift in Sweden's policy toward the United States, a policy that extended through the entire Cold War era.

Sweden's support of Britain and the United States from mid-1943 was a reversal of what happened while the Germans were winning. The border with Norway became more and more porous, allowing Norwegian resistance fighters to move back and forth. Sweden became the training ground for some 5,000 Danish and 13,000 Norwegian "police," who were prepared to step in to maintain order and disarm German troops stationed in their countries when the war ended. Courier flights by specially designated, noncombat B-24's were permitted between Stockholm and England. These operated out of Bromma Airport and carried Norwegian resistance personnel and equipment as well as Allied aircrews that had been forced to land in Sweden. Special Operations (OSS) activities linked with the Norwegian resistance were increased and a base for these set up in Stockholm. Downed

Allied aircraft were repaired in Sweden and then allowed to return to Britain. A network of "field control" posts was established along the northern Swedish-Norwegian border, staffed by OSS personnel; and a special air base was set up near Luleå to support the Norwegians. In July 1944 a virtually intact V2 rocket that had crashed in Sweden was turned over to the Allies for inspection. Finally, in 1945 fifty P-51 Mustang fighters and nine B-17 bombers were supplied to the Swedish airforce by the United States. All these actions placed the Swedes in a favorable position regarding postwar security, set a pattern of cooperation with the United States that continued after the war, and worked in Sweden's favor in terms of membership in the United Nations.

Against this backdrop of tightrope diplomacy, the people of Sweden carried on their lives during the war in increasingly tight circumstances. The life of every Swede was changed. Government became involved in more and more aspects of life through price and production controls, labor market management, rationing, and information control. Private automobiles almost disappeared because of the lack of gasoline and rubber. Military and emergency vehicles were allocated what little gasoline there was. Wherever possible, public transportation switched to electrical power, and increasing numbers of people took to using these means regardless of social class. Some Swedes met this situation with a clever solution that drew upon the one plentiful source of fuel they had—wood. Cars, trucks, and buses were converted to run on gas (mostly hydrogen) generated in special cookers using charcoal or wood as fuel and gas source and mounted to the vehicle or on a trailer. The use of bicycles also increased. Heating fuels were in short supply, and this meant cooler houses and apartments in the winter. There were restrictions on the use of hot water to conserve fuels, and people took fewer baths—or more group ones. Air raid shelters, often made of huge concrete pipes or sandbags, appeared in the streets of towns and cities. Blackout shades on windows and special curtained entrances were required, and cities were darkened at night. An elaborate civil defense organization was created. Diets changed, as many foods disappeared from the market. Rationing began in March 1940, and during the worst year, 1942, it seemed that almost everything was rationed, including sugar, coffee, tea, meat, eggs, soaps, liquor, shoes, textiles, electricity, and coal. Some things simply disappeared from the shop shelves. Conservation and recycling were encouraged. Old tires, shoes, metal goods, and other materials were collected. Newspaper articles showed women how to make jackets from skirts or children's outfits from worn adult garments. Swedes became wearers of paper clothing and wooden-soled shoes. They ate rabbit, drank liquor made from wood, and rode bicycles.

The war had many effects. Diets actually became healthier. Swedes got more exercise. They learned to work together for a common good. Social-class differences blurred. Even language became more egalitarian. Women also benefited from the conflict. They were vital in the rearmament and civilian defense programs. They also served as nurses, cooks, drivers, non-combat pilots, observers, and spotters. In almost every civilian occupation they stepped in to replace men called into the armed forces. They worked on farms and in factories and offices. They took over as tram and train conductors—but not engineers. These experiences gave a boost to the women's movement in Sweden and made women less willing to return to traditional home roles once the war was over. They did not, however, give women the equality they deserved. Sweden remained a gender-divided society for several more decades.

An intense propaganda campaign was mounted to unite the country behind these measures and to stiffen morale and tighten security. A blue-and-yellow-striped tiger became the symbol of wartime Sweden. The image was a pun because in Swedish *tiga* means "be silent" (for security reasons), whereas *tiger* (the same as in English) is the dangerous hunter on watch for traitors and spies. Everyone learned the favorite wartime song "Någonstans i Sverige" (Somewhere in Sweden). Overall, the wartime experience, though difficult and sometimes harsh, did much to create a united people, a people who suffered and worked together with less regard to social class or political party. This experience played an important part in shaping postwar policies and politics, and the passing of the generations that experienced the war in the late twentieth century significantly affected contemporary attitudes and developments.

In the postwar years, and especially toward the end of the century, Sweden was often criticized for what it did not do or what it did too late with regard to the Nazis' persecution of Jews and other groups. The German campaign against Jews was certainly no mystery to many Swedes: They knew about the anti-Jewish laws of the 1930s, the destruction of Jewish property —"Crystal Night," 9–10 November 1938—and the emigration of many Germany Jews. Although they later claimed ignorance, many Swedes also knew about the concentration camps and Adolph Hitler's Final Solution (the extermination of all Jews).

Many Swedes were anti-Semitic. Sweden's population was among the most homogenous in Europe, with the roughly seven thousand Jews in the country were concentrated in Stockholm and Göteborg. A few people believed in the radical anti-Semitic ideas of the period; many lumped Jews with virtually all foreign groups and saw them simply as outsiders. Although not subject to legal discrimination, Jews were often victims of social isolation and occasionally the targets of physical attacks or press diatribes by the far right. One suspects that most Swedes were, like so many other people elsewhere, disengaged and preoccupied with their own concerns.

Security realities certainly determined what the Swedish Government was willing to do. Again, as the course of the war changed, so did the country's policies. From 1943 Sweden was active in extending help to victims of Nazi oppression. Swedes were absolutely essential to the rescue of almost all of Denmark's nearly 8,000 Jews. Berlin ordered their roundup in late September 1943, the Jews of Denmark were forewarned and went into hiding. Over the course of a few weeks, they were transported across the Sound to Sweden, where they lived under generally good conditions for the rest of the war. Sweden took great risk in this, and the Germans were outraged. Then there were the efforts of Raoul Wallenberg, Per Anger, and their colleagues at the Swedish legation in Budapest to help Hungarian Jews in the summer of 1944. Here, too, a roundup and transport to the death camps had been ordered. Special passports were issued to Hungarian Jews making them temporary Swedish citizens, and safe houses were maintained. Wallenberg acted as an agent in these activities. At great personal risk he harassed the Germans and their Hungarian Arrow Cross allies to impede their efforts and met with leaders to try to convince them to call off the operation. Thousands of Hungarian Jews perished in the Holocaust despite Swedish efforts. In a time of "terrible evil," the Swedes' efforts gave some comfort to the Jews in Budapest and may have saved as many as 5,000.

There is a second tragic side to this story. On 17 January 1945 Raoul Wallenberg and a driver, Vilmos Langfelder, went to the suburbs of Budapest to meet the commander of the advancing Soviet forces. They never returned from this meeting. It is believed both were taken to Moscow, imprisoned, probably tortured, and tried as a spies. Most historians now accept the Russian admission that Wallenberg was executed in 1947. There are, however, tantalizing bits of information that filtered out of the former Soviet Union's political prison system or *gulags* that have him alive much later; thus a measure of uncertainty remains about his fate. In the years since Wallenberg's disappearance the Swedish Government has come under repeated criticism because little was done to obtain Wallenberg's release. It certainly appears as if he was a victim of Swedish Cold War security fears.

There are also many other examples of Swedish humanitarian aid during the war. Between 1939 and summer 1944 a small number of Swedes were in regular contact with members of anti-Nazi resistance groups in Germany. They provided useful military and political information to Sweden through meetings in Berlin and Stockholm. The Swedish Government was aware of resistance hopes and plans, and Sweden became a meeting place for members of the resistance and Allied representatives. Sweden was also a site for floating various peace feelers during the war as well as a center for espionage activities by both sides. Folke Bernadotte and the Swedish Red Cross organized the release of Danish and Norwegian internees from concentration camps in the Reich and in their special "white buses" transported several thousand people to safety. Thousands of Finnish children were given asylum in Sweden during the war. Perhaps as many as 30,000 Baltic people fled to Sweden in September and October 1944. By late that year it is estimated that over 91,000 refugees had entered the country. Most of these returned to their homelands following the war. Some stayed. Tragically, others, including over 150 Baltic army personnel, were returned to Soviet-occupied territory, where they probably were executed.

6

The Contemporary Era

The last half-century has been one of the most dynamic in all of Sweden's long history. To someone who lived through this period, the Sweden of 2001 is very far from that of 1945. In political life a culture of consensus-based democracy has become firmly established, the parliament is now unicameral, a new constitution has been adopted, the power of the monarchy has been reduced, new political parties have appeared on the scene, and voter behaviors have changed. Foreign and defense policies followed old lines of nonalignment and independence throughout the period, but involvement in international organizations increased. One of the most extensive and generous social welfare systems in the world was developed. Social-class differences blurred, and the population became more ethnically and culturally diverse. Women gained greater equality. Industrial growth, the expansion of the public and private service sectors, and an ongoing process of adaptation to a changing world economy characterized the country's economic history. Culturally, Sweden continued to be a leader in many fields, but new impulses from abroad and the influence of a huge number of immigrants and refugees worked to transform what it means to be Swedish. In many ways Sweden became an ideal place: environmentally beautiful, intellectually and culturally stimulating, egalitarian, prosperous, and safe.

124   The History of Sweden

Table 6.1

Kings since 1945

Gustav V	1907–1950
Gustav VI Adolf	1950–1973
Carl XVI Gustaf	1973–

Governments since 1945

Per Albin Hansson	July 1945–October 1946	Social Democrat
Tage Erlander	October 1946–October 1951	Social Democrat
Tage Erlander	October 1951–October 1957	Social Democrat-Farmer
Tage Erlander*	October 1957–October 1969	Social Democrat
Olaf Palme	October 1969–October 1976	Social Democrat
Thorbjörn Fälldin	October 1976–October 1978	Moderate-Liberal-Center
Ola Ullsten	October 1978–October 1979	Liberal
Thorbjörn Fälldin	October 1979–May 1981	Moderate-Liberal-Center
Thorbjörn Fälldin	May 1981–October 1982	Center-Liberal
Olaf Palme**	October 1982–February 1986	Social Democrat
Ingvar Carlsson	March 1986–October 1991	Social Democrat
Carl Bildt	October 1991–October 1994	Moderate-Center-Liberal-Christian Democrat
Ingvar Carlsson*	October 1994–March 1996	Social Democrat
Göran Persson	March 1996–	Social Democrat

*retired
**killed

Source: SNS. Studieförbundet Näringsliv och Samhälle. www.const.sns.se/swedish politics/govts.htm

There were darker sides to this period as well, however. For some the welfare state went too far and cost too much. Instead of creating an environment in which the individual could develop fully, some believed, a stifling uniformity had been created. Others were troubled by the long years of Social Democrat control (1932–1976) or by the overwhelming influence in the economy of a handful of very wealthy families. The economy proved difficult to change, and painful adjustments were forced on it in the last decades of the twentieth century. Environmental problems arose. Crime and drug use increased. Some Swedes turned against the ethnically different. Protests erupted against the new Sweden and the new global economy, and one of these turned terribly violent.

POLITICS

The constitutional elements of the Swedish political system changed in several critical ways in the last half of the twentieth century. First, a measure to replace the two-house parliament with a unicameral system was adopted in 1968–1969 and went into effect in 1970. Initially the new Riksdag had 350 seats, but a problem with this number quickly became apparent. The 1970 election returned an equal number of socialist and nonsocialist representatives, and in some instances decisions had to be reached by drawing lots. In 1976 the number of seats was reduced to 349. Accompanying the new structure were changes in the voting system. National and local elections were now to take place on the same day, the third Sunday in September—every three years until 1994 and every four years since then. Proportional representation and multiple-member constituencies (twenty-nine of them) were maintained. In an effort to make the composition of the assembly reflect the election outcome as accurately as possible, 310 of the parliament's seats are allocated from the constituencies; the remaining are distributed on the basis of party percentages of the total vote. In order to prevent the proliferation of political parties, vote thresholds were set. A party had to receive 4 percent of the national vote or 12 percent in a constituency in order to qualify for a seat. The voting age is eighteen. Third, the reforms also changed the committee structure in the Riksdag, which is now based on sixteen standing committees, with the membership on each reflecting the distribution of seats among the parties in the assembly. It is in the committees that the real work of designing legislation occurs. Input from special commissions, members, and interest organizations helps to shape bills. Once a measure reaches the floor of the parliament, its fate is usually assured.

By the 1970s the 1809 Constitution had been modified by formal amendment so many times that its original clarity was lost. A new constitution went into effect in January 1975 that incorporated all these changes. It also contained language that reduced the power of the crown to a ceremonial level. Although still nominally "head of the state," the monarch lost all direct influence in policy formulation and was no longer responsible for forming governments. That power moved to the Speaker of the Riksdag. Finally, in 1980 the Succession Law was made gender-blind, and the heir to the throne is now Victoria, the eldest child of Carl XVI Gustaf and Sylvia.

The years since the end of World War II can be divided into political periods in a number of different ways. On the basis of party predominance, there are two periods: 1945–1976 and 1976 to the present. During the first of these, which was in many ways an extension of the period beginning in

1932, the Social Democrats were in control. Alone or in cooperation with the Farmers until the late 1950s and then with the Communists, they enjoyed working majorities in the parliament and the power to push through major legislative programs. Since 1976 no one party has predominated and there have been four swings of power between the socialist and nonsocialist parties. When in power during this period, the Social Democrats tended to form minority governments and then build voting majorities in the Riksdag, usually with the Left Party. On four occasions the nonsocialist parties managed to put together coalitions, but they were not always stable, and when Ola Ullsten formed a Liberal Party minority government in 1978, he could count on just thirty-nine votes in the parliament (see Table 6.1 on p. 124). An alternative periodization approach is to create a divide at 1957, which is when the Farmers' Party stopped supporting the Social Democrats. Since then socialist and nonsocialist party blocs have tended to cooperate—though not always. The period may also be divided into an era of stability and predictability that ended in 1976 and a less stable time since, or into a segment when just five political parties played on the political stage (down to 1988) and one when there were seven or more.

A number of other general trends help to define the period. One has been the renaming of parties. The Communists became the Left Party Communists (*VpK*) in 1967 and then simply the Left Party (*Vänsterpartiet*) in 1990. The Farmers' Party became the Center Party (*Centerpartiet*) in 1958. The Conservatives changed their label to the Moderates (*Moderata Samlingspartiet*) in 1969. Usually this was done for obvious political reasons such as to emphasize the broadening of an older party's base, as was the case with the Farmers' Party, or to separate the group from historical stigma, as when the *VpK* dropped "Communist" from the party name following the collapse of the Soviet Union. A second trend, beginning in 1964, has been the development of new parties. The oldest and most successful of these is the Christian Democrats (*Kristdemokraterna*), a group that mixes the ideals of Christian ethics with capitalism. They first ran for parliament in 1964 but did not secure seats there until 1991. A second new party was the Greens (*Miljöpartiet de Gröna*). Its concerns are with environmental degradation, energy consumption, and nuclear proliferation. The party first fielded candidates in 1982 and won its first seats in 1988. The third of these new parties was the New Democrats (*Ny Demokrati*), founded by industrialist Ian Wachtmeister and Bert Karlsson. It took up a place on the far right. Under the slogan "A party for the private individual, not for the collective," its leaders advocated strict controls on immigration, assimilation of foreigners, and sweeping reductions in government regulations and taxes. The New Democrats won twenty-five seats in the 1991 election and played a key role in providing or denying the Bildt Government a majority. Their fall was a rapid as their rise, however. In 1994, discredited by their own intolerance and bad behavior, they mustered only 1.2 percent of the vote. By mid-2000 they were reported to be bankrupt. (Wachtmeister left the party and in 1998 founded another, *The New Party* (*Det Nya Partiet*), whose program is pro-business but also includes planks that favor assimilation of the immigrants and sending refugees back to their homelands. In addition, there are at least seventeen other minor parties such as the Freedom Front, the Freethinking Party, the Consumers' Party, the Natural Law Party, and the Pensioners' Interest Party. None of these has reached either voter threshold to win seats in the parliament.

In addition to the above structural changes in the system a striking change in voter behavior has occurred, especially since the 1970s. Basically, the nature of voter alignment and decision making has been transformed. This is reflected in a decline in voter loyalty to a single party, the weakening of the identification of political parties with particular social classes, the increasing mobility by voters from party to party, and the growing importance of issues in voter decisions. At the very least it seems that significant numbers of voters move from party to party or bloc to bloc across elections. At the same time the importance of the media, especially television, in campaigns has expanded as more emphasis is being placed on personality rather than substance in many campaigns.

During the thirty-one years the Social Democrats were in control, a new Sweden was consciously created. In part the transformation was based on a new party program, "The Twenty-Seven Points," developed in the last years of World War II. The language of this program was less confrontational and less explicitly anticapitalist than statements from the 1930s, but its contents argued for remaking society. Whereas "nationalization" had been an earlier keyword in Social Democratic rhetoric, now the favored term was "economic planning." Full employment, material prosperity, the end of poverty, a greater voice for workers in the production processes, income equality for farmers, and reduced class distinctions were some of the goals to be achieved through direct, active government involvement. The economy was to be manipulated for the social good, but capitalism was to remain. Nationalization might happen, however, in cases where businesses were blatantly inefficient or socially unfair.

The program was the basis for a body of legislation that defined the welfare state in late twentieth-century Sweden and included comprehensive national health care, dental insurance, regular and supplementary pensions, unemployment protection, job retraining and relocation, daycare, child allowances, parental leaves to care for newborn children, free education from

Table 6.2
Party Strength in Selected Elections in (%)

	1944	1958	1968	1976	1982	1991	1994	1998
Left (Communists)	10.3	3.4	3.0	4.8	5.6	4.5	6.2	12.0
Social Democrats	46.7	46.2	50.1	42.7	45.6	37.7	45.3	36.4
Center (Farmers)	13.6	12.7	15.7	24.1	15.5	8.5	7.7	5.1
Folk Party (Liberals)	12.9	18.2	14.3	11.1	5.9	9.1	7.2	4.7
Moderates (Conservatives)	15.9	19.5	12.9	15.6	23.6	21.9	22.4	22.9
Christian Democrats			1.5	1.4	1.9	7.1	4.1	11.7
Green Party					1.7	3.4	5.0	4.5
New Democrats						6.7	1.2	0.2

Source: Center for Business and Policy Studies, SNS Swedish Politics. Election Results at
www.const.sns.se/swedishpolitics/votes.htm

Table 6.3
Seats in Parliament in Selected Years

	1976	1982	1991	1994	1998
Left (Communists)	17	20	16	22	43
Social Democrats	152	166	138	161	131
Center (Farmers)	86	56	31	31	18
Folk Party (Liberals)	39	21	33	26	17
Moderates (Conservatives)	55	86	80	80	82
Christian Democrats			26	15	42
Green Party				18	16
New Democrats			25		

Source: Center for Business and Policy Studies, SNS Swedish Politics. Election Results at
www.const.sns.se/swedishpolitics/seats.htm

preschool through university, guaranteed vacations (rising from three to five weeks by end of the century), high-standard housing, low-cost public transportation, and well-subsidized arts and cultural programs. On the costs side, all this was to be paid for by some of the highest taxes in the West on incomes, property, capital gains, estates, consumption, and businesses.

The welfare state was not built simply because one party had its way, however, and there are other reasons for the Social Democrats' success in this area. One was the highly favorable economic context. With the exception of a brief recession in the 1950s, Sweden enjoyed nearly three decades of growth and prosperity. This provided the economic resources necessary for the building of the welfare state. Another factor was the broad consensus that this transformation enjoyed. It was not just the Social Democrats and their Farmer or Communist allies who advocated these developments. Although differing on degree or extent, they had the support of all Sweden's political parties. This consensus was carefully crafted within the context of Sweden's decision-making processes that involved the inclusion of interested and affected groups along the way. Third, the troubles of the 1930s and the shared experiences of the war had done much to build a sense of national community among the generations of Swedes who had lived through these times. Finally, public responsibility for social problems has an long history in Sweden. Care of the poor, the sick, and the elderly was an obligation that involved families, local communities, and the Church. In the late nineteenth century, however, the state became more involved with issues of health, old age, and working condition. In a way the growth of the welfare state after World War II was the third stage in a process initiated years earlier.

Two very different men led the country through this period. The first was Tage Erlander, who took over as prime minister and head of the Social Democratic Party following Per Albin Hansson's unexpected death in October 1946. A tall, lanky man who was frequently the target of political cartoons that exaggerated his height, Erlander was relatively unknown. He quickly developed into an astute and able politician, however, and successfully ran the country for twenty-three years. His style was personal and nonconfrontational, and he made effective use of private meetings at Harpsund, an idyllic country estate near Flen, west of Stockholm, to ease tensions and create compromise. The second was Olof Palme, who stepped in when Erlander retired in 1969. Palme was a man of intelligence and passion who never shied from confrontation and often invited it, especially in international affairs. During the late 1960s and early 1970s he repeatedly criticized the United States for its war in Vietnam and its exploitation of third world countries. He also attacked the Soviets for their invasion of Afghanistan in 1979. He belonged to a new generation of leaders in the party who wanted to move ahead, to change Sweden and the world.

A number of contentious issues arose during the Erlander-Palme years. Generally they were over the extent of state influence or the scope of programs. The fight over supplementary pensions in the late 1950s was one of the most heated. The existing basic pension program provided for small payments and was supported by worker contributions. The Government advocated an additional program that would, at the time of retirement, raise the level of benefits to something approaching a person's income before retirement—or during the best-paying years of his or her career. This program would be paid for through the establishment of investment funds based on employer payments. In 1957 a national referendum, in which three options were presented, was held over the issue. The outcome gave a plurality to the

Social Democrats' plan, and the Government pushed ahead. The so-called ATP supplemental pension program went into effect in 1960.

The two-component system remained the basis for pensions in Sweden until the early twenty-first century, when costs, slow economic growth, and the aging population issue forced reassessment and revision. Study of the problems began in the 1980s, a proposal for reform was put forward in 1994, and the basic elements of a new program were adopted by the parliament in 1998. Under the new system, which should go into effect sometime after 2000, workers and employers will divide contribution costs. The equivalent of 16 percent of an individual's wages will go into the "pay-as-you-go" portion of the system in which each worker will have an "account" that will earn interest until retirement. Another 2.5 percent will be invested in a general fund. The first part of the system will be publically managed; the investment fund will be in private hands. In keeping with the fundamental ideals of the welfare state, a basic pension will be guaranteed to everyone regardless of his or her contributions. Some interesting rewards built into the new system are intended to encourage people to retire later and thereby keep costs down. First, the longer individuals work, the higher their retirement benefits. Second, individuals will receive larger retirement payments if they have raised children. There will, however, be a ceiling on benefits, and contributions drop to half the set levels when income passes a certain amount (about $40,000 per year). Plans are to have the system phased in over a number of years.

A second important issue was education. Despite earlier reforms Sweden's system remained essentially elitist. The children of the working class tended to leave school early or go through the trade school option, and they remained in the working class. The university-educated elite tended to perpetuate itself in a similar pattern. The Government sought to merge social groups in the basic school years and then expand the opportunities for higher education. A 1962 reform provided for a common, nine-year basic school (*grundskolar*) experience. In 1966 a three-line plan for secondary schools was introduced that provided preparation for trade, professional, or university higher-education options. Three years later a testing system for admission to those options was added. In the 1990s the secondary curricular system was changed again. The line options were dropped in favor of seventeen programs. At the same time a stream of other educational reforms flowed from the parliament aimed at issues like curricular uniformity, gender equality, minority programs, vouchers for private schools, administrative decentralization, local independence in curricula, and teacher training. In addition, during these decades the university choices were expanded. Initially new universities, one in the far north at Umeå and the other at Linköping, were added, and several university branch campuses were created such as those at Växjö in Småland and at Karlstad in Värmland. Expansion continued, and by 2001 there were nine universities, fourteen university colleges, eight specialty colleges, and four technical schools distributed across the country. Higher education also went through administrative changes and degree-program reorganization.

The prosperity bubble in Sweden and much of the West burst in the early 1970s. Inflation, rising production costs, falling productivity, and energy issues were some of the problems. The Organization of Petroleum Exporting Countries (OPEC) oil embargo in 1973 had an enormous impact on Sweden, for half the country's energy came from petroleum products. At the same time discontent with the Social Democrats was increasing. They were blamed for the economic problems and criticized for their inability to fix them quickly. Their four decades in power had created a system opponents viewed as arbitrary, excessive, and inflexible. Time had also helped to create an entrenched army of bureaucrats who administered programs that accounted for one-third of the GDP. In the 1976 election campaign nonsocialists attacked the excesses, the loss of personal choice, and the costs of the system.

The Social Democrats stood on their record in 1976 and even argued for expanding the welfare system. They also introduced a highly controversial program, the so-called wage earner funds, into the campaign. Proposed by Rudolf Meidner, an economist at LO, the funds were seen as a way to increase worker influence in the production sphere. Employers would be required to put a proportion of their after-tax profits into funds, which would then be used to purchase stock shares in Swedish companies. The concept dovetailed nicely with other efforts by the Social Democrats and LO to increase worker democracy that had involved labor input in management decisions. For the nonsocialists the funds looked like a way to achieve ownership. Over time the workers would obtain majority control through share purchases. A quiet, creeping revolution of the economic system would occur. A surprisingly heated campaign developed, and the opposition parties even organized public protests against the funds.

The Social Democrats left office following the 1976 election; but when they returned to power in 1982, Olof Palme revived the wage earner funds issue and pushed a bill through the Riksdag. Five regional funds were set up in 1984. Conservative fears were not realized, however. The new version of the program was far less aggressive than earlier, and this helped to quiet concerns. Also, once the funds were in place, money tended to be invested in public companies. Still, the funds remained unpopular with nonsocialists and were liquidated in the early 1990s.

The outcome of the 1976 election, though far from a sweeping victory for nonsocialists, was a watershed event in Sweden's political history. The Social Democrats and Communists together lost just 1.5 percent in the popular vote that fall, but it was enough to tip the balance in the Riksdag to the nonsocialist parties. An era ended. Palme stepped down and a three-party coalition headed by Center Party leader Thorbjörn Fälldin took office.

The nonsocialist parties held on to power for six years in four different governments. They really had no answers to Sweden's problems, some of which were global and unsolvable by a single nation. The domestic or internal troubles offered no easy solution. This was illustrated by the debate over nuclear power. Sweden had built its first nuclear generating plant in 1972, and by the 1980s had a dozen in operation. About half the country's electricity came from these plants. The accident at Three Mile Island, Pennsylvania, in March 1979 alarmed everyone. The Center Party and the Communists took a strong environmentalist position and even advocated shutting down Sweden's facilities. The Social Democrats, who favored a policy of gradually replacing the nuclear stations, found allies in the Moderates and the Liberals. Economics lay at the heart of the debate. Closing plants without alternative sources of power in place could lead to serious economic problems. In 1980 three options for phasing out the existing plants were presented in a national referendum. The outcome favored running the current set of nuclear stations through their predicted life spans. The Government and parliament responded with a program to stop any new building and to complete a phase-out by 2010. The problem was far from solved, however. A seesaw array of decisions followed. After the Chernobyl disaster in 1986 that sent radioactive fallout over Sweden, it was decided to push ahead with these plans. Yet, nothing really happened. A special Energy Commission report in 1995 stated that it would be impossible to follow through on the closure plans, but it added that one plant could be shut down by the end of the decade. The Social Democratic, Left, and Milieu parties pushed an agreement through the parliament in 1997 to target the two reactors at Barsebäck, on the west coast just north of Malmö. The first of these was closed and plans were set to shut down the second. A storm of opposition was created by these actions, and the staggering costs and troubling environmental trade-offs related to a nuclear power phase out were made very clear. Replacing the power generated at this one station was predicted to double the unit cost of the electricity, involve hundreds of millions of dollars in compensation to the power company in charge (*Sydkraft*), and create serious environmental problems. Although some electricity would come from wind and hydroelectric facilities, much of it would be generated by new fossil fuel plants. Numerous public opinion polls from around the turn of the century indicated that about 80 percent of the Swedes favored running the remaining nuclear plants through their predicted life spans, which might mean for another thirty years in some cases.

In dealing with the broader problems facing Sweden in the 1980s, the Social Democrats were no more successful than their opponents. In part, of course, ideological commitments prevented them from taking any radical steps to reduce public expenditures or lower taxes. In addition, the public in general was unwilling to give up the benefits the system provided. Sweden was at the mercy of the world economy upon which it had become so dependent. In the slowdown of the 1980s, Sweden's competitive position worsened. High labor costs and generous sickness and unemployment benefits compounded to reduce productivity and market competitiveness. Devaluations of the Krona helped in the short run, but more fundamental structural changes were needed. Government debt soared as borrowing rose to meet fixed expenditures.

Popular frustration resulted in another swing of power in the 1991 election. This time the Social Democrats and their Communist allies lost over 6 percent in the popular vote, and nonsocialists moved into the majority. The new nonsocialist coalition was headed by Moderate leader Carl Bildt, a charming and popular public figure who many compared with Ronald Reagan or Margaret Thatcher. The Government's policies centered on cutting costs and taxes, searching for efficiencies in the public sector, and taking modest steps to privatize parts of the welfare system. In other words, they moved toward a return to the deflationary policies of the 1920s. In fact, however, they could not do very much. Public attitude had not changed, and as much as people might complain about the high costs of the welfare system, few actually wanted to do away with it. The Government did make some headway, though. Small fees were imposed for some services. People were given more freedom to chose their doctors. Taxes were cut. The maximum rate was fixed at around 50 percent for middle-income earners and the so-called marginal tax rates (the tax imposed on the proportion of income over a certain level) were cut back. Corporate taxes were also reduced. But Bildt and his colleagues could not win. The economy remained sluggish. Unemployment rose to over 10 percent—but it was actually closer to 15 percent when those in job-retraining programs were included. National debt ran around 70 percent of GDP. On the positive side the initial steps toward joining the European Union were taken. Application was made in 1991, and negotiations covering the terms of membership were conducted during Bildt's tenure. Overall, however, discontent with the nonsocialists' management of Sweden's affairs guided the voters in 1994. The Social

Democrats share of the vote rebounded from 37.7 percent to 45.3 percent, and they returned to power.

The Governments of Yngve Carlsson and Göran Persson, which led Sweden after the 1994 and 1998 elections, followed a course that earned them the label "neoliberal" from some observers. It seemed the Social Democrats had become champions of free-market capitalism. Following the November 1994 national referendum on membership in the European Union, in which over 83 percent of the voters participated and which resulted in a 52.3 percent yes vote, they presided over the country's entry in January 1995. They also risked making minor cutbacks in welfare programs. For example, workers would no longer receive full pay for the first day off the job because of illness. The trade unions were pressured to hold back on wage demands, and this helped keep costs down and increase the country's competitiveness. Productivity rose. Unemployment fell to below 6 percent, which was considered acceptable. In addition, interest rates came down, which encouraged investment. Finally, rising tax receipts helped to reduce the national debt.

Despite the improved economic conditions, in the 1998 election the Social Democrats polled only 36.4 percent of the vote, their lowest return since 1921. The only thing that kept them in power was the six-point rise in the Left Party's strength. The rebadged Communists, led by Gudrun Schyman, were now the third largest party in the parliament. This shift within the socialist bloc reflected the new mobility of voters. Former Social Democratic voters, disgruntled with policies or leadership, seem to be moving left and giving their support to the Left Party. (The September 2001 Norwegian election showed similar results. There the Labor Party fell from 35 percent of the vote to just over 24 percent, while the Socialist Left Party moved up from 6% to 12.4%.) Polls from summer 2001 showed that had an election been held then, the outcome would have been much the same as three years before. The Communists, Liberals, and Moderates would have gained a little, the Social Democrats would have lost a little, and the Greens might have fallen below the 4 percent threshold. Overall, the balance would have remained.

Whichever bloc or party comes out ahead in the near future, it will have a familiar list of problems to face, including public expectations built up over more than half a century, a hugely expensive welfare system, an enormous public sector, high taxes, an aging population, a structured economy that is difficult to change, and intense global competition. Thirty years of wrestling with many of these issues have not produced any long-term successes.

INTERNATIONAL RELATIONS

Historical traditions, the postwar international environment, external events, and domestic resources and capabilities all worked to shape Sweden's foreign and security policies after 1945. Although staying out of World War II had involved a complicated tight rope act and frequent compromises of neutrality—and noninvolvement had aroused vehement criticism from within the country as well as from neighbors and the belligerents—the possibility of neutrality, however illusionary, had been confirmed. So too had the wisdom of nonparticipation in Great Power conflicts. Whereas much of the rest of Europe lay in ruins, Sweden emerged unscathed. The country suffered almost no damage to its territory, relatively small external material losses, and few human casualties. At the same time the immediate postwar years seemed to offer hope for general world peace and continued cooperation among the Allies. The Cold War had not yet begun, at least in its fullest sense, and there were high hopes that the United Nations would be an effective agent of peace.

In the first five years or so after the war, Sweden opted for an independent, multifaceted policy. It joined the United Nations in 1946 and encouraged East-West cooperation in Europe. The breakdown of cooperation among the former Allies and the hardening of Soviet control in the Baltic states, Poland, and the rest of central Europe led to some policy reassessment in Sweden. This was made more important when the Soviets pressured the Finns into signing the Treaty of Friendship, Cooperation, and Mutual Assistance (FCMA) in 1948, which, in effect, severely restricted Finland's freedom in foreign and security policy directions. Nonalignment and the capacity to preserve that policy now seemed all the more important. It was in this context that Sweden looked toward building an independent neutral block with Denmark and Norway, backed by a defensive alliance. This idea failed in 1949. The Danes and Norwegians, whose views were influenced by their having been invaded and occupied during the war, as well as by a lingering resentment over Sweden's unwillingness to help them in the early years of occupation, had far less faith in a partnership and Scandinavia's ability to defend neutrality in the event of a major conflict. At the same time Europe's far north became more and more important to the Super Power blocs. Both favored the creation of a situation there that would make control of the region relatively easy to establish and worked against a Nordic pact. For example, the United States and Great Britain linked weapons' purchases and manufacturing licenses to alignment with the West. Faced by these conditions, Denmark and Norway abandoned the idea and opted for membership in the North Atlantic Treaty Organization

(NATO), and Sweden went its own way in the Nordic region. During the Cold War era Sweden's leaders followed an overt policy of nonalignment in peacetime that would allow them to be neutral in a war. This was articulated by postwar foreign minister Östen Undén and virtually all his successors. At the same time the Swedes worked to reduce East-West tensions in Scandinavia and the Baltic, bolstered their own defenses, and from 1968 advocated maintaining Scandinavia as a nuclear-free zone.

In a global context Sweden has been a champion of peace and the small nations throughout the postwar period. It joined the United Nations in 1946 and has consistently been an active member. Dag Hammarskjöld was the UN secretary general from 1953 until his tragic death in the Congo in 1961. The country participated in UN peacekeeping operations in Korea, the Middle East, Africa, and the Balkans. For three times during the 1990s, Moderate leader Carl Bildt acted as a peace negotiator in the Balkans. Sweden has also been committed to the principal of contributing an amount equal to 1 percent of its annual GDP to development and relief projects, but actual contributions have run around 0.5 percent. These engagements have involved human and material costs and have occasionally created long-term and unexpected problems for Sweden. A particularly sensitive case involved Folke Bernadotte, a nephew of King Gustav V and a man known for his efforts to help Jews at the close of World War II. Bernadotte and a colleague, Andre Serot, were murdered in September 1948 while on a UN peace mission to the Middle East. The reasons for the killing, probably organized by an extreme Zionist group called Lehi, are complex but seem to include what the group believed were Bernadotte's personal attitudes toward the Palestinians and the UN's efforts to bring peace to the region. Some sources claim that Yitzhak Shamir, later Israeli prime minister, was a member of the group that arranged the murder, and the event has colored Swedish–Israeli relations ever since.

Other cornerstones of Swedish foreign policy have been Nordic and European cooperation. The former is symbolized by the Nordic Council, founded by Denmark, Norway, Sweden, and Iceland in 1952 (with Finland joining in 1956), and the Nordic Council of Ministers, founded in 1971. These groups are not concerned with defense or security issues but, rather, focus on economic development, labor exchanges, education, culture, and the environment. They work through an assembly composed of representatives from the Nordic parliaments, in meetings of ministers from like branches of government, and through a permanent secretariat in Oslo.

In terms of European cooperation, the postwar era falls into two periods; before Sweden joined the European Union in 1995 and since. During the first of these, Sweden maintained a certain distance from European affairs and organizations that might compromise nonalignment. It joined the Organization for European Economic Cooperation (OEEC) and enjoyed the benefits of the Marshall Plan. As the Common Market took shape in the 1950s, Sweden joined with Austria, Great Britain, Denmark, Norway, Portugal, and Switzerland to form the European Free Trade Association (EFTA) in 1960. (Finland was added in 1961.) Unlike the Common Market this organization had no political, foreign policy, or defense elements. Its focus was on creating a tariff-free market among its members and developing links with the emerging European Community. Denmark and Great Britain left it to join the European Community in 1973. The remaining members concluded the European Economic Area (EEA) agreement with the European Union in 1993–1994, thereby merging their economic markets. The end of the Cold War and the collapse of the Soviet Union weakened the argument in Sweden that joining the European Union meant joining the Western bloc. In the negotiations leading up to EU membership, Sweden was able to secure a number of concessions. For one thing, it could continue to preserve its autonomy in foreign policy and defense. (So far, Sweden's leaders have said they will not participate in a European army, and the country is only an observer in the West European Union.) Further conditions of membership included the preservation of Sweden's higher environmental standards, securing regional development assistance, protection for Swedish farmers and fishermen, continuation of the country's controls on alcohol marketing, and even the survival of the country's bad habit of using snuff (in this context, chewing tobacco). In terms of monetary cooperation, Sweden is part of the European Monetary Union but has withheld commitment to adopting the common currency, the EURO. In 2001 the Persson Government expressed its preference for moving in this direction, perhaps by 2005; it announced that a referendum would be held on the question following the 2002 elections. Popular opinion, however, was not running with the Government. In polls conducted in summer 2001, only 31 percent supported full participation in the European Monetary Union and adoption of the EURO.

A final element in Sweden's international relations is the nurturing of strong regional links. This is a relatively recent trend, and it is being repeated in other parts of Europe. Two areas are particularly important here: The first is the development of what one analyst calls a "super region" that includes eastern Sweden, Finland, western Russia, and the independent Baltic republics. In this regard, Sweden has shown especially strong interest in Estonia, Latvia, and Lithuania, where extensive economic, political, cultural, and educational cooperation has developed.

The second regional system being encouraged, labeled the Öresund area, encompasses the Danish island of Sjælland and southwest Sweden. This area's population is nearly 3.5 million, and at its core are the cities of Copenhagen, Helsingör, Helsingborg, Malmö, and Lund. (The Swedish parts of this region were under Denmark's control until 1658.) The region is tied together by the Öresund Bridge, a $3.7 billion project completed in July 2000. Begun in the early 1990s, the project is an amazing engineering feat. Over 7.8 km long (from Kastrup airport to Lernacken near Malmö), it includes a 4 km tunnel and a manmade peninsula and island on the west end. The central suspension bridge is over 1,000 m long, including a 490 m cable-supported span to allow for open sea traffic below it. This new "fixed link" carries car, truck, and train traffic across one of the busiest sealanes in Europe. Its capacity is far greater than the old system of ferries. Hopes are high that the bridge will nurture strong economic, cultural, and educational development, and that the region will be better able to compete with some of the large metropolitan centers on the continent. Although bridge use has not reached expected levels and there remain a number of problems, such as the limits of the current commuter rail system, the trends are promising. For example, a consortium of eleven postsecondary schools in the area have established Öresund University, a move that greatly increases the resources available to students and faculty.

SECURITY AND DEFENSE

A strong, independent defense capability has been a fundamental corollary of Sweden's foreign policy of nonalignment. This was inherited from the World War II experience. Following the war the nation's security planners continued to argue that although Sweden could never hope to defeat a concerted attack by a Great Power, it could present defenses so costly to overcome that any attacker might think twice. Sweden would fight back and inflict what leaders hoped would be unacceptable losses. This determination was based on a very expensive military establishment. In 1998 the defense budget accounted for $5 billion or 2.3 percent of GDP. Small permanent contingents of enlisted personnel and officers in the army, navy, and airforce are supplemented by recruits drawn from a compulsory military service system. Virtually every Swedish male is eligible for military service, and today about one in every three (c.18,000) is drafted and trained each year. The length of training depends on branch and service specialization. Women are not drafted, but the officer corps of all three branches of the armed services have been open to them since 1980. Conscientious objection is an option, and alternative service assignments are made to respect this. Those not drafted go into what the Swedes vaguely call a "manpower pool." The system gives the country about 180,000 men easily and quickly mobilized, plus about 70,000 in the so-called Home Guard. The reserve depth is far greater but would take more time to mobilize. In the event of an attack, the first option is to prevent invading forces from establishing a presence in the country. Failing that, plans for conducting ongoing defensive and guerilla actions are in place.

The three branches operate on the principle of decentralization, with units and equipment stationed at crucial places around the country, often in secure and very well camouflaged sites. The national road system has been constructed with defense in mind, and some of the country's major highways have sections designed to double as landing fields. The navy specializes in coastal defense, submarine and antisubmarine warfare, and mining operations. Their principal ships are generally relatively small, fast, and maneuverable.

In order to strengthen the credibility of Sweden's nonalignment policy and to enhance the country's independence, military equipment is designed and built domestically whenever possible. Small arms, artillery, personnel transport vehicles, tanks, communications and detection equipment, missiles and guidance systems, aircraft, and naval vessels are all produced in Sweden. As a result of this policy, Sweden's armaments industry has become an important contributor to the national economy, and the country has become a player in the global weapons market.

A highly visible example of Sweden's military industrial complex is the country's military aircraft industry. Between the 1950s and 2000, three highly capable jet platforms were developed, the Drakken, Viggen, and JAS39–Gripen. Each of these was competent, up to date, and competitive for its time. Although often identified as SAAB products, they were national efforts and engaged many Swedish companies including Volvo (engines), L. M. Ericsson (computers), and Bofors (armaments). Development of the latest of these so-called platforms, the Gripen, was initiated in the mid-1980s. Although the project encountered considerable opposition because of costs and had some early problems, the aircraft has entered production and about one hundred had been delivered by late 2000. Foreign customers or potential customers include South Africa, Hungary, the Czech Republic, Poland, Austria, and Brazil.

Although there is a relatively strong consensus about the country's security policy and defense system, there are critics. Some have argued that the money spent on defense did not buy security. During the Cold War few experts believed one of the two Super Powers would hesitate to attack Sweden if need be. In addition, it was widely thought the country's defenses would collapse quickly to avoid casualties, despite war plans and rhetoric.

Then there was the nuclear card, which if played by a Super Power would be disastrous for Sweden. No amount of defense spending could protect Sweden then. Another line of criticism held that the system as established was really ineffective. During the 1980s the navy was embarrassed by frequent alleged incursions by submarines into Swedish waters. The worst of these was when a Soviet "whiskey class" sub ran aground in October 1981 outside of Karlskrona, the country's main naval base, and was discovered by a fisherman. There were other incidents, and it appeared that Sweden's territorial waters, including Stockholm harbor, were regularly being violated by submarine operations probing Sweden's detection effectiveness. Thirteen years of expensive searches with the latest high-tech equipment, pursuits, and depth charging by the navy led only to an admission in 1995 that most of the subs were probably mink, otter, or other marine mammals. Also, there were those who argued that Sweden's system, which was largely traditional in its response planning, would not be able to deal with a covert initial attack that could paralyze the country by shutting down its highly vulnerable electrical power grid. Finally, there is good evidence to support the criticism that this system was neither truly independent nor nonaligned. Beginning during the closing years of World War II, Sweden became a covert member of the Western bloc. Its defense establishment was there to hold off an attack from the Soviet Union until U.S. and NATO help could arrive. This is evidenced, in part, by the compatibility or "interoperability" of Swedish weapons with those of NATO.

A special chapter in the history of Sweden's postwar defense strategies involves the country's nuclear weapons development program. For over twenty years following World War II, Sweden worked independently to create a small number of atomic weapons. Central to this was a company called *Atomenergi*. It linked the building of a number of nuclear electrical power stations with the production of the plutonium necessary for a bomb. The program was supported by the Government, the military, and the public until the mid-1960s. Strategically, it was seen as a component of national defense. Weapons could be used to strike at invasion forces or in "forward" defensive actions against an aggressor. The airforce was designated as the primary branch for the use of these weapons. When the project began, there were relatively few atomic weapons. The Soviet Union tested its first atomic device in 1949. The United States and the U.S.S.R. did not have hydrogen bombs until 1952 and 1953, respectively. Mutually assured destruction (MAD) was not yet possible. The expansion of the Super Powers' nuclear arsenals and the development of intercontinental ballistic missiles (ICBMs) in the 1960s radically changed the context in which Sweden's program operated. In the new setting, to use the two or three atomic bombs Sweden might build against the Soviet Union would be to invite annihilation. Support for the project evaporated in the 1960s, and with the unanimous support of the parliament, the Government announced its halt in 1968. Sweden joined the group of sixty-two nations that signed the Nuclear Non-Proliferation Treaty the same year. Since then Sweden has worked closely with its Nordic neighbors to keep nuclear weapons out of the region.

SOCIAL DEVELOPMENT

Between 1945 and 2000 Sweden's population grew from around 6.7 million to about 8.8 million. What was exceptional about this growth was that a very high percentage (45 percent between 1944 and 1978, for example), resulted from immigration. Birth rates, in fact, were low; and assuming a number of factors remained constant, there would have been almost no increase in population without this influx of new people.

Immigration has repeatedly influenced the composition of the country's population, language, high and popular cultures, economy, and politics. Birka was a cosmopolitan place during the Viking Age. The Conversion brought in English, Frankish, German, and Slavic peoples. Medieval trade and dynastic development involved significant migration by Germans. Gustav I Vasa relied on German political advisors. The dynamic development of the country's economy in the seventeenth century was, in part, based on Dutch, Walloon, and other western European entrepreneurs or technical experts. The armed forces were often multiethnic in composition,

Table 6.4
Immigrants, Emigrants, and Net Immigration Selected Individual Years

Year	Immigrants	Emigrants	Net+
1945	21,126	8,261	12,865
1950	27,940	12,860	15,080
1955	30,069	12,675	17,394
1960	26,143	15,138	11,005
1965	49,586	15,977	33,609
1970	77,326	28,653	48,673
1975	44,133	27,249	16,884
1980	39,426	29,839	9,587
1985	33,127	22,036	11,091
1990	60,048	25,196	34,852
1995	45,887	33,984	11,903
2000	58,659	34,091	24,568

Source: SCB. Statistiska centralbyrån. http://www.scb.se

with French, German, English, and Scottish migrants making up important elements of the officer ranks. A look at the names of many of Sweden's old noble families, such as De Geer, De la Gardie, Maclean, and Wachtmeister, reveals this diversity. Finns have frequently been a source of labor or were brought in to clear new farms from the forests. Overall, the number of immigrants coming to Sweden before the late twentieth century has been small, and the population has been very homogeneous. Those who were different, including gypsies, Jews, and the Sami people, were obviously so, and they were often set apart and faced criticism and abuse. The flood of refugees and labor migrants who entered the country after World War II contributed to a demographic revolution in Sweden, and their influences on the country will continue to be felt for decades.

The "new Swedes" fall primarily into three, often indistinguishable groups: refugees, labor migrants, and their dependents. Toward the end of the war and in the years just following, many of the people who came to Sweden were refugees from one of the other Nordic countries, Germany, or the Soviet-occupied Baltic states. They made up most of the 134,000 immigrants who arrived in the 1940s. During the 1950s the nature of the migrants changed. A common labor market was created for Denmark, Finland, Norway, and Sweden in 1954, and this opened the door to a flow comprised mainly of Finns. During the 1960s, additional foreign workers drawn to Sweden by high wages and generous social benefits migrated from Greece, Turkey, and the former Yugoslavia. The labor market tightened in the late 1960s and early 1970s, and this led to stricter labor migration controls. A 1967 law required a person to obtain a work permit *before* coming to Sweden. At the same time the flow of refugees increased. As many as 30,000 persons a year sought asylum in Sweden, and the country's open-door policies made it an attractive choice. Also, once a small group of refugees from a particular country became established, it acted as a magnet to others. The newcomers made up a remarkable group and included Iranians, Iraqis, Kurds, Chileans, Eritreans, and Southeast Asians. In the late 1980s and 1990s many of the refugees were from the wartorn Balkans. By the close of the 1990s, about one-ninth of the population was foreign born, and one of every eight Swedes was either foreign born or the child of an immigrant parent. Among the largest of the foreign-born groups were Iranians (c. 33,000), Turks (c. 22,000), Poles (c. 16,000), and Chileans (c. 13,000), but the diversity of the new Swedes was better measured by the fact that some fifty languages were now being taught to immigrant children in the schools.

Many cities, but especially Stockholm, Göteborg, and Malmö, became strikingly multiethnic. To anyone familiar with the history of immigration and ethnicity in the United States, Australia, or elsewhere, predictable pat-

terns appeared. Individual ethnic groups developed distinct neighborhoods or communities where their native cultures could thrive in a
self-contained setting. Often these ethnic communities were located in one
of the large suburban apartment complexes built in the 1970s. A network of
organizations, businesses, restaurants, entertainment outlets, churches,
and publications appeared for each group, all of them having as at least one
of their purposes the preservation of cultural identity. Typically an immigrant group retains much of its homeland culture through the first generation. Identity then shifts, and the second generation tries hard to lose at
least the obvious aspects of its foreignness. The third generation gives the
appearance of having been completely assimilated. In fact, however, some
of those in that third generation are caught in limbo. They feel they do not
really belong to either the new culture or the culture of their origins. In Sweden, these struggles of assimilation have appeared.

Official policy toward the new Swedes was two-dimensional and costly.
It aimed at encouraging both cultural retention and assimilation, and programs were developed to facilitate both. On the side of retention, legislation provided for immigrant language instruction in the schools, support to
organizations, and funds for the publication of newspapers and books in
the immigrant languages. On the assimilation side the government tried to
mix ethnic with native Swedes in housing situations, created job opportunities that would enhance adaptation, and provided child and adult
Swedish-language programs. Employers were required to give immigrant
workers time off with pay to attend language classes.

Becoming Swedish and gaining acceptance from the Swedes will take
time. These transitions have been easier for many of the early labor migrants and northern European refugees because they are closer to Sweden
culturally and historically and because they blend into the population in
terms of their physical appearance. Southern European labor migrants and
the more recent refugees from the Middle East, Africa, Asia, and South
America have had a much more difficult time. Their appearance, dress, cultures, and religions make their differentness obvious. Many encounter
discrimination. A particular problem has been that although some refugees
were highly trained professionals in their homelands, in Sweden they
lacked the language skills and often failed to meet the country's licensing
standards. The result was that, for example, engineers drove taxi cabs or
waited on tables. The economic troubles of the last decades of the twentieth
century made the situation for many of the new Swedes worse. An ugly xenophobia surfaced in Sweden in the 1990s. The New Democrats rode a brief
wave of popularity based on this. Discrimination in the job market, social

isolation, beatings, knife attacks in schools, murders, defacing of property, and acts of arson were some of the things the minorities faced.

Sweden's governments pursued an activist role in response to various anti-immigrant attacks. In the late 1990s new legislation was passed aimed at encouraging greater acceptance on the part of the "native" Swedes. Young people, especially, were targeted with informational programs, and a policy of no tolerance of racial discrimination was introduced into the schools. New regulations were imposed to open more job opportunities and encourage nondiscriminatory hiring, and a special office for hearing and settling job-related problems for minorities was created.

Crime

Although little attention has been paid to it in this volume, crime has long been a part of Swedish history. The earliest law codes were devoted, in part, to how accusations against individuals were to be brought, trials conducted, and criminals punished. The earliest Swedish state emerged partly from a chaotic society in search of order and internal peace. Until the mid-eighteenth century, actions against accused criminals followed procedures that would shock twenty-first-century observers, actions such as the frequent use of torture to extract confessions. Punishments were horrific. The death penalty was applied to a wide range of crimes, including treason, murder, military desertion, thievery, and adultery. The young noble who murdered Gustav III in 1792 was punished in the usual fashion: his right hand was struck off and then he was beheaded. For lesser crimes the punishments might actually have been worse. A servant who fled his or her contracted master could, for example, be sentenced to several years at hard labor. If the work did not kill the person, then disease, malnutrition, or exposure to the elements often would.

Reform of legal proceedings and prisons took place during the eighteenth and nineteenth centuries. Torture was abolished, and fewer crimes called for the death penalty. Sentences were reduced and prison conditions improved. Around the middle of the nineteenth century, reformers succeeded in radically changing the nature and purpose of Sweden's prisons. The principles of solitary confinement and prisoner rehabilitation were applied. A prison became a place where the accused could contemplate his or her crime and listen to uplifting messages about how to be a good and productive citizen. After World War II a new series of reforms gave Sweden one of the world's most humane penal systems. Living conditions were improved, socialization allowed, and job training and experience provided. Inmates were even allowed leaves and visits by spouses or partners. Critics likened the new system to a network of pleasant camps.

Overall, Sweden has had some of the lowest crime rates in the West for much of the modern period; even as crime became an increasing problem in other parts of Europe and in the United States, Sweden continued to enjoy a kind of idyllic detachment. This changed abruptly and shockingly on a quiet winter night in 1986. On 28 February Prime Minister Olof Palme was murdered in central Stockholm while walking home from a movie with his wife. This was an event that simply could not take place in Sweden, yet it had. To make matters worse, the police investigation seemed, according to one source, more like the bungling of Inspector Clouseau, Peter Sellers's famous character. The arrest, release, rearrest, and then acquittal of one suspect, who many believe to be the actual murderer, seemed to make a mockery of Sweden's police and criminal law system. The case remains open and unsolved, and there are countless theories about it. Iraqis, Iranians, Serbs, and the South African secret police are all on the list of possible killers. Later events continued to shock the Swedes. In January 1995 four people were gunned down at a Stockholm disco by an enraged youth in what was called the "Stureplan massacre." In June of the same year, an enraged off-duty army weapons instructor shot and killed seven people in Falun. In what is the worst of these tragedies, a fire was set in a Göteborg disco leased by a Macedonian immigrant association in October 1998, and in the stampede to escape the blaze sixty-three young people died and another 210 were injured. Four teenagers were convicted of "gross arson" for the crime. In 1999 the number of murders in all Sweden was 173, down from a high of 199 in 1996. Many U.S. cities have higher figures.

Crime in contemporary Sweden goes beyond murders, of course. The number of rapes and robberies have climbed in recent decades. In 1999 over 57,000 assaults were reported. There were more than 34,000 drugs arrests the same year. Clearly Sweden has its own war to wage on drugs. Racial xenophobia, often unleashed by neo-Nazi groups, has resulted in assaults on and killings of ethnic minority members. A person used to be able to feel safe wandering the streets of any Swedish city day or night, but not any more. Stockholm's subway stations are frequently the scenes of muggings. Gangs, including Sweden's versions of America's Hell's Angels, have developed, and their activities range from the relatively harmless spreading of graffitti to local warfare.

Following the development of crime in Sweden is made easier because the country keeps remarkably good track of its people and their behaviors—far more so than many other countries. Sweden conducted the first population census in Europe in the mid-eighteenth century and has some of the best demographic and genealogical records in the world. Caution needs to be taken when using many of the numbers available, however, especially when comparing or ranking. Swedes report and record crimes with far greater care than do other nations. Further, the numbers need to be seen in the context of a total population of about 8.8 million.

Women

Sweden is a leader in the modern women's movement. Progress in attaining legal rights was made in the late nineteenth century, essential political equality was gained in the 1920s, and sexual and reproductive rights were achieved in the 1930s and soon after World War II. Progress was made in equal educational opportunities in the 1920s and especially in the 1960s. All these changes were legislated reforms, however; they did not necessarily involve any changes of attitudes. True gender equality means that fundamental assumptions, behaviors, and expectations have to be changed, too. This is what has certainly begun to happen in the postwar era. That women are truly perceived as the equals of men in politics, intellectual pursuits, management settings, the armed forces, and so on, has made great progress in Sweden. Numbers demonstrate theses advances. Over 40 percent of the representatives in the *Riksdag* are women. Women head the Left, Center, and Green parties. The first woman cabinet minister was Karin Kock-Lindberg, who served in the late 1940s. Carl Bildt's Government in the early 1990s had eight women. Ten members of Göran Persson's Government from 1998 are women, and not all of them in what are considered to be the traditionally female ministries such as social security or education. Lena Hjelm-Wallén is assistant prime minister, Anna Lindh is minister of foreign affairs, Margareta Winberg is minister of agriculture, and Mona Sahlin is second in command of the Commerce Department. This pattern is repeated at the county and communal levels of government, as well as in the universities and other levels of education. More and more women are in the professions and in management. More go on to higher education. Many of Sweden's leading writers are women, including Kerstin Ekman and Marianne Fredriksson. Internationally, Sweden ranks fourth in the number of women in management, third in the number in government, and first in a UN category called "gender empowerment."

Do these patterns of change and numbers mean women have achieved full equality in Sweden? No, they do not. In occupational distribution women are still clustered in traditional educational and care-giving fields such as teaching, nursing, and social work. Women still face employment discrimination and income disparities. Although women have found their way into the offices of management, they have not reached the top in the largest and most powerful companies. Whereas Denmark has a queen (Margrethe II), Finland has a woman president (Tarja Halonen), and Norway had a woman prime minister (Gro Harlem Brundtland), a woman has yet to lead Sweden. Mona Sahlin came close in the late 1990s but was removed from the running by a rather silly scandal involving her use of a government credit card. Also, old attitudes about parenting and domestic duties remain deeply ingrained, and many women who work are still expected to perform traditional domestic duties as well. Equal sharing of those responsibilities has not been achieved.

ECONOMIC DEVELOPMENT

Sweden's economic history in the postwar period may be divided in two broad periods. One extends from 1945 to the late 1960s, a time of sustained growth in the private and public sectors, increasing income and material prosperity, and growing regional and global economic integration and interdependence. The second period began in the late 1960s and extends to the present, a time of instability, uncertainty, and often painful adjustments to domestic and global economic realities.

Sweden's industrial economy experienced a "golden age" in the first three decades after the war. Fearing a recession like the one that followed World War I, the Government was cautious and maintained many of the wartime controls, including wage and price regulations, supply allocation restrictions, and rationing. There was no recession, however, and all of western Europe, including Sweden, recovered with remarkable speed. By the early 1950s most of the wartime restrictions had been removed. Annual GDP growth was around 3.4 percent for much of the decade, then swelled to over 5 percent annually in the early 1960s and dropped to around 4 percent for the last half of the decade. Import and export trade grew at even faster rates. Output in most branches of the industrial sector increased, driven by new technologies and investment. There was especially vigorous expansion in the motor vehicle, shipbuilding, machine, and electrical appliance areas. In what is a comparatively tiny country, two independent automobile manufacturers, SAAB and Volvo, and a major producer of household appliances, Electrolux, developed. Much of this growth was fed by consumer demand. The Swedes, along with much of western Europe and the United States, bought their way to prosperity. New *things* flooded the retail market. They were mass produced in Swedish and foreign factories and consumed by a public deluged by advertising. Automobiles, televisions, vacuum cleaners, refrigerators, washing machines and dryers, radios, hi fi's and then stereos, and fashions were available and desired. Former luxuries became necessities. In the public sphere expenditures on highway, bridge, and public transportation facilities soared. Stockholm launched the first phase in the construction of its subway system in the early 1950s. Private home or apartment ownership was vigorously promoted, and the building trades boomed. New rings of planned suburbs, each with its own housing complexes, stores, services, schools, and recreation areas, were built around old urban areas.

In this dynamic economy unemployment was low, real incomes rose, and the disparities between the highest and lowest paid were reduced. It was also the ideal setting in which to build the welfare state. The newly affluent Swedes were psychologically prepared and willing to pay the taxes needed to fund the new or expanded social programs. The public sector's spending on the welfare state was an important component of the booming economy, especially from the mid-1960s on, and it came to account for about one-third of the GDP.

Mobility and demographic change were other aspects of this dynamic postwar economy. The labor immigration described earlier was part of this. Another involved the continued depopulation of the agricultural regions of the country. Mechanization became widespread in Swedish farming after the war, and this reduced the demand for labor. Some of the surplus moved to smaller, regional industrial centers; some of it gravitated toward the cores around Stockholm, Göteborg, and Malmö. By the mid-1960s over half the country's population lived in a band that stretched across the middle of the country from east to west. The further mechanization of the forest sector and falling demand for Sweden's iron ore had similar impacts. In some parts of the far north and west there was concern about the viability of these areas to survive economically and still provide the necessary services for their declining populations. Government regional development policy in the later decades of the century helped to reverse some of this drift.

The bubble of seemingly endless growth and prosperity burst in the late 1960s, and since then Sweden has experienced a series of ups and downs, most of them paralleling world trends. The initial downturn was characterized by a decline in exports and was caused by the rising prices of Swedish goods and services. High wages, high taxes, and inflation drove costs up. Swedish products became less competitive in the global markets. By the early 1970s the country was in a recession; the situation was made worse by the OPEC oil embargo in 1973 and the resulting rise in petroleum prices. In this context the wisdom of the Social Democrats came under question and the labor market, which had remained largely peaceful since 1938, experienced a series of wildcat strikes. No quick solutions were offered by Olof Palme and his colleagues, who followed traditional Keynesian method of spending to maintain economic vitality and reduce unemployment and paying for its programs through borrowing. The result was a soaring national debt. Enough voters turned to the nonsocialist parties in 1976 to tip the balance in the parliament, but the new coalition government did no better. Their answer to the competitiveness problem was to devalue the Krona—which they did four times between 1976 and 1981. At the same time they tried to shore up particularly troubled industries, including mining, steel, and shipbuilding, through subsidies and nationalization. Iron-mining operations were consolidated in the old, state-owned *Luossavaara-Kiirunavaara AB (LKAB)*. In 1977 Kockums in Malmö, Götaverken in Göteborg, and Uddevallavarvet, all major shipbuilders that were in crises, were merged into a state-controlled concern, *Svenska Varv*. A 45 percent state-owned steel company, *Svenskt Stål* was built by uniting the works at Domnarvet, Luleå, and Oxelösund. These moves forced rationalization on old and noncompetitive businesses. In some cases operations were shut down. In others, specialization helped to save them. For a time the Götaverken works shifted its production to oil-drilling platforms. Kockums in Malmö turned to building submarines.

When the Social Democrats returned to power in 1982, their answer to the economic problems, labeled the "third way" between Keynesian spending and Margaret Thatcher's government economies and an unleashed free market, was to force wage restraint on the unions and devalue the Krona by 16 percent. Conditions did improve by the late 1980s, but new troubles developed as the economy "overheated." An investment spree, funded on credit, contributed to new growth, but fundamental problems, including Sweden's high labor costs, high taxes, and aging manufacturing sector, were ignored. To cool things down the finance minister, Kjell-Olof Feldt, proposed a package of measures, including a freeze on wages, strikes, and tax levels in spring 1990. In what was referred to in the press as "the war of the roses," the Social Democratic Party and *LO* argued over the package, and it was defeated in the parliament. Discredited, Feldt was replaced in a Government restructuring. The nonsocialists returned to power the next fall, but Carl Bildt's program of tax cuts and limited welfare service privatization was no more successful. Particularly alarming was the growing national debt. When the Social Democrats returned in 1994, their economic policies were either more successful or they were lucky and rode the general global upswing of the late 1990s.

There is a lot of gloom and doom in the contemporary literature about Sweden's economy, some of which is justified. The country has serious issues to address. One is the level of taxation on individuals and corporations. Personal income tax rates, when local and state taxes are combined, run as high as 60 percent. Corporate profits are taxed at around 28 percent. The value-added tax on most goods is 25 percent. Capital gains taxes on Swedish shares is 30 percent—up from 12.5 percent in a Government move to discourage profit taking and capital flight. Labor and interest costs are high. Sweden is an expensive place to live and do business, and it has fallen to fifteenth on the list of countries with the highest standards of living. In a few well-publicized cases of the absurd, individual Swedish businessmen have received tax bills in excess of their incomes. In the international market for managerial and technical talent, Sweden has trouble competing, and many Swedish companies have moved their corporate offices out of the country.

There is a brighter side to the general economic picture. Many of the country's companies have undergone important transformations with positive results. *Rationalization, concentration, specialization,* and *globalization* are words that help to sum up these changes. Clearly competition and technological developments have forced many of the noncompetitive and often older companies to close or else change what they produce and how they do business. In the process Sweden has become less and less a country of natural resources, raw materials, and primary industries like textiles or heavy machinery. As we have seen, the mining, shipbuilding, and steel branches have been propped up by nationalization, an option rarely taken in Sweden. (Despite the predominance of the Social Democrats in this period, only about 10 percent of the country's economy has ever been state owned.) Others have merged to create viable new companies. From the late 1990s buyouts by foreign-owned companies or mergers with foreign companies have also been important. Among these are Stora's, the old copper and forest products company, merger with Finland's ENSO, pharmaceutical giant ASTRA's joining with Britain's Zeneca, Nobel Industries' purchase by Dutch Akzo, SAAB's purchase by GM, Volvo's sale of its automobile division to FORD, and agricultural equipment maker ASEA's merger with Swiss Brown Boveri. Adaptation to the changing global markets has also been a technique for success in Swedish business. Volvo and SAAB provide interesting examples. The automobile-manufacturing divisions of both companies moved up market in stages. When their cars entered the United States' market in the late 1950s, for example, they were odd looking but practical, interesting from an engineering perspective, and relatively inexpensive. The Volvo PV544 looked like a car from the mid-1940s, and in many ways it was. It developed a reputation as reliable and even somewhat sporty. The SAAB 93 was one of the few front-wheel- drive cars on the market at the time and was powered by a smoking, unique-sounding, 2-cycle engine. Twenty years later Volvos and SAABs were viewed as safe, solid, reliable, and conservative. By the end of the century both manufacturers had moved into the "near luxury" market and had radically transformed both their products and their images. Similarly, SAAB's aircraft division, in addition to making military aircraft, found a profitable niche in the commuter airplane business. L. M. Ericsson moved into the wireless telecommunication sector early and became a major producer of cellphones.

Another trend has been the conscious effort by government to revitalize declining parts of the country. Planning and money have been focused on the timber industry areas of the north and west, for example. Government administrative service offices have been intentionally relocated in these areas, and new business development has been encouraged. In January 2001 the Swedish National Board for Industrial and Technical Development was split into three new agencies to encourage the founding and growth of new enterprises in lagging regions of the country.

Certainly one of the most important events in Sweden's history in this period, from perspectives that reach beyond the economic, was the country's entrance into the European Union in January 1995. This decision followed years of study and hesitation. Most of Sweden's trade partners from EFTA, including Great Britain, Denmark, Austria, and Finland, had either joined the new Europe or wanted to do so. Sweden had participated in the community through the Europe Economic Area agreement since 1993–1994. The business community, "Sweden incorporated," supported membership. Among the political parties the Greens, the Left, and the New Democrats were opposed. Opposition also came from other groups concerned about lower EU standards on a wide range of goods and services, agricultural and fishing policies, labor migration, Sweden's traditional foreign policy and nonparticipation in military blocs, special and regional interests, and costs. As we have seen, some of these concerns were addressed in the final membership agreements.

As Sweden entered the twenty-first century, many economic indicators looked promising and predictions were cautiously optimistic. In 2001 growth in GDP was slowing and expected to be just under 3 percent; the state's budget was in surplus, and the national debt was being paid down. Inflation was expected to run around 2.5 percent; unemployment was around 5 percent. Less promising were the weakness of the Krona, negative reports from important companies, including L. M. Ericsson, SAS, and bearing manufacturer SKF, and the economic downturn in the United States and elsewhere.

Not every Swede agrees with or supports Sweden's European and global connections. This became shockingly clear in mid-June 2001, when the streets of Göteborg erupted in protest on the occasion of the meeting of the EU commissioners and the visit of U.S. president George W. Bush. Among the concerns of the demonstrators were issues of third world debt, the European Monetary Union, and the Americans' rejection of the Kyoto Agreement on global warming. Most of the protestors were well organized around what they called the Freedom Forum (*Fritt Forum*). They planned to conduct discussions, informational meetings, and peaceful demonstrations during the EU conference. Representatives from these groups met with Prime Minister Göran Persson, who was then serving a six-month term as president of the European Union. An estimated 20,000 people were involved. Unfortunately, events took an ugly turn. Some people blamed the riots on a small minority of so-called black-dressed ruffians or "anarchists" intent on violence for its own sake. Several areas in central Göteborg turned into war zones. Mounted police officers were used to try to keep order, but the authorities were unprepared for the scale of the demonstrations and for the violence that developed. Windows were smashed, barricades erected, and paving stones thrown at the police. Hundreds were arrested, and there were many injuries. In one incident police shot and wounded three of the demonstrators, one young Swede critically. One account called the Göteborg events "the worst street riots in Sweden in modern times." (*Dagens Nyheter*, 16 June 2001) The intensity of the demonstrators brought back memories of the 1960s, when anti-Vietnam War and anti-American protests in Stockholm were frequent and when, on one occasion, the U.S. ambassador was pelted with eggs. Several things emerged from these events. First, the law enforcement community was wholly unprepared for what occurred. This was understandable only because of Sweden's relatively peaceful history. Such things just do not happen there. Second, many young people are not in agreement with the policies of their government or of the European Union. They represent a voice little heeded by the forces behind the European Union. These were not the first protests, nor would they be the last.

CULTURAL DEVELOPMENTS

The last half-century has witnessed the continuation of many cultural trends set in the years between the world wars, and many leaders served in both periods. Swedish, Scandinavian, or Nordic modern architecture and design remained important, at least until the 1970s, and contributed to an international school that emphasized functionalism, simplicity, and integration with the setting. Although a so-called postmodern eclecticism has become increasingly important, many designers still work in this style. Traditional high culture enjoys enormous popularity. Stockholm is the home of the country's "national" theater, ballet, opera, and symphony, all of which date from the eighteenth century. The wonderful eighteenth-century theater at Drottningholm continues to be a center for productions, including Ingmar Bergman's version of *The Magic Flute*. But high culture is not confined to Stockholm. Göteborg opened a spectacular new opera house in the 1990s. Regional centers support many excellent if less prestigious performing centers and ensembles.

In literature many of the leading authors of the old generation continued to write until well into the postwar period. Three of these, Pär Lagerkvist (1951), Harry Martinson (1974), and Eyvind Johnson (1974) won Nobel Prizes in Literature. Vilhelm Moberg (1898–1973) produced his best-known works, the four-volume historical novels on emigration from Småland and settlement in the United States between 1949 and 1959. Ivar Lo-Johansson (1901–1990), whose writing career spanned some fifty years, published cutting critiques of social problems in novels such as *The Pensioners' Sweden* (*Ålderdoms Sverige*) and in his ongoing autobiographical series. Per Anders Fogelström belonged to a group of authors who emerged in the late 1960s to describe the lives of ordinary people. Beginning in 1962, he wrote a connected group of eight novels about the lives of the working classes of Stockholm from the mid-eighteenth to the late twentieth centuries At the same time a new generation of writers emerged: P. O. Enquist's carefully researched documentary-style novels, such as *The Legionnaires* (*Legionärarna*) (1968) and *The Royal Physician's Visit* (*Livläkarensbesök*) (1999) and his screenplay for *Hamsun*, tell important and often controversial stories about the past. Kerstin Ekman has laid bare the landscapes and the conflicted lives of the people of far northern Sweden through mysteries like *Black Water* and *Under the Snow*; whereas Marianne Fredriksson has focused on gender, generational, and cultural conflicts in novels such as *Hanna's Daughters* and *Simon's Family*. Both women are internationally known best-selling authors. One of the more interesting aspects of recent Swedish fiction is the appearance of immigrant authors, some of them writing in their native languages. Others, like Theodor Kallifatides, who describes growing up in his native Greece in *Peasants and Masters* (*Bönder och herrar*), write in Swedish. There is also an exciting new generation of poets.

The Swedish film industry has been making high-quality films since the 1920s, and many of them have received international acclaim. Since the war Ingmar Bergman has been the country's best-known director and screenplay writer, with over fifty film projects to his credit. But there are other fine directors in Sweden. Jan Troel directed the film versions of Moberg's emigrant-immigrant series and a stunning production on the life of Norwegian author Knut Hamsun. Bo Widerberg, an established novelist, became internationally known for *Elvira Madigan* (1962). His political voice was expressed in *Ådalen 31*, about the strike and demonstration in 1931 that resulted in five deaths, and *Joe Hill*, about the Swedish-born labor activist in the United States. Lasse Holmström's *My Life as a Dog* (*Mitt liv som hund*), from 1985, is a wonderfully sensitive treatment of the trials of a boy trying to cope with his mother's dying and his own adolescence. In the 1990s Lukas Moodyson, whose *Give Me Love* became widely popular among young people, emerged as a one of the most promising young directors in Sweden. The country has also produced many fine screen and stage actors. The best known internationally are Greta Garbo, Ingrid Bergman, and Max von Sydow. Each of their careers reflects the actor's own talents and the internationalization of the film industry. Von Sydow, for example, starred in many of Ingmar Bergman's films and was Karl Oskar, the Småland farmer, in Troel's emigration epics. American audiences know him better from his appearance in films like *Dune*, *The Exorcist*, and *Flash Gordon*.

Swedes have also made their contributions to popular music. ABBA burst on the scene in 1974, and the foursome was for a time Sweden's "second leading export"—behind Volvo cars. Today ABBA founders Benny Andersson and Björn Ulvaeus have teamed up to write and produce two successful musicals: *Kristina from Duvemåla*, based on Moberg's emigrant novels, and "*Mamma Mia*," based on ABBA's career. The latter opened in London in 1999. Later performers who reached some measure of international recognition and popularity in several popular music styles were the Göteborg foursome Ace of Base, Roxette, Kent, and The Cardigans. Connected with their own success in popular music, Swedes have been able to attract star performers from all over the world. Stockholm has become a popular site for making music videos. Other musical genre have also flourished in Sweden. Jazz is enormously popular, and there are excellent clubs in the major cities. Also, Stockholm was a pioneering center in the development of electronic music, with state-of-the-art facilities and an international cast of performers and composers.

Closing a survey history like this is never easy. There is always something else to say or some event that happened just yesterday that needs to be included. Perhaps as good a way as any to conclude is to revisit the many-faceted contributions of the "new Swedes," for they, as much as politics or international developments or economic change, are helping to create the Sweden of tomorrow. Swedish "culture" has never been homogeneous. Class and regional differences have existed for centuries. Today one must add ethnic differences to the mix. Everything from foods to fashions to folk customs is being affected. To tour contemporary Sweden is to take part in an international parade of peoples—peoples with varied faces and costumes and languages. Traditional cultural symbols like Maypoles, crayfish, bonfires, akvavit, and Lucia's are being joined by the icons of the new cultures in Sweden. To eat there is to partake of an incredibly diverse *smörgåsbord* (table arrayed with a wide range of sandwiches and other dining choices).

Only a few decades ago restaurant fare was monotonous and overwhelmingly Swedish. Today the options are truly international. Ethnic restaurants abound, often in close proximity to the familiar *konditori* (pastry shops) and curbside *korv* (sausage) stands. On a summer day many urban market squares and avenues are stages for ethnic performers. Particularly striking to this writer was a day several years ago when the buildings along *Drottninggatan* in downtown Stockholm provided a wonderful echo-chamber for a South American pipe band and a folk troupe from the northern province of Dalarna.

Notable People in the History
of Sweden

The following does not contain every name mentioned in the text. Many of the monarchs and prime ministers have been excluded. Lists of the rulers appear in Chapters 3 and 4. Lists of prime ministers may be found in Chapters 5 and 6.

Asplund, Gunnar (1885–1940). An architect and a leading figure in the development of the "Swedish modern" style in the 1930s. Among his best-known projects are the Stockholm City Library and Stockholm Exposition Hall.

Bergman, Ingmar (1918–   ). Perhaps the best-known Swedish film director and screenplay author of the late twentieth century. His career began before World War II and continues into the twenty-first century. Since 1944, he has been involved in at least fifty film projects.

Bildt, Carl (1949–   ). The head of the Moderate Party and prime minister in the early 1990s, he gained international prominence when he repeatedly served as chief negotiator in UN efforts to bring peace and stability to the Balkans between 1995 and 1999.

Birger Jarl (c.1203–1266). A thirteenth-century leader, advisor to kings, and founder of a royal dynasty, he is also traditionally credited with establishing Stockholm in 1252, which is true only in that he helped to increase activity in an already established town.

Birgitta Birgersdotter, Saint (1303–1373). Swedish noble woman who, after living a secular life for nearly forty years, turned to the Church. She founded an order for women, the Birgittines, at Vadstena, and was canonized in 1391. Her *Revelations* are important sources on medieval religious mysticism.

Boye, Karin (1900–1941). A novelist, short story writer, poet, and feminist of the younger generation of writers during the 1920s and 1930s. Trained as a teacher, Boye made her mark as a writer. She helped to found a literary magazine, translated T. S. Eliot into Swedish, and produced a significant body of her own work. Deeply troubled by depression, she underwent psychoanalysis in the 1930s. Her death was probably a suicide. One of her most important novels, *Kallocain*, is available in English.

Branting, Hjalmar (1860–1925). A leading figure in the founding and early growth of the Social Democratic Party. His political career spanned more than three decades, and he helped to shape his party's ideals and policies and make it the largest single party in the parliament. He was prime minister three times.

Bratt, Ivan (1878–1956). A physician and temperance advocate, he developed the "Stockholm System" of liquor rationing before World War I that was applied nationally in 1917.

Bremer, Fredrika (1801–1865). A novelist, traveler, and early advocate of women's rights. Around the mid-nineteenth century she penned a series of novels that focused on the lives of women. Her travel descriptions introduced many Swedes to such places as Cuba, the American South, and Minnesota. Several of her works have been translated, including the novel *The Colonel's Family* and the account of her travels in North America and Cuba, *Homes in the New World: Impressions of America*.

Carl XVI Gustaf (1946–   ). The current king of Sweden. He succeeded his grandfather, Gustav VI Adolf, in 1973. Despite his playboy reputation and occasion gaffs, he has done well in the role of ceremonial leader spelled out for the king in the 1975 Constitution. His principal duty has been to represent the country at home and around the world.

Christian August (1768–1810). A Danish prince chosen as heir to the Swedish throne in 1809, following the deposition of Gustav IV. When he came to Sweden early the following year, he took the name **Karl August**. His sudden death in May 1810 unleashed a new succession crisis. His funeral in Stockholm turned very ugly, and an uncontrolled mob murdered one of the country's senior nobles, Axel von Fersen.

De Geer, Louis (1587–1652) ("the Elder"). A Dutch entrepreneur, industrialist, and supporter of the state, he came to Sweden in the 1620s and soon became one of the richest men in the country. He became involved in virtually every facet of Sweden's economic life and was particularly important in international commerce, private and public finance, and the iron and weapons industries.

De Geer, Louis (1818–1896) ("the Younger"). A political leader, cabinet member, and advisor to Karl XV. A moderate nineteenth-century liberal, he authored the 1865 parliamentary reform bill.

Ekman, Carl Gustav (1872–1945). A Liberal leader in the interwar years. Twice prime minister and often the engineer of legislative successes or failures, he was nicknamed "the weigh master" for his skills in putting together voting majorities in the 1920s. Ekman was an strong supporter of prohibition and contributed to the split of the Liberal Party in 1923. He was forced to resign as prime minister in 1932, when he was implicated in the collapse of Ivar Kreuger's financial empire.

Ekman, Kerstin (1933–   ). A late-twentieth-century Swedish author of novels that deal with the far north of the country. Among her works in translation are *Black Water, Under the Snow*, and *Witches' Rings*.

Engberg, Arthur (1888–1944). A Social Democrat and minister of education during the 1930s.

Ericsson, John (1803–1889). A brilliant engineer and inventor, he is credited with the development of the screw propeller, water turbines, and electrical generators. In the United States he is best known as the inventor of the Union warship *The Monitor*.

Fogelström, Per Anders (1917–1998). The author of a remarkable series of novels in which he described the history of the lower classes in Stockholm from the mid-eighteenth century to the 1960s. Only one of these, *City of My Dreams*, is available in English, but translation of others in the series is planned.

Fredriksson, Marianne (1927–   ). One of Sweden's best-selling late-twentieth-century novelists. Her works reflect on the clashes between the past and the present, especially in the lives of women, and on changes in Swedish society since the late nineteenth century. Among her novels in translation are *Hanna's Daughters, Simon's Family*, and *Two Women*.

Günther, Christian (1886–1966). Foreign minister during World War II, he is often either praised or criticized for negotiating deals with the Germans that were intended to keep Sweden out of World War II. Among these was the so-called transit traffic that allowed the Nazis to transfer troops on Swedish railroads to and from Norway.

Gustav I Eriksson Vasa (c.1494–1560). King of Sweden, 1523–1560. He is considered by some to be the maker of the early modern Swedish state. By others he is viewed as a tyrant. He rallied support against the Danes, was elected king by the parliament, secured the country's exit from the Kalmar Union, supported the Lutheran Reformation, and organized central government. He also cruelly punished any and all who opposed him.

Gustav II Adolf (Gustavus Adolphus) (1594–1632). King of Sweden, 1611–1632. Like his grandfather, Gustav is seen by some as one of the great rulers of the country and one of history's greatest military leaders. By others he is viewed as a warmonger and a tyrant. He contributed to the development of political peace at home, fought the Poles to a standstill, imposed many important reforms on the Swedish military, and took Sweden into the Thirty Years' War—all undertaken at great cost. He died at the Battle of Lützen in 1632.

Gustav III (1746–1792). King of Sweden, 1771–1792. A confusing and paradoxical figure, he saw himself as an enlightened ruler who wanted to restore Sweden's greatness. He made lasting contributions to the country's cultural life and tried to modernize the economy. He also abused his powers, waged an illegal and costly war with Russia, and aroused considerable animosity, especially among the nobility. He was assassinated in 1792.

Gustav IV (1778–1837). King of Sweden, 1792–1809. He was an assertive but not very able ruler who ignored his advisors and the parliament, behaved autocratically, and took the country to war against Napoleon. Because of his actions Finland was lost to the Russians, and he was deposed by a peaceful coup in 1809. Exiled from Sweden, he lived on the continent as "Colonel Gustafsson."

Gustav V (1858–1953). King of Sweden, 1907–1953. A man of many talents and interests, he was the last king to "rule" in Sweden. He accepted the development of parliamentary democracy in 1917 and adapted to the changing role of monarch in the country.

Hammarskjöld, Dag (1905–1961). An economist, statesman, and UN leader. The son of Hjalmar Hammarskjöld (prime minister during World War I), this remarkable person held degrees in the humanities, economics, and law. Between the world wars he served as secretary of the Unemployment Commission and as an undersecretary in the Finance Ministry. He is said to have coined the term *planned economy* and authored much of Sweden's early welfare state legislation. Following the war he was Sweden's delegate to the Organization for European Economic Cooperation and the United Nations. From 1953 until his death he was secretary general of the United Nations. He died in a plane crash while on a peacekeeping mission to the Congo in 1961 and was awarded the Nobel Peace Prize the same year, posthumously. Among his writings is *Markings*, a deeply spiritual book based a journal he kept of his personal conversations with himself.

Hansson, Per Albin (1885–1946). The child of a house painter, Hansson grew up to become a journalist and leader in the Social Democratic Party. He succeeded Hjalmar Branting as head of the party in 1925 and was prime minister from 1932 to 1946, except for the summer of 1936. He was a leading figure in the development of the concept of the "people's home" and the legislative program of Sweden's emerging welfare state, and he led Sweden through the difficult times of World War II.

Hedin, Sven (1865–1952). An adventurer, explorer, author, and nationalist, he conducted expeditions into central Asia, which he described in lively published accounts: *Through Asia* (1899) and *My Life as an Explorer* (1925). He was an outspoken nationalist, supporter of the monarchy, and pro-German during World War I. In 1902 he became the last person to be ennobled in Sweden.

Horn, Arvid (1664–1742). A conservative and cautious aristocrat who led Sweden for most of the period 1718–1738, he was an architect of the documents that redefined Sweden's political system during the so-called Era of Liberty, 1719–1772, and worked to rebuild the country after the Great Northern War.

Johansson, Albin (1886–1968). The head of the central cooperative organization, KF, from the 1930s to the 1950s. He was important in the growth and extension of the movement into production areas that helped to break several monopolies. He was also active in regional and international cooperative organizations.

Karl XII (1682–1718). King of Sweden, 1697–1718. He was an absolutist and gifted military leader. He spent almost his entire adult life fighting the Great Northern War. The circumstances surrounding his death make for one of the great mysteries of Swedish history. He died of a gunshot wound to the head in November 1718. Although he may have been killed by fire from the fortress at Frederikshald (Norway), it is very likely he was murdered by his own officers.

Karl XIV Johan (1762–1844). King of Sweden, 1818–1844. This man's biography is remarkable. The son of a lawyer, Jean Baptist Bernadotte rose to become a marshal in the armies of imperial France under Napoleon. Chosen as heir to Karl XIII in 1810, he subsequently turned on France, joined the alliance against Napoleon, and contributed to his defeat in 1813–1814. As king he was a relatively conservative throwback to the pre-French Revolutionary era.

Key, Ellen (1849–1926). A writer, social critic, feminist, and teacher. Her *Century of the Child* is available in English.

Kristina (1626–1689). Queen of Sweden, 1632–1654. The daughter of Gustav II Adolf, Kristina was a fascinating and paradoxical figure. Intelligent, intellectual, and emotional, she converted to Roman Catholicism, abdicated her throne, and left Sweden to live in Rome for most of the last thirty-five years of her life.

Linneaus (Linné), Carl von (1707–1778). An eighteenth-century botanist and naturalist, he developed the binomial system for classifying plants. He and his students, who were dispatched across the globe, were important in identifying, naming, and illustrating a phenomenal range of the world's plant life.

Lundborg, Herman (1868–1943). An advocate of eugenics in the early twentieth century, he served as the first director of the eugenics institute established at Uppsala University in the 1920s and sought through his research to "define" the Swedish population in terms of its physical characteristics.

Magnus Eriksson (1316–1374). King of Sweden, 1319–1356/65. He was important in the development of the monarchy and the creation of a unified law code for the country. Open rebellion against him erupted in 1356, and he was declared deposed nine years later.

Margrethe (I) (1353–1412). A daughter of Denmark's Valdemar IV and wife of Norway's king, Haakon VI. When her husband and then her son, Olof, died, she became the de facto ruler of all Scandinavia. She was a leading force in the creation of the Kalmar Union that linked Denmark, Norway, and Sweden together in 1397.

Milles, Carl (1875–1955). An internationally known twentieth-century sculptor, he worked for many years at Cranbrook Academy in Michigan. Many of his works are on display at the museum that was his studio, *Millesgård*, in Stockholm.

Moberg, Vilhelm (1898–1973). A journalist, critic, dramatist, and novelist. His series on nineteenth-century emigration is a classic, but his other works included critiques of Sweden during World War II and descriptions of the lives of the inhabitants of Småland. He set out to write a history of ordinary Swedes in which he was highly critical of the kings who had been made heroes in nationalist histories. For example, he referred to Gustav I as "Tyrant II." He completed two volumes before his death. Many of his works have been translated, including *The Emigrants, Unto a Good Land, The Settlers, Last Letter Home, A History of the Swedish People* (two volumes), and *Ride Tonight*.

Myrdal, Alva (1902–1986). A scholar, author, political leader, ambassador, and advocate of peace and international cooperation. This extraordinary women teamed up with her husband, Gunnar Myrdal, to write the very important study of Swedish population issues in the 1930s. She was an advocate of social welfare programs, served in the Swedish parliament, was ambassador to India, worked with UNESCO, and received the Nobel Peace Prize in 1982. In translation, her writing includes *On Equality* (a statement of Swedish Social Democratic Party ideals) and *Women's Two Roles: Home and Work*.

Myrdal, Gunnar (1898–1987). An attorney, professor, scholar, author, and political leader, he worked with his wife, Alva Myrdal, during the 1930s as an advocate of social welfare reform. His study of race relations in the United States, *The American Dilemma: The Negro Problem and Modern Democracy*, remains a standard work on the subject. He was minister of commerce after World War II and turned his scholarship and teaching attention to international economics. In 1974 he was awarded the Bank of Sweden Prize in Economics (in memory of Alfred Nobel).

Möller, Gustav (1884–1970). A Social Democrat, minister of social affairs under P. A. Hansson, and architect of many social programs in the 1930s and after World War II.

Nobel, Alfred (1833–1896). A chemist, inventor, entrepreneur, and philanthropist, he developed dynamite in 1867 (a form of nitroglycerin that is relatively safe to handle) and went on to invent smokeless gunpowder and other explosives. He built an international explosive-manufacturing empire and was one of the wealthiest men of his day. In the late nineteenth century he became a strong supporter of world peace, and his will established the Nobel Prizes in the Sciences, Literature, and Peace.

Olaus Petri (Olof Petersson) (1493–1552). A leader of the Reformation in Sweden, he converted to the Lutheran faith in the early 1520s and was influential in bringing the Reformation to Sweden. He translated the Bible into Swedish and was an advisor to Gustav I Vasa.

Ottesen-Jensen, Elise (1886–1973). A Norwegian-born advocate of women's rights and especially birth control, she headed a campaign to improve the lives of working-class women by helping them limit the size of their families.

Oxenstierna, Axel (1583–1654). A nobleman, chancellor to Gustav II Adolf, and regent and then chancellor to Kristina. Some think he was the most important person in the first half of the seventeenth century in Sweden, as he had worked with these two rulers to build early modern Sweden's government and economy.

Palme, Olof (1927–1986). Succeeded Tage Erlander as leader of the Social Democratic Party and prime minister in 1969. He served in the latter capacity until 1976 and then again from 1982 until his murder on 28 February 1986. Some call him the best-known Swedish political leader of the twentieth century—a deserved reputation, given his sharp tongue, strong leadership, and committed involvement with international assistance.

Saint Ansgar (801–865). Archbishop of Hamburg-Bremen and a ninth-century missionary to Sweden. Although he was largely unsuccessful in his efforts, he is traditionally viewed as the person who first brought Christianity to Sweden.

Sandler, Rickard (1884–1964). Social Democrat, intellectual, prime minister in the 1920s, and foreign minister through much of the 1930s—until December 1939, when he was removed because of his belief that Sweden should resist German pressures to compromise the country's neutrality. He remained politically active after World War II and headed the commission formed in 1954 to develop recommendations for a new constitution.

Segerstedt, Torgny (1876–1945). Editor of *Göteborgs Handels-och Sjöfarts tidning* and an outspoken critic of Sweden's compromises with the Germans during World War II.

Strindberg, August (1849–1912). Probably Sweden's best-known author. A playwright, novelist, social critic, and artist, he wrote naturalistic and intensely psychological works that are still widely studied and performed. He also wrote a set of historical plays about Gustav I, Olaus Petri, Gustavus Adolphus, Kristina, and Gustav III that present these heroes of traditional Swedish history in very personal and critical ways.

Wallenberg, André Oscar (1816–1886). A naval officer, banker, financier, and politician, he is best known as the founder of Stockholms Enskilda Bank in 1856. For over two decades before this he was a naval officer. From the 1850s he turned his attentions to business, banking, and industrial development. He was an outspoken advocate of savings-and-loan–based banks and joint-stock companies, and he used the press to spread new economic ideas. In the parliament, where he served for over thirty years, he was a liberal champion of reforms, including women's property rights.

Wallenberg, Raoul (1912–?). A member of a wealthy Swedish banking family, he was educated at the University of Michigan and worked for a time in a bank in Palestine. In early summer 1944 he was sent to Budapest, where he worked with Per Anger and the Swedish embassy staff to help Jews threatened by German extermination policies. In January 1945 he disappeared into the Soviet Union, and the full story of his fate remains a mystery.

Wigforss, Ernst (1881–1977). An economist, Social Democrat, and minister of finance for much of the period 1932–1949. An advocate of the deficit finance ideas of John M. Keynes, he developed many of the financial aspects of Sweden's welfare state.

Bibliographic Essay

Swedish history, in the broad perspective, has been well covered by scholars writing in English, at least since the beginning of the twentieth century. Every new generation has produced one or more good overview histories. In terms of coverage of specific topics, however, Sweden is less well served in English sources. "Spotty" is a word that describes what is available. There are, for example, many works on the Vikings, the Vasa kings of the sixteenth century, the Swedish empire of the seventeenth century, Gustavus Adolphus, Charles XII, overseas emigration, and the welfare state. Yet, there is almost nothing on women, popular culture, everyday life, or education. There are a number of good biographies, but they are mostly of the Early Modern Period's national-hero monarchs. Without a knowledge of Swedish, anyone seeking to delve deeply into most subjects will quickly run up against a complete lack of sources.

GENERAL HISTORIES

Franklin D. Scott, *Sweden: The Nation's History* (with an epilogue by Steven Koblik) (Carbondale: Southern Illinois University Press, 1988) is the best and most extensive of the more recent English-language histories. A new overview is Lars O. Lagerkvist, *A History of Sweden*, published by the Swedish Institute in Stockholm in 2001. Ingvar Andersson's *A History of*

Sweden (New York: Praeger, 1956) and Stewart P. Oakley's *A Short History of Sweden* (New York: Praeger, 1966) are reliable but dated. Vilhelm Moberg began to write the history of Sweden from the perspective of ordinary people and completed two volumes (up to about 1540) before his death in 1973. See *History of the Swedish People: Prehistory to the Renaissance* and *From Renaissance to Revolution* (New York: Pantheon, 1971 and 1973, respectively). Byron J. Nordstrom's *Scandinavia since 1500* (Minneapolis: University of Minnesota Press, 2000) provides a current overview in the broader Scandinavian context. Also useful in seeing Sweden in the context of the Baltic region are David Kirby's two works, *Northern Europe in the Early Modern Period: The Baltic World, 1492–1772* (New York: Longman, 1990) and *The Baltic World, 1772–1993* (New York: Longman, 1995). For topically arranged reference works see Irene Scobbie, *Historical Dictionary of Sweden* (Metuchen, NJ: Scarecrow Press, 1995), and Byron J. Nordstrom, *Dictionary of Scandinavian History* (Westport, CT: Greenwood Press, 1986). Excellent statistical sources are *Statistical Yearbook of Sweden* (Stockholm: Statistiska centralbyrån, annually) and *Yearbook of Nordic Statistics* (Copenhagen: Nordic Council, annually). On geography see Axel Sömme, *Geography of Norden* (New York: Wiley & Sons, 1961), and William R. Mead, *An Historical Geography of Scandinavia* (New York: Academic Press, 1981).

VIKINGS AND MEDIEVAL SWEDEN

Else Roesdahl, *The Vikings* (New York: Penguin Putnam, 1998), and Colleen Baley, Helen Clarke, R. I. Page, and Neil S. Price, with James Graham-Campbel editor, *Cultural Atlas of the Viking World* (New York: Facts on File, 1994), are current in their scholarship, well written, and illustrated. Birgit and Peter Sawyer, *Medieval Scandinavia* (Minneapolis: University of Minnesota Press, 1993), is brief, but includes coverage of more than political themes.

EARLY MODERN PERIOD

The works of Michael Roberts are among the best in any language for the Early Modern Period. They include *The Age of Liberty: Sweden, 1719–1772* (Cambridge: Cambridge University Press, 1985), *The Early Vasas: A History of Sweden, 1523–1611* (London: Cambridge University Press, 1968), *Essays in Swedish History* (Minneapolis, University of Minnesota Press, 1967), *From Oxenstierna to Charles XII: Four Studies* (Cambridge, Cambridge University Press, 1991), *Gustavus Adolphus* (London: Longman, 1992), *Gustavus Adolphus and the Rise of Sweden* (London: English University Press, 1973), *Sweden as a Great Power, 1611–1697* (New York: St. Martin's Press, 1968), and *The Swedish Imperial Experience, 1560–1718* (Cambridge: Cambridge University Press,

1979). On international relations see Jill Lisk, *Struggle for Supremacy in the Baltic, 1600–1725* (Birmingham, UK: Minerva Press, 1968). There are many interesting works about Gustav II Adolf's daughter, Kristina (Christina) including: Faith M. Mackenzie's *The Sibyl of the North: The Tale of Christina, Queen of Sweden* (Boston: Houghton Mifflin, 1931), Sven Stolpe's *Christina of Sweden*, edited by Sir Alec Randall and translated by Sir Alec Randall and Ruth M. Bethell (New York: Macmillan, 1966), Georgia Masson's *Queen Christina* (New York: Farrar, Straus & Giroux, 1969), and Susanna Åkerman's *Queen Christina of Sweden and Her Circle: The Transformation of a Seventeenth Century Philosophical Libertine* (New York and Leiden: E. J. Brill, 1991). On Sweden's colony in North America, Amandus Johnson's *The Swedish Settlements on the Delaware* (Philadelphia: University of Pennsylvania, 1911) remains a standard. More current works include Stellan Dahlgren and Hans Norman's version of Johan Rising(h)'s diary from his years in the colony, *The Rise and Fall of New Sweden* (Uppsala: Uppsala University, Acta Universitatis Upsaliensis, 27, 1988), and *The Age of New Sweden* (Stockholm: Royal Armoury, 1988), which includes articles on the colony and Sweden by Sven Nilsson, Allan Ellenius, Gunnar Eriksson, Arne Losman, and Margaret Revera. The best biography of Charles XII is by Ragnhild Hatton (New York: Weybright and Talley, 1968), but an interesting perspective is also provided by Francois Voltaire, *Voltaire's History of Charles XII, King of Sweden*, translated by Winifred Todhunter (New York: E. P. Dutton, 1912). August Strindberg's historical dramas about the rulers of this period are also interesting. See: *Queen Christina, Charles XII,* and *Gustav III* (one volume), translated and introduced by Walter Johnson (Seattle: University of Washington Press, 1955); *Gustav Adolf*, translated and introduced by Walter Johnson (Seattle: University of Washington Press, 1957, and *The Vasa Trilogy: Master Olaf, Gustav Vasa, Erik XIV*, translated and introduced by Walter Johnson (Seattle: University of Washington Press, 1959). Although historically inaccurate in many ways, the 1934 motion picture *Queen Christian* (MGM), starring the Swedish-born actress Greta Garbo, reveals some aspects of this fascinating and complicated personality. Exploring a very different theme, H. A. Barton's *Northern Arcadia: Foreign Travelers in Scandinavia, 1765–1815* (Carbondale: Southern Illinois University Press, 1998) includes descriptions and evaluations of many aspects of the late-eighteenth and early-nineteenth centuries as seen by foreign travelers to Sweden, Denmark, Norway, and Finland.

PARLIAMENT

There are two excellent recent books on Sweden's parliament: Stig Hadenius, *The Riksdag in Focus: Swedish History in a Parliamentary Perspec-*

tive (Stockholm: Swedish Parliament, 1997), and Michael Metcalf, ed., *The Riksdag: A History of the Swedish Parliament* (New York: St. Martin's Press, 1987).

NINETEENTH CENTURY

H. Arnold Barton includes detailed sections on Sweden from about 1760 to 1815 in *Scandinavia in the Revolutionary Era* (Minneapolis: University of Minnesota Press, 1986). Economic history is covered briefly in Lennart Jörberg, "The Nordic Countries, 1850–1914," in *The Emergence of Industrial Societies*, Part II, edited by Carlo M. Cipolla (New York: Harvester Press, 1976). The mass migration has been extensively researched by scholars in Sweden and the United States since the 1960s, and the literature has grown. A very good introduction to the many aspects of this subject is Hans Norman and Harald Runblom, eds. *From Sweden to America: A History of the Migration* (Minneapolis: University of Minnesota Press, 1976). To delve deeper into the subject, see the work of H. Arnold Barton, Ulf Beijbom, or Dag Blanck. Also, every year since 1977, the October issue of *The Swedish-American Historical Quarterly* has published a bibliography of new works on Swedish-American history. Vilhelm Moberg's emigrant novels (*The Emigrants, Unto a Good Land, The Settlers*, and *Last Letter Home*) are very good historical fiction, but they deal only with one part of Sweden and then only during the early stages of the mass migration in the late 1840 and 1850s. Raymond Lindgren's *Norway-Sweden: Union, Disunion, and Scandinavian Integration* (Princeton: Princeton University Press, 1959) is dated but still a very good survey of this topic.

TWENTIETH CENTURY

Stig Hadenius, *Swedish Politics during the Twentieth Century* (Stockholm: Swedish Institute, 1985), provides a good overview of the last century. On World War I Steven Koblik's *Sweden: The Neutral Victor* (Stockholm: Läromedelsförlag, 1972) stands alone, and it deals mainly with the diplomacy of the last two years of the war. Gunnar Broberg and Nils Roll-Hansen, eds., *Eugenics and the Welfare State: Sterilization Policy in Denmark, Sweden, Norway, and Finland* (East Lansing: Michigan State University Press, 1996), covers the fascinating topic of eugenics. Broberg authored the chapter on Sweden. On World War II, general policies and actions are covered by W. M. Carlgren, *Swedish Foreign Policy during the Second World War* (New York: St. Martin's Press, 1977). Steven Koblik's *The Stones Cry Out* (New York: Holocaust Library, 1988) and Paul Levine's *From Indifference to Activism: Swedish Diplomacy and the Holocaust* (Uppsala: Uppsala University, 1996) deal with what Sweden knew and did regarding the Holocaust. The Swedish political system is described in many books. Joseph Board, *Government and Politics in Sweden* (Boston: Houghton Mifflin Co., 1970), is a good place to start. Although now long out of date, Nils Andrén provides a good introduction to foreign policy in *Power-Balance and Non-Alignment* (Stockholm: Almqvist and Wiksell, 1967). Christine Ingebritsen has surveyed the policies of each of the Nordic countries with regard to the European Union in *The Nordic Countries and European Unity* (Ithaca: Cornell University Press, 1998).

WELFARE STATE

The welfare state is one of the most intensively covered themes in modern Swedish history, and the literature is extensive. A classic on the early stages of the welfare state and the context in which it grew is Marquis Childs, *Sweden: The Middle Way* (New Haven: Yale University Press, 1936). Good surveys include Eric Einhorn and John Logue's *Modern Welfare States: Politics and Policies in Social Democratic Scandinavia* (New York: Praeger, 1989) and Henry Milner's *Sweden: Social Democracy in Practice* (Oxford: Oxford University Press, 1989). A powerful critique of the Swedish system can be found in Roland Huntford, *The New Totalitarians* (New York: Stein and Day, 1972). On the Social Democrats see Klaus Misgeld, Karl Molin, and Klas Åmark *Creating Social Democracy: A Century of the Social Democratic Labor Party in Sweden* (University Park: Pennsylvania State University Press, 1988).

PERIODICALS

Historisk tidskrift is the quarterly journal of Sweden's society of professional historians. It has been published since 1881. Although most of the articles and reviews are in Swedish, they often have English summaries. The professional historical societies of the Nordic countries publish the English-language *Journal of Scandinavian History*, and many fine articles have appeared there. The English weekly *The Economist* provides regular reports on economic activity, covers some aspects of current events, and occasionally publishes lengthy articles on Sweden or the Scandinavian region. (See, for example, "A Survey of the Nordic Countries," *The Economist*, 23 January 1999, special insert following page 50.) Occasionally there are articles on Swedish history in *Scandinavian Studies*, the journal of the Society for the Advancement of Scandinavian Study. On Swedish-American history see *Swedish-American Genealogist* and *The Swedish-American Historical Quarterly*.

THE INTERNET

Many excellent sources of information about Sweden and Swedish history can be found on the Internet, and new ones are constantly coming on-line. Some sites are in Swedish, but they offer an English-language option. Four good places to start are www.si.se (the home page of the Swedish Institute in Stockholm), www.sweden.se (VirtualSweden), www.markovits. com/nordic/ (Nordic Pages), and www.web.com/sis/ (the home page of the Swedish Information Service in New York). Each of these provides access to many sources of information and windows into dozens of other sites. Every branch of the government, as well as all the organizations, political parties, and most of the businesses mentioned in this book have extensive websites. GOOGLE is a very good search engine for locating materials. Of course, as with all sources, one must be careful to assess the reliability of web-based information.

Index

Håga mound, 17
Hague International Peace Confer-
    ences of 1899 and 1907, 90
Halland, 48
Hammarforsen power station, 112
Hammarskjöld, Dag, 136
Hammarskjöld, Hjalmar, 71; govern-
    ment, 94; World War I, 95
Hanse. *See* Hanseatic League
Hanseatic League, 38, 41, 57–58
Hansson, Per Albin: background, 106;
    death, 129; government's record,
    107; succeeds Branting, 106; vision
    of the People's Home, 106; World
    War II, 117
Härjedalen, 48
Hats, 44–45
Hedeby, 23
Hedin, Sven, 71
Helgö, 20
Herredag, 36
Hertha (Bremer), 82
Hierta, Lars Johan, 66
History: nineteenth century histories,
    87; shaping factors, 10
Hjelm-Wallin, Lena, 146
Höglund, Zeth, 106
Holm, Erik, 110
Holmström, Lasse, 153–154
Holocaust, 121
Horn, Count Arvid, 44
Housing: medieval, 28; public support
    in the 1930s, 107
Hven, 48

Ibn Fadlan, 22
Ibsen, Henrik, 82
I dag (Segerstedt), 116
Immigrants: authors, 153; Dutch, 57;
    post–World War II, 141–145, 148
Immigration, 4, 60; government poli-
    cies, 143–144; labor migration, 148;
    nature of post-World War II, 142;
    post–World War II, 141–144
Imports: early modern, 59; Viking
    Age, 23–24; World War II, 117

Industrial development: Industrial
    Revolution, 75; 1930s, 109–110;
    post–World War II, 147, 149–151
Industrial working class, nineteenth
    century, 78
Industries: automobile, 147; copper,
    55–56; overview, 3; shipbuilding,
    149. *See also* Armaments industry;
    Iron industry; Paper industry
International Order of Good Templars
    (IOGT), 85
International relations: nineteenth
    century, 87–92; post–World War II,
    135–138. *See also* Foreign policy
Inter-war years, 97–113: architecture,
    112; cultural developments,
    111–113; design, 112; fashion,
    112–113; politics, 97–107; popular
    culture, 112–113
Iron Age, 12, 18–21; subperiods, 12;
    trade, 19–20; written sources, 19
Iron industry: early modern, 56–57;
    early modern entrepreneurs, 57;
    late twentieth century, 149; nine-
    teenth century, 76–77
Iron mining, 149
Iron ore, export to Germany in World
    War II, 117

Jagellonica, Katarina, 47
Jämtland, 48
Jazz, 154
Jews, Nazi persecution of, in World
    War II, 120–121
Johan III, 42; empire, 46
Johnson, Eyvind: post–World War II,
    153; World War II, 111
John III, 42
Josefina of Leutchenburg, 65–66

Kallifatides, Theodor, 153
Kalmar, 39; early modern trade, 58
Kalmar Union, 39, 58; end of, 40
Karl August. *See* Kristian August
Karlsborg fortress, 89
Karlskrona, 140
Karlsson, Bert, 126. *See also* New Dem-
    ocrats

About the Author

BYRON J. NORDSTROM is Professor of History and Scandinavian Studies at Gustavus Adolphus College. He is the author of *Dictionary of Scandinavian History and Scandinavia Since 1500,* as well as articles about Swedish and Swedish-American history.